The Apostolic Church Order

The Greek text
edited and translated
with an introduction and notes

Revised edition

Alistair C. Stewart

SCD Press
2021

*The Apostolic Church Order. The Greek text,
edited and translated, with an introduction and notes*
(Early Christian Studies, 10, revised edition)
By Alistair C. Stewart© 2006, 2021

SCD Press
PO Box 1882
Macquarie Centre NSW 2113
Australia
scdpress@scd.edu.au

All rights reserved. No part of this book may be reproduced or transmitted in any form or by any means, electronic or mechanical, including photocopying, recording or by any information and storage system without permission in writing from the publishers.

ISBN-13: 978-1-925730-27-2 (paperback)
ISBN-13: 978-1-925730-28-9 (ebook)

Layout and design by: Lankshear Design Pty Ltd
Printed and bound by: Ingram Spark

The Apostolic Church Order

the Greek text
edited and translated
with an introduction and notes

Revised edition

Alistair C. Stewart

SCD Press
2021

Early Christian Studies 10

SCD Press Editorial Board

Professor Diane Speed

Professor James R. Harrison

Professor Peter G. Bolt

Additional Series Editors

Professor Pauline Allen (Australian Catholic University)

Professor Wendy Mayer (Australian Lutheran College)

Professor Bronwen Neil (Macquarie University)

Early Christian Studies

1. Jan Harm Barkhuizen, *Proclus Bishop of Constantinople. Homilies on the Life of Christ* (2001).
2. Robert C. Hill, *Theodoret of Cyrus. Commentary on the Song of Songs* (2001).
3. Johan Ferreira, *The Hymn of the Pearl* (2002).
4. Alistair Stewart-Sykes, *The Life of Polycarp. An anonymous vita from third-century Smyrna* (2002).
5. Daniel Van Slyke, *Quodvultdeus of Carthage. The Apocalyptic Theology of a Roman African in Exile* (2003).
6. Bronwen Neil & Pauline Allen, *The Life of Maximus the Confessor. Recension 3* (2003).
7. George Kalantzis, *Theodore of Mopsuestia. Commentary on the Gospel of John* (2004).
8. Rudolf Brändle, *John Chrysostom. Bishop – Reformer – Martyr* (2004).
9. J. Mark Armitage, *A Twofold Solidarity. Leo the Great's Theology of Redemption* (2005).
10. Alistair Stewart-Sykes, *The Apostolic Church Order. The Greek Text with Introduction, Translation and Annotation* (2006, 2021).
11. Geoffrey D. Dunn, *Cyprian and the Bishops of Rome: Questions of Papal Primacy in the Early Church* (2007, 2018).
12. Pauline Allen, Majella Franzmann, & Rick Strelan (eds.), *"I Sowed Fruits into Hearts" (Odes Sol. 17:13). Festschrift for Professor Michael Lattke* (2007).
13. David Luckensmeyer & Pauline Allen (eds.), *Studies of Religion and Politics in the Early Christian Centuries* (2010).
14. Oliver Herbel, *Sarapion of Thmuis: Against the Manicheans and Pastoral Letters* (2011).

15. Raymond Laird, *Mindset, Moral Choice and Sin in the Anthropology of John Chrysostom* (2012, 2017).
16. Alexander L. Abecina, *Time and Sacramentality in Gregory of Nyssa's Contra Eunomium* (2013).
17. Johan Ferreira, *Early Chinese Christianity: The Tang Christian Monument and Other Documents* (2014).
18. Wendy Mayer & Ian J. Elmer (eds.), *Men and Women in the Early Christian Centuries* (2014).
19. Silouan Fotineas, *The Letters of Bishop Basil of Caesarea: Instruments of Communion* (2018).
20. Andrey Romanov, *One God as One God and One Lord. The Lordship of Jesus Christ as a Hermeneutical Key to Paul's Christology in 1 Corinthians (with a special focus on 1 Cor 8:6)* (2021).
21. Hyueng Guen Choi, *Charity and the Letters of Barsanuphius and John of Gaza* (2020).
22. Alistair C. Stewart, *The Canons of Hippolytus. An English version, with introduction and annotation and an accompanying Arabic Text* (2021).

To my friend and brother presbyter
Noel Burke
Canon of the Cathedral of St Michael
in the island Diocese of Barbados

Preface to the revised edition

Since completing the first edition of this work at the end of 2005, scholarship on K has been enriched by a new textual witness, and by Allie Ernst's study on Martha. In the meantime I have myself completed works on the development of Christian office and on the *Testamentum Domini*, both of which have proved to cast significant new light on this text.

The original edition is long out of print. By happy chance, having taken over publication of the Early Christian Studies series from Australian Catholic University, the Sydney College of Divinity had lost the typeset version, while I still had possession of the original files from which the book was set. Thus I am delighted that the SCD has agreed to issue a revised version of the original work. My thanks to Diane Speed, and particularly to Peter Bolt who oversaw the new publication and lent encouragement, and to Joy Lankshear who has redrawn the diagrams.

The text is not much different from that published in 2006. Nor is the translation, though there are some new notes, and a couple of significant changes, suggested to me by David Hunter, who gave the final push to getting this revised work underway. My thanks to him.

Some of the introduction is unaltered, particularly in the section regarding the two ways. However, the latter part of the introduction is entirely revised, and as a result of my reading of Ernst, and my work on *Testamentum Domini*, I have reconsidered the context of the polemic against female ministry, and as a result significantly revised the date I originally assigned to the final redaction of this document, which I now see as somewhat later than the sources employed. These reconsiderations have, however, made me certain of its Cappadocian or Phrygian locale.

I have, since 2005, been transplanted from a country vicarage in Dorset to an urban one in Slough. However, ties with Barbados are still strong, and I rejoice to report that Canon Burke remains συμμύστης καὶ συνεπίμαχος. Fr Austin Milner passed to his reward in 2010, though not before returning to Oxford and celebrating his golden jubilee. Oret pro nobis.

St Peter's Parsonage, Chalvey, Slough
On the feast of St Andrew, 2019

Preface

I was first introduced to this work by Fr Austin Milner, then of Jamaica, in a conversation in Barbados concerning the state of study of the church orders generally. I am not ashamed to admit that at the time I had never come across the work owing to the neglect which it suffered for the greater part of the last century but being interested in Christian prophecy, and female prophecy in particular, I was intrigued at Fr Milner's description of a church which supported two widows who had revelations. It seemed to me that some publication should reawaken study of this text.

Although the seed of the work was found in the Caribbean it was not possible to plant it there. I had hoped to begin the work after moving to the USA but events conspired to prevent this happening and so the present work was grown entirely in Dorset soil and is the product of a country parson's leisure, therefore coming forth over ten years after its first inception.

The purpose of this work is an attempt to bring this church order to renewed scholarly attention. As such I feel that no particular apology is required, for as Faivre, one of the few scholars to have paid any serious attention to this work, remarks: "Depuis sa dernière édition... son abandon est quasi-total." (Faivre, "Apostolicité", 22). A context for this remark may be provided by the observation that this last edition was published in 1914. Others have likewise lamented the neglect of this church order and so, even should my conclusions in the introduction, in which I essay a date rather earlier than that usually offered, a *Sitz im Leben* for the redaction of the text, and an exploration of the sources employed, be found entirely wanting by the scholarly community, and even should the text I have produced be utterly scorned, I would claim nonetheless to have done a service by rescuing this church order from undeserved obscurity.

An apologia, however, needs to preface the text. Indeed, this is the eighth edition of the Greek text, the text having previously been edited by Bickell, Pitra, Lagarde, Hilgenfeld, Funk, Harnack and Schermann, as well as receiving attention from Wilamowitz-Moellendorff and Hennecke. I am therefore moving somewhat hubristically in exalted company. The Greek text is extant in its entirety in but one MS; in addition there are MSS of the Epitome, a work related to the Apostolic Church Order, and another abbreviated version of the two ways section in a further MS. Beyond this there are versions of the whole in Syriac, Sahidic, Arabic and Ethiopic and a substantial fragment in Latin, which are of varying value in determining the Greek text.

Thus when I come to present the text, not every variation between the versions is given, as at some points the text is clear, and at others the versions diverge so widely from the Greek that they are clearly attempts to impose a meaning comprehensible to the reader upon an obscure text. As such they are interesting for the *Nachleben* of this living literature, but not useful for the exercise of establishing the original. Likewise not every suggested emendation from the editors is listed, nor every obvious error in the Greek MSS, the sole criterion being worth of due consideration in the reconstruction of the Greek text.

Because of the complexity of the task I have employed annotation rather than a conventional apparatus, attempting to show the rationale by which I have concluded each disputed point so that others may more readily disagree, especially as I am by no means convinced of the correctness of every reading printed.

Beside a text and an introduction I have provided an English translation for the convenience of readers. As far as I can tell this is the first time that a translation of the entire Greek text into a modern language has been published. Readers are nonetheless warned that the translation is made on the basis of the text presented here, which diverges significantly at several points from earlier texts, and may therefore be entirely misleading, as much depends on conjecture. I have, however, signaled some of the more radical points of departure from the received text. Annotation beyond this has been fairly minimal because most points of particular interest are covered in the introduction and since much of the material is parallel to the Didache, on which many excellent commentaries are already available, and is therefore left without comment to avoid duplication of what is already available.

The most pleasant duty, however, is to acknowledge those who have assisted me in this task. First mention must of course be given to Fr Milner. However special thanks must be accorded to Philip Purchase, once of my parish but now a classicist in far-off places, Allen Brent, and Wendy Mayer, each of whom have read the MS and suggested corrections and improvements. Subsequently Gilles Dorival most graciously made me welcome in Aix en Provence and gave me access to the papers of the late Pierre Nautin. There, on the feast of SS Timothy and Titus this year, I thought that the work had been completed. However, Allie Ernst subsequently gave me cause to reconsider many points—though here I may state that I have not accepted all the suggestions that I have received and must be held responsible at the last for any error. In the closing stages of the work, Christine Trevett was gracious in sharing material and ideas with me and finally David Luckensmeyer and Dinah Joesoef at the Centre for Early Christian Studies brought order to unruly tables and apparatus.

The dedication is to a fine priest, a former student, and true friend; that he hardly embodies the characteristics demanded in this text of a presbyter, but rather those of bishop and deacon, says more about the history of the text than about his exercise of his sacred office.

Sturminster Marshall Vicarage:
St John's day, 2005

Contents

Introduction		1
The Apostolic Church Order		1
1.	**The two-ways section**	3
1.1	The two ways section of K and E	4
1.2	The relationship between K, D, and B	16
1.2.1	The additional material in D	17
1.2.2	The relationship between B and D	18
1.2.2.1	B as reordering of D	18
1.2.2.2	D as reordering of TWT preserved by B	21
1.2.2.3	D and B as independent variants of TWT	25
1.2.3	The replacement of the Haustafel in K	26
1.2.4	The additional material in K	28
1.2.4.1	K material with B parallels	29
1.2.4.1.1	The commandment to love God	30
1.2.4.1.2	Loving one's teacher as the apple of an eye	32
1.2.4.1.3	The eschatological conclusion	35
1.2.4.1.3.1	K revised in the light of B	35
1.2.4.1.3.2	The eschatological conclusion as inherent in TWT	36
1.2.4.1.3.3	K as having a source independent of B	36
1.2.5	Some conclusions on the relationship between B, D and K	40
1.3	Two-ways material in K which is not found elsewhere	41
1.3.1	Gendered demons	42
1.3.2	The support of teachers	44
1.4	Conclusions on the TWT in K	45

2. The epistolary opening and apostle list ... 46
- 2.1 The apostle list ... 46
- 2.2 The epistolary opening ... 49
- 2.3 Conclusions on the opening of K ... 53

3. The sources and redaction of the church-order of K ... 54
- 3.1 Harnack's two ancient sources ... 54
- 3.2 Bartlet's hypothesis of a double revision ... 57
- 3.3 Interim conclusion ... 64
- 3.4 K24–28 ... 64
  - 3.4.1 Jesus as teacher ... 64
  - 3.4.2 The presence of Mary and Martha ... 65
  - 3.4.3 The offering of the Body and Blood ... 68
  - 3.4.4 The redaction of 24–28 ... 69
- 3.5 The redaction of K22 and K29 ... 79
- 3.6 The conclusion to K ... 80
- 3.7 The ancient church order lying behind K ... 80
  - 3.7.1 κκ as a qualification list ... 82
  - 3.7.2 The bishop and presbyters in κκ ... 84
  - 3.7.3 The reader ... 93
  - 3.7.4 The deacons ... 99
  - 3.7.5 The widows ... 103
  - 3.7.6 The text of κκ ... 104
  - 3.7.7 The date and origin of κκ ... 106

4. The extent of K's editorial work ... 107
- 4.1 K1–3 ... 107
- 4.2 The assignment to apostles ... 109
- 4.3 K's engagement in TWT ... 110
- 4.4 K16–23 ... 111
- 4.5 K24–30 ... 114
- 4.6 Conclusions on K's editorial work and his sources ... 115

4.7	The date and provenance of K	116
4.7.1	Harnack's dating of K	116
4.7.1.1	The division of the regulations among the apostles	117
4.7.1.2	The clerical degrees are formed according to the type of heavenly things	117
4.7.1.3	The appointment of the presbyters	117
4.7.1.4	The offering of the Body and Blood	118
4.7.1.5	The nature of the use of D	118
4.7.2	Conclusions on the date of K	118
4.7.3	The provenance of K	120

5. K among the church orders ... 122
    5.1   The apostolic attribution of K ... 122
    5.2   K and the Didascalia ... 124
    5.3   K and Testamentum Domini ... 130

6. Conclusion ... 132

Text, Textual Commentary, and Annotated Translation ... 134

Appendices ... 176
    Appendix 1: The text of E ... 177
    Appendix 2: K14 with parallel B material ... 184
    Appendix 3: A synoptic arrangement of TWT in D, K, E and B ... 185

Bibliography ... 199

Indices ... 206

Abbreviations

Beyond standard abbreviations, the following are employed:

B	Epistula Barnabae
β	An hypothetical source for B, derived from TWT
D	The Didache
δ	An hypothetical source for D, derived from TWT
E	The Epitome of apostolic commands (a derivative, it is argued, of κ)
K	Apostolic church order (apostolische Kirchenordnung)
κ	A hypothetical source for K derived from TWT
κκ	A hypothetical source for K, containing church order material
L	The Doctrina apostolorum
TWT	The two ways tradition

See also the abbreviation list preceding the text and textual commentary.

Introduction

The Apostolic Church Order

This church order was first published in Greek in 1843 by Bickell under the name of *Die apostolische Kirchenordnung*.[1] Although it has received a variety of names, that given by Bickell is as good as any, and is employed here in its accepted English translation. This is abbreviated to K, for *Kirchenordnung*, following Schermann, whose system of abbreviation is largely followed.[2]

Although several editions were published in the nineteenth century, K was eclipsed in scholarly attention by the discovery of the *Didache*.[3] It was in his monograph on the *Didache* that Harnack determined that K was a late and secondary work,[4] the product of Egypt in the fourth century and, although he recognized that ancient sources lay behind the church order, it is his conclusion on date and provenance which is remembered. Harnack's work thus concluded the process of investigation, and ushered in the virtual end of the serious study of K.

Although Harnack's conclusion that K was a late and secondary work is that which is remembered, Harnack did make some effort to determine the redactional history of the church-order and to determine older sources which lay behind it. Since we may now see church-orders as "living literature" we may study both

---

1   In his *Geschichte des Kirchenrechts* I. This was the first edition of the Greek text, though the Ethiopic version was published with a Latin translation by J. Ludolfus (Leutholf) in his *Commentarius*, 304–314.
2   Schermann, *Elfapostelmoral*.
3   For further introductory comments regarding the discussion before Harnack, see Harnack, *Lehre*, 193–209, and Steimer, *Vertex Traditionis*, 60–63. However, particular mention must be given to Krawutzcky, "Altkirchliche Unterrichtsbuch", 359–445, to which Harnack was particularly indebted.
4   Harnack, *Lehre*.

the sources and the manner of their redaction in evaluating the historical value of the work and so give attention once again to the ancient sources lying behind the work, as well as revisiting Harnack's conclusions. Such is the purpose of this introduction.

The work is clearly composite. After an epistolary opening describing the gathering of the apostles there follows an ethical section consisting of the two-ways material, similar to that found in the *Didache*, in which different sections of the material are attributed to different apostles. After this there is a section concerning ministries, beginning with directions for the election of a bishop, and then a discussion of the ministries of women, which follows dialogically from the discussion of ministries more generally. Lemoine thus sees the work built up of different sections, and suggests that the work was extended in sections in different centuries, the first being the dialogical construction of the two ways in the second century, the second the discussion of ministries and the elaboration of a threefold order which excludes women (in the third) and finally the redaction of the introductory material later in the third century.[5] Frankly this is too simple; within the sections there are signs of expansion and the composite nature of the completed work indicates that the sections had independent life before their redactional juncture. The starting point for the discussion is therefore that of Harnack, who assumes that the document was built up redactionally from distinct and ancient sources and who went on to reconstruct and to discuss these sources.

Harnack determined that there were three main sources employed by the redactor, a document of the two-ways type, which he first identified as the *Didache*,[6] and subsequently as a

---

5 Lemoine, "Étude". This conclusion is provisionally stated at 12, and subsequently elaborated.
6 *Lehre*, 210-211.

prior edition of the two-ways material used by the didachist,[7] and two ancient sources on office and ordination. Beyond that he suggested that the redactor had an apostle list of some antiquity and the *Epistle of Barnabas*, which he employed in the construction of the two-ways section of K.[8] Although we will discover some differences with Harnack, his discussion provides a useful starting point. However, in determining the complex redactional history of K we may well begin with the two-ways material, in that there are other versions of the material which, once the order of relationships is established, can be employed as comparative material which enables us to discern the hand of various redactors.

1. The two-ways section

The first section of K is taken up with the ethical discourse which is known as the two-ways tradition (henceforth TWT). This same discourse is also found in the *Didache* (henceforth D), in a Latin translation known as the *Doctrina apostolorum* (henceforth L) and in the *Epistle of Barnabas* (henceforth B). The origin of this discourse in Jewish ethical discourse is widely recognized. Thus, as examples, we may observe *Testament of Levi* 19: "Choose for yourself light or darkness", and the statement of ethical dualism which states the existence of two ways which God has granted at *Testament of Asher* 1.[9] Most pressing of the parallels, however, is that noted by Audet between the Christian TWT and that of the Qumran *Community rule*.[10] The TWT material of K thus has a long ancestry; our concern here is less the origin of the material, or its subsequent spread, but its history as far as K is concerned.

---

7 Harnack, *Sources*, 1.
8 *Lehre*, 210–215.
9 Note the discussions of Niederwimmer *Didache*, 57–58, 84–87; Rordorf and Tuilier, *La doctrine*, 24; van de Sandt and Flusser, *Didache*, 57–58.
10 Audet, "Affinités".

1.1 The two ways section of K and E

As already noted, TWT material is found in D and B as well as in K. The first issue, therefore, which this section of K throws up is the literary relationships obtaining between these various versions. Before this set of relationships can be discussed, however, it is necessary to determine the relationship between K itself and a further version which is found in three MSS and which describes itself as the epitome of the rules of the apostles (E).[11] This is the closest version of TWT to K, in that the material is divided in the same way between the same eleven apostles. As Wengst points out, a literary relationship is evident not simply in that both contain the way of life divided among the same eleven apostles in the same manner, but in view of their agreements against D.[12] Among them we may note:

D: ἡ μὲν οὖν ὁδὸς τῆς ζωῆς ἐστιν αὕτη· πρῶτον ἀγαπήσεις τὸν θεὸν τὸν ποιήσαντά σε...

K: ἡ μὲν οὖν ὁδὸς τῆς ζωῆς ἐστιν αὕτη· πρῶτον ἀγαπήσεις τὸν θεὸν τὸν ποιήσαντά σε **ἐξ ὅλης τῆς καρδίας** σου...

E: η οὖν τῆς ζωῆς ἐστιν αὕτη· πρῶτον ἀγαπήσεις τὸν θεὸν τὸν ποιήσαντά σε **ἐξ ὅλης τῆς καρδίας**

---

11 ἐπιτομὴ ὅρων τῶν ἁγίων ἀποστόλων.
12 Wengst, *Schriften*, 7–8.

οὐ ποιήσεις σχίσμα, εἰρηνεύσεις δὲ μαχομένους, κρινεῖς δικαίως, οὐ λήψῃ πρόσωπον ἐλέγξαι ἐπὶ παραπτώμασιν.	οὐ ποιήσεις σχίσματα, εἰρηνεύσεις δὲ μαχομένους, κρινεῖς δικαίως, οὐ λήψῃ πρόσωπον ἐλέγξαι **τινὰ** ἁμαρτόντα ἐπὶ **παραπτώματι**, οὐ γὰρ ἰσχύει πλοῦτος παρὰ κυρίῳ· οὐ γὰρ ἀξία προσκρίνει οὐδὲ κάλλος ὠφελεῖ, ἀλλ᾽ **ἰσότης ἐστι** πάντων **παρ᾽ αὐτῷ**	οὐ ποιήσεις σχίσμα, εἰρηνεύσεις δὲ μαχομένους, κρινεῖς δικαίως, οὐ λήψῃ πρόσωπον ἐλέγξαι **τινὰ** ἐπὶ **παραπτώματι**, **ἰσότης** γὰρ **ἐστι παρὰ** θεῷ

Whereas Harnack suggested that E was an abbreviation of K,[13] Schermann argued that E was not derived from K but actually a source of K, interpreting the title, namely ἐπιτομὴ ὅρων τῶν ἁγίων ἀποστόλων καθολικῆς παραδόσεως, as stating that E was a compendium of apostolic teaching, rather than an abbreviation of the apostolic canons (namely K).[14] Further to this he points out that the apostle lists of E and K are different, in that K includes Jude the son of James, who is added to this list in order to make up the number of twelve, whereas there is no part for him in the two-ways material. He therefore suggests that the list of eleven apostles to whom the material is attributed is the more original, as one would expect a later correction to make twelve.[15] The list preceding K must therefore be secondary, and on this basis he suggested that E was one of the sources of K.

There are certain factors which speak in favour of seeing E as a source of K. For instance there are several points at which K is more extensive in its treatment than the corresponding point in E, and this might be seen as an expansion of an earlier source; in this light Wengst suggests that such material, had it been avail-

---

13 Lehre, 204.
14 Schermann, Elfapostelmoral, 19–20.
15 Schermann, Elfapostelmoral, 21–22.

able to E, would not have been omitted.[16] Although this is possible, it is not a secure argument; if E is seen as an abbreviation there is no reason why the omission of this secondary material might not be seen as part of the abbreviating technique. Wengst further argues that at several points when K follows D, E appears to preserve a more original reading.[17] As an example we may take:

D: ὁδοὶ δύο εἰσί, μία τῆς ζωῆς καὶ μία τοῦ θανάτου, διαφορὰ δὲ πολλὴ μεταξὺ τῶν δύο ὁδῶν.

K: ὁδοὶ δύο εἰσί, μία τῆς ζωῆς καὶ μία τοῦ θανάτου, διαφορὰ δὲ πολλὴ μεταξὺ τῶν δύο ὁδῶν.

E: ὁδοὶ δύο εἰσί, μία τῆς ζωῆς καὶ μία τοῦ θανάτου, καὶ διαφορὰ πολλὴ μεταξὺ τῶν δύο

With this one exception, however, all of Wengst's more original readings are absences from E of material which is in D, which, once again, may be seen as the result of the process of abbreviation. However, the concluding speech, that of Bartholomew, which in E is a *Haustafel* parallel to D, is entirely different in K, which has a concluding eschatological exhortation with a close relationship to B. The text of this eschatological conclusion is shown at Appendix 2 in a synoptic arrangement with the parallel B material.

Given the significant departure here then, were E derived from K, as Harnack and the majority of scholars have assumed, then it would have to be assumed that E had determined to leave K at this point and to follow D, which seems improbable given the otherwise close reliance on K. If E is directly dependent upon D, however, and K, in turn, on E, then there is no difficulty in accepting that K, which expands material elsewhere, has determined at this point to follow another source. This may be classed as a major agreement of D and E against K. There are, moreover,

---

16 Wengst, *Schriften*, 8.
17 Wengst, *Schriften*, 9.

other minor agreements of D and E against K, which would suggest that E, and not K, is the document directly derived from D, and that K is derived from E.
First is that occurring in Nathanael's speech:

D: οὐχ ὑψώσεις σεαυτὸν οὐδὲ δώσεις τῇ ψυχῇ σου **θράσος. οὐ κολληθήσεται** ἡ ψυχή σου μετὰ ὑψηλῶν, ἀλλὰ μετὰ δικαίων καὶ ταπεινῶν ἀναστραφήσῃ.

K: οὐχ ὑψώσεις σεαυτὸν, οὐδὲ δώσεις τῇ ψυχῇ σου μετὰ ὑψηλῶν, ἀλλὰ μετὰ δικαίων καὶ ταπεινῶν ἀναστραφήσῃ.

E: οὐχ ὑψώσεις σεαυτὸν οὐ δώσεις τῇ ψυχῇ σου **θράσος**, οὐδὲ **κολληθήσῃ** τῇ ψυχῇ σου μετὰ ὑψηλῶν ἀλλὰ μετὰ δικαίων καὶ ταπεινῶν

Here E is here much closer to D than to K; against K, D and E both contain the statement οὐ(δὲ) δώσεις τῇ ψυχῇ σου θράσος and include forms of the verb κολλάω.
In Thomas' speech we read:

D: μνησθήσῃ **νυκτὸς καὶ ἡμέρας,** τιμήσεις **δὲ** αὐτὸν ὡς κύριον·

K: μνησθήσῃ αὐτοῦ νύκτα καὶ ἡμέραν, τιμήσεις αὐτὸν ὡς τὸν κύριον.

E: μνησθήσῃ **νυκτὸς καὶ ἡμέρας,** τιμήσεις **δὲ** αὐτὸν ὡς κύριον·

D and E have νυκτὸς καὶ ἡμέρας, as opposed to K's νύκτα καὶ ἡμέραν, and both, moreover, contain the statement τιμήσεις δὲ αὐτὸν ὡς κύριον· as opposed to K's τιμήσεις αὐτὸν ὡς τὸν κύριον.
Next, close to the beginning of TWT, we may note:

D: ἡ μὲν **οὖν** τῆς ζωῆς ἐστιν αὕτη

K: ἡ μὲν γὰρ ὁδὸς τῆς ζωῆς ἐστιν αὕτη

E: ἡ **οὖν** τῆς ζωῆς ἐστιν αὕτη

οὖν is present in D and E, but not K. Harnack and Schermann, however, read οὖν here, without MS evidence for K and against the versions.[18] Part of the problem with assessing the extent of agreement between K, D and E is the problem of text, and the extent to which E should be counted as a textual witness for K. Another is thus less textually secure:

| D: **δεύτερον** τὸν πλησίον σου ὡς σεαυτόν | K: δευτέρα δέ· ἀγαπήσεις τὸν πλησίον σου ὡς ἑαυτόν | E: **δεύτερον** ἀγαπήσεις τὸν πλησίον σου ὡς ἑαυτόν |

Although the text is not secure, again it seems that editors wishing to read δεύτερον, against the δευτέρα of the MSS,[19] are attempting to conform K to D and E.

Finally we may note in Kephas' speech:

D: οὐ ποιήσεις σχίσμα   K: οὐ ποιήσεις **σχίσματα**   E: οὐ ποιήσεις σχίσμα

Against these minor agreements, however, must be set the many agreements both of E and K against D and D and K against E, which imply that K, and not E, is the middle term. As an example we may take Nathanael's speech in which minor agreements of D and E against K occur: words appearing in boldface are instances where K agrees with D or E against the other. Clearly these vastly outnumber the minor agreements; in addition there are several omissions of words in K, where a word appears either in D or in E but not in both; these are likewise agreements in which K is the middle term, though they cannot readily be marked as such.

---

18   See the textual commentary ad loc.
19   See the textual commentary ad loc.

D	K	E
τέκνον μου, μὴ γίνου ψεύστης, ἐπειδὴ ὁδηγεῖ τὸ ψεῦσμα εἰς τὴν κλοπήν, μηδὲ φιλάργυρος μηδὲ κενόδοξος· ἐκ γὰρ τούτων ἁπάντων κλοπαὶ γεννῶνται.	**τέκνον μου,** μὴ γίνου ψεύστης, **ἐπειδὴ ὁδηγεῖ τὸ ψεῦσμα ἐπὶ τὴν κλοπήν,** μηδὲ φιλάργυρος, μηδὲ κενόδοξος: ἐκ τούτων ἁπάντων κλοπαὶ **γεννῶνται.**	μὴ γίνου ψεύστης, μηδὲ φιλάργυρος, μηδὲ κενόδοξος: ἐκ τούτων ἁπάντων κλοπαὶ γίνονται
τέκνον μου, μὴ γίνου γόγγυσος, ἐπειδὴ ὁδηγεῖ εἰς τὴν βλασφημίαν, μηδὲ αὐθάδης μηδὲ πονηρόφρων· ἐκ γὰρ τούτων ἁπάντων βλασφημίαι γεννῶνται.	**τέκνον μου,** μὴ γίνου γόγγυσος, **ἐπειδὴ** ἄγει **πρὸς τὴν βλασφημίαν, μηδὲ** αὐθάδης, **μηδὲ** πονηρόφρων: ἐκ γὰρ τούτων ἁπάντων βλασφημίαι **γεννῶνται.**	μὴ γίνου γόγγυσος, μὴ θυμώδης, μὴ αὐθάδης, μήτε πονηρόφρων· ἐκ γὰρ τούτων ἁπάντων βλασφημίαι γίνονται.
ἴσθι δὲ πραΰς, ἐπεὶ οἱ πραεῖς κληρονομήσουσιν τὴν γῆν.	ἴσθι δὲ πραΰς, **ἐπειδὴ** πραεῖς κληρονομήσουσι τὴν **βασιλείαν** τῶν οὐρανῶν.	ἴσθι δὲ πραΰς, ἐπειδὴ πραεῖς κληρονομήσουσι τὴν βασιλείαν τοῦ θεοῦ
γίνου μακρόθυμος καὶ ἐλεήμων	γίνου μακρόθυμος, ἐλεήμων, **εἰρηνοποιός, καθαρὸς τῇ καρδίᾳ** ἀπὸ παντὸς κακοῦ,	γίνου μακρόθυμος, ἐλεήμων, εἰρηνοποιός, καθαρὸς τὴν καρδίαν,
καὶ ἄκακος καὶ ἡσύχιος καὶ ἀγαθὸς καὶ τρέμων τοὺς λόγους διὰ παντός, οὓς ἤκουσας. οὐχ ὑψώσεις σεαυτὸν οὐδὲ δώσεις τῇ ψυχῇ σου θράσος. οὐ κολληθήσεται ἡ ψυχή σου μετὰ ὑψηλῶν, ἀλλὰ μετὰ δικαίων καὶ ταπεινῶν ἀναστραφήσῃ. τὰ συμβαίνοντά σοι ἐνεργήματα ὡς ἀγαθὰ προσδέξῃ, εἰδὼς ὅτι ἄτερ θεοῦ οὐδὲν γίνεται.	ἄκακος **καὶ** ἡσύχιος, ἀγαθὸς **καὶ φυλάσσων** καὶ τρέμων τοὺς λόγους **οὓς ἤκουσας.** οὐχ ὑψώσεις σεαυτόν, οὐδὲ δώσεις τὴν ψυχήν σου μετὰ ὑψηλῶν ἀλλὰ μετὰ δικαίων καὶ ταπεινῶν **ἀναστραφήσῃ.** τὰ δὲ συμβαίνοντά σοι ἐνεργήματα ὡς ἀγαθα προσδέξῃ, εἰδὼς ὅτι ἄτερ θεοῦ οὐδὲν γίνεται.	ἄκακος, ἥσυχος, ἀγαθὸς, φυλάσσων καὶ τρέμων τοὺς λόγους τοῦ θεοῦ. οὐχ ὑψώσεις σεαυτὸν οὐ δώσεις τῇ ψυχῇ σου θράσος, οὐδε κολληθήσῃ τῇ ψυχῇ σου μετὰ ὑψηλῶν, ἀλλὰ μετὰ δικαίων καὶ ταπεινῶν. τὰ συμβαίνοντά σοι ἐνεργήματα ὡς ἀγαθὰ προσδέξῃ, εἰδὼς ὅτι ἄτερ θεοῦ οὐδὲν γίνεται.

Schermann explains K as a middle term by suggesting that E is an independent derivative from TWT, independent, that is, from D. But in this case he has to explain the absence of so much TWT material from E. Because of the presence in K of the material which is absent from E, he has to assume that D, as well as E, is a source of K, thus making K the middle term in the way that Mark is the middle term in the Griesbach hypothesis.

There are, moreover, several points at which K and D agree against E, where K/D clearly preserve the more original reading. For Wengst this is compelling evidence that E is not the immediate source of K. These are as follow:

D: ὅθεν γὰρ ἡ κυριότης λαλεῖται, ἐκεῖ κύριός ἐστιν.	K: ὅθεν γὰρ ἡ κυριότης λαλεῖται, ἐκεῖ κύριός ἐστιν.	E: ὅθεν γὰρ Ἰησοῦς Χριστὸς λαλεῖται, ἐκεῖ κύριός ἐστιν.
ἐὰν ἔχῃς **διὰ** τῶν χειρῶν σου, **δώσεις λύτρωσιν** ἁμαρτιῶν σου.	ἐὰν ἔχῃς **διὰ** τῶν χειρῶν σου, **δώσεις λύτρωσιν** τῶν ἁμαρτιῶν σου.	ἐὰν ἔσται ἔχειν σε ἀπὸ τῶν χειρῶν σου, δὸς εἰς ἄφεσιν ἁμαρτιῶν σου.
...οὐ φονεύσεις, οὐ μοιχεύσεις, οὐ παιδοφθορήσεις, οὐ πορνεύσεις, οὐ κλέψεις, οὐ μαγεύσεις, οὐ φαρμακεύσεις, οὐ φονεύσεις τέκνον ἐν φθορᾷ,...	οὐ φονεύσεις, ου μοιχεύσεις, οὐ πορνεύσεις, οὐ παιδοφθορήσεις, οὐ κλέψεις, οὐ μαγεύσεις, ου φαρμακεύσεις, οὐ φονεύσεις τέκνον ἐν φθορᾷ...	...οὐ φονεύσεις, οὐ ποιήσεις ἁμαρτίαν τινὰ τῇ σαρκί σου, οὐ κλέψεις, οὐ μαγεύσεις, ου φαρμακεύσεις...

Wengst suggests that it is possible that D was the basis of the appearance of these phrases in K; but rightly notes that, if K is following E, it would be hard to explain a sudden reversion to D.[20]

Finally, and perhaps most critically, if E is an independent

---

20 Wengst, *Schriften*, 9.

document, as Schermann's theory must suppose, then the rationale for the apostolic speeches is entirely absent, for as it stands E makes no sense. Were K the source of E then E can be seen as an abbreviation of K, in which the apostolic speeches are part of an organized fiction by which the apostles are directing the church, but a presentation of the two-ways material shared out between apostles, with no prior account of a meeting of the apostles, is inconceivable. Thus E is not a source of K, as it is unlikely ever to have been a freestanding document; rather it is a summary abbreviation.

However the problems posed by the final chapter, by the expansion of the apostle list in K, and by the minor agreements, remain. If E is derived from K, then E must have turned to D for the final section. If we reject the simultaneous redaction of two documents by K we must do the same for E.

This impasse may be solved by suggesting that E does not derive from K as it stands, but must derive from an earlier recension of K, which we may call κ. A similar suggestion is made by Wengst, though on different grounds,[21] and Niederwimmer likewise describes the relationship between K and E as dependent upon a common original.[22] The alternative explanation is that E is an abbreviation of K, but that it is in some way contaminated through the memory, or through the oral transmission, of TWT closer to D than to K. This, however, still does not explain the final chapter of E, with the replacement of K's eschatological conclusion with the *Haustafel* found in D. Although the existence of κ is inevitably hypothetical, there is some evidence that such a recension of TWT existed as Rufinus refers to a work which he calls "duae viae vel iudicium Petri."[23] Neither K nor E

---

21 Wengst, *Schriften*, 10.
22 Niederwimmer, *Didache*, 63. See 1.2.2.2 below for further discussion of Niederwimmer's genealogy of TWT.
23 Rufinus *Expositiones in symbol. apost.* 38.

can be called *duae viae* as only one way is described in each, but the inclusion of Peter's name indicates that some apostolic attribution was made, which excludes any other version of TWT beyond the branch represented by K and E; thus a document attributing elements of the TWT to different apostles which is not presently extant must have existed. This may well have been κ. We may explain the title in E, moreover, by suggesting that κ was headed as ὅροι τῶν ἁγίων ἀποστόλων.

If we accept the possibility of a κ-redaction, then we may suggest that κ contained a final chapter close to that of D, which K has altered. The same explanation may be used to account for the minor agreements noted above. For instance, whereas there is no obvious reason why K should choose to recast the speech in the mouth of Nathanael, it may readily be seen as a recasting, and the minor agreements attributed to such an editorial process. In support of this we may note that the phrase οὐ δώσεις τῇ ψυχῇ σου θράσος, which was recast in K but is intact in D and E, also appears in B, and therefore stood somewhere in TWT; thus the recasting of the phrase must be the work of K. The minor agreement noted above in Thomas' speech, in which the article is included, may be read as a strengthening of the precept, in that the teacher is not to be obeyed simply as a master but as the Lord, in the context of a strong statement concerning the place of leadership in the church, which may be assigned, as will be argued in more detail below, to the K redactor. Finally we may readily see that, as Schermann suspected, the list of twelve apostles is secondary and does not belong to the speeches by eleven of them, but that K has made the list of eleven into a list of twelve.

There are thus two possible explanations of the relationship of K and E.

That of Schermann is as follows:

Diagram 1

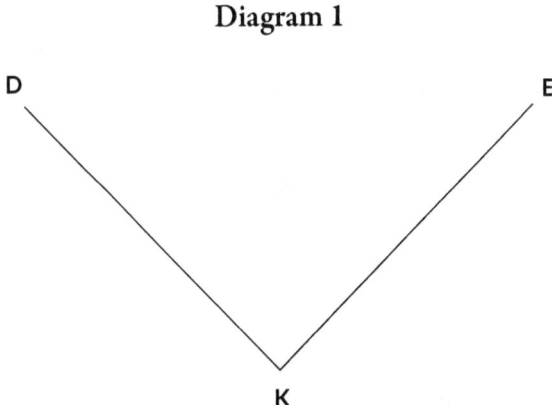

Whereas this is possible, it is difficult to envisage, in part because it assumes a complex redactional effort by K, and in part because the independent existence of E is unlikely; it makes no sense as a document.

The relationship suggested instead is:

Diagram 2

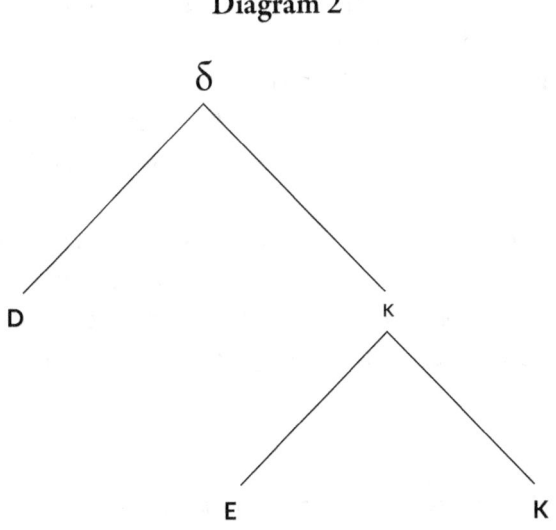

Here δ signifies not the extant D but the version of the two ways which was incorporated into D. The rationale for this will transpire below.

Although we have argued against his reconstruction, we should nonetheless note the suggestion of Wengst.[24]

Diagram 3

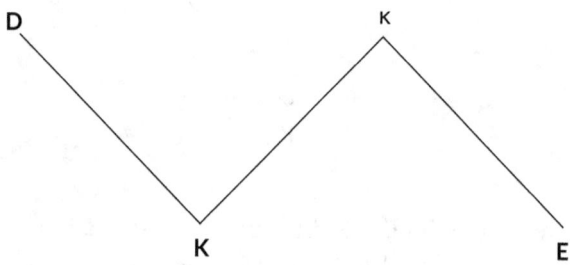

Although this is conceivable, it assumes a complex redactional task on the part of K which is unnecessary if we postulate a reception of the δ tradition. It does not, moreover, explain the presence of B parallels in K, to which we will turn presently, and assumes a proximity of κ to E.[25] One of the objections to the priority of E was that it would make no sense as a document in itself as it gives no rationale to the apostolic attribution of the commandments; the list should stand independently of the attribution of different speeches. The same objection must be raised to any view of κ as proximate to E in this regard.

What positively has been gained is that when there is disagreement between E and K in content it is possible to see that E is reflecting κ more closely than K; where there is agreement, then we can be assured that this material was present in κ. The

---

24 Wengst, *Schriften*, 22.
25 As is explicitly stated by Wengst at *Schriften*, 10.

text of E may be found in Appendix 3, in a synoptic arrangement with D and K, as well as B.

If E is a summary of κ, we may also note the existence of other "epitomae" of the material, namely those contained in a Codex from Moscow (Mosq.)[26] and as part of a collection of texts in a codex from Mount Athos (A).[27] A is much reduced, but contains no significant material which is not in K. There are some minor additions, for instance the addition of κύριον in the first commandment, and minor deviations, such as the rearrangement of the statement regarding the law and prophets, as may be noted from the table below. These may be attributed to citation from scribal memory. As such we cannot say whether A is a derivation of κ or of K, and so it is hard to assess its value as a witness to K.

K: Ἰωάννης εἶπεν· ὁδοὶ δύο εἰσί, μία τῆς ζωῆς καὶ μία τοῦ θανάτου, διαφορὰ δὲ πολλὴ μεταξὺ τῶν δύο ὁδῶν. ἡ μὲν γὰρ ὁδὸς τῆς ζωῆς ἐστιν αὕτη· πρῶτον ἀγαπήσεις τὸν θεὸν τὸν ποιήσαντά σε ἐξ ὅλης τῆς καρδίας σου καὶ δοξάσεις τὸν λυτρωσάμενόν σε ἐκ θανάτου, ἥτις ἐστὶν ἐντολὴ πρώτη. δευτέρα δέ· ἀγαπήσεις τὸν πλησίον σου ὡς ἑαυτόν, ἥτις ἐστὶν ἐντολὴ δευτέρα, ἐν οἷς ὅλος ὁ νόμος κρέμαται καὶ προφῆται.

A: Ἰωάννης εἶπεν ὁδοὶ δύο εἰσὶν, μία τῆς ζωῆς καὶ μία τοῦ θανάτου. καὶ ἡ μὲν τῆς ζωῆς ὁδὸς ἐστὶν, πρῶτον ἀγαπήσεις κύριον τὸν θεόν σου ἐξ ὅλης τῆς καρδίας σου, καὶ δοξάσεις αὐτὸν τὸν λυτρωσάμενόν σε ἐκ θανάτου, ἥτις ἐστὶν ἐντολὴ πρώτη. δευτέρα δὲ ἐντολὴ ἐστὶν, ἀγαπήσεις τὸν πλησίον σου ὡς ἑαυτόν, ἐν οἷς ὅλος ὁ νόμος καὶ οἱ προφῆται κρέμανται.

26 Codex Mosquensis 125 (ed. Gebhardt et al.), XXIX-XXXI.
27 Athous, Koutloumousiou 39 f. 79va, l. 16-79vb, l. 3 (ed. Lincicum).

Turning to Mosq., we may observe that the Bartholomew material (the eschatological conclusion found in K but not in E) is found herein, albeit out of sequence. This is a clear indication that this scribe was working from K, and not from κ. As such it is a better textual witness to K than E, though the extent of its abbreviation reduces its value. It has further peculiarities; the Bartholomew material appears after Simon, instead of that assigned to Nathanael, which is missing, and Peter appears twice, once with the same speech assigned to him in K/E, and again taking the material which the other versions assign to Kephas. This indicates some attempt on the part of the editor to correct the list of apostles found in the original, identifying Peter and Kephas, and combining Nathanael with Bartholomew. Moreover, it does not contain any significant material not found in K; the largest divergence is in the Peter/Kephas speech, where οὐ ποιήσεις σχίσμα(τα) (K and E) is recast as οὐ ποιήσεις συνάψαι τινὰ μάχην πρὸς ἕτερον.

We cannot know the reason why this material was epitomized three times; possibly it was a school exercise, which might give some indication of its continued use in catechesis. The material is to be found in a synoptic format in Appendix 1; readers may reach their own conclusions.

1.2 The relationship between K, D, and B

Using K, rather than E, as the base, we can now go on to explore the relationship of K with the other documents containing the two-ways tradition. In this introduction we are solely concerned with K, rather than the whole history of TWT, and will in particular not give consideration to the precise relationship between L and D. It is quite possible that L reflects δ very closely,[28] but in that case need not detain us further.

---

28 So Goodspeed, "Didache," 228–237; Van de Sandt and Flusser, *Didache*, 61–63; Hennecke, "Grundschrift".

A synoptic arrangement of D, K, E, and B is found at Appendix 3. A glance at this synopsis reveals the following salient features:

1. There is material in D which does not appear in any other version.
2. B is entirely independent of the other three documents, as the order of material is entirely different, whereas D and K, whatever their other divergences, contain substantially the same material, and this material is arranged in the same order in both documents. There is, moreover, a large block of material in both D and K which is not present in B.
3. As already noted, there is a significant diversion between K and D (and E) at the conclusion of the two-ways material; an eschatological conclusion is found instead of the *Haustafel*.
4. There is substantial material in K which does not appear in the other versions.

We must explore the implications of each of these features in turn.

1.2.1 The additional material in D

As has been observed there is a substantial section of D which does not appear in K or B. This means either that D has inserted this into its source, or that the other versions have consciously omitted it. Harnack at first believed that this material was deliberately omitted by K, but subsequently changed his mind. The overwhelming consensus, given the absence of this material in L, is that this is an insertion in the tradition,[29] which means that K

---

29 According to Funk, *Doctrina*, XXIX. Massebieau was first to suggest this, in *Revue d'Histoire des religions* 1884, 168. It could be seen as the consensus by Harnack, *Apostellehre*, 26, by 1886! More recently see van de Sandt and Flusser, *Didache*, 62.

(and L) are not directly dependent on D but on an earlier version of the material which was subsequently redacted by the didachist.[30] This we have labelled δ.

1.2.2 The relationship between B and D

As has already been suggested, K is in a literary relationship with D, but on the basis of the different order of material, B is not in the same relationship. On the basis of its order, B is

i. a deliberate re-arrangement of the TWT as received by D, or
ii. the form of TWT as received by D, which D has reordered, or
iii. a different and independent form of TWT.

We consider each of these possibilities in turn.

1.2.2.1 B as reordering of D

That B is a reordering of D was suggested by Goodspeed, and has received recent support from van de Sandt and Flusser, as well as being cautiously suggested by Draper.

Goodspeed's argument centres on seeing B as an improvement on D. In observing the omission of material in B he suggests:

> ...a closer examination of Barnabas' great omission... shows that much of it—murder, lust, enchantment, magic, lying, avarice, grumbling,—are covered elsewhere in Barnabas... mostly in *positive* command, adjusted to a loftier plane of Christian living.... Anger, murder, enchantment, magic and grumbling are covered either generally or specifically in Barn. 19:3–11. It is a mistake to suppose Didache superior to Barnabas in its presentation of the Two Ways material; Didache is in fact inferior, for it contains some repetitions which Barnabas strips off... Moreover Barnabas

---

30   Van de Sandt and Flusser, *Didache*, 65.

presents not so much vices to be shunned as virtues to be cultivated... The average Christian then as now does not so much need to be told not to murder... as to be kind, generous, pure and true.[31]

Attractive as this argument is, it does not really hold up. If this is B's plan it not consistently applied, for not only does B positively assert that Christians are not to fornicate, but many of the D passages which do not appear in B are warnings that lesser foibles may turn to greater sins.

Whereas Goodspeed's argument is based on seeing B as an improvement on D, the argument of van de Sandt and Flusser derives from a view of B as inferior! Their argument is the essentially negative one that it is hard to imagine how the ordered form of D (and L, which they see as an even more primitive form of TWT than D) might emerge from B. B is "chaotic", and so the ordered form of paraenesis in D can hardly have been created by unravelling the form in B.[32] In answer we might say that, if D is such a reasonable and rational presentation, it is even harder to see why B should wish to confuse it.

Something of an answer to this is offered by Draper, who suggests that B is a hostile witness to D, and that B is an ironic presentation of the catechetical material of the D community. D is essentially still Jewish Christian, whereas B is virulently anti-Jewish.[33] However, even if this were demonstrable,[34] it would explain only why the TWT is relegated to an appendix in B, but would not explain the distinct order of presentation.

However, an interesting point in Draper's study, which will

---

31 Goodspeed, "Didache", 235-236.
32 Van de Sandt and Flusser, *Didache*, 60.
33 Draper, "Barnabas".
34 For a brief critique of Draper, which suggests that Draper does not demonstrate what he has set out to prove, see Carleton Paget, *Barnabas*, 50-51. Bestmann, *Geschichte*, 136-153, suggested, on similar lines to Draper, that B is a gentile response to the Jewish Christian D.

prove pertinent to the use of TWT by K, is the suggestion that TWT is transformed by B from a baptismal catechesis to advanced teaching. That D uses TWT as baptismal catechesis is confirmed by the instruction to baptize following the presentation of TWT, but B presents this teaching as for the advanced. To an extent it might be suggested that literary documents present material only to those who are literate and, moreover, that D is also addressed to those who are advanced, in that it is addressed to those who are to undertake the baptism of those who are catechized using TWT. But it remains the case that this material, albeit mediated, is addressed to catechumens, whereas B presents this material as additional to the substantive teaching which has already been given. So, in comparison to K, we may note that there is a difference in the address of the eschatological conclusion which in K is addressed to "brothers" but in B is addressed to those in positions of leadership—though, of course, this begs the question of the addressees of K.

This may be an indication that B has removed the material from its catechetical frame, as Draper suggested. There may, moreover, be some truth in Draper's contention that this relates to the divergent attitudes of D and B towards Judaism, but this is not germane to the present study. What is germane is that there is no proof here that B reorders D, as even if there is a relationship, the reordering of the material is not what distinguishes the uses to which it is put.

Critical for anyone wishing to argue for B as a rearrangement of D is the "great omission" to which Goodspeed refers. Kraft and Niederwimmer explain the presence of material which is present in both D and K but not B, namely the *teknon* sayings, by suggesting that they were added as a group either by D or at an earlier level of redaction of D which we may term δ.[35] This means that,

---

35   Niederwimmer, *Didache*, 63; Kraft, *Apostolic fathers*, 146.

unless we were to postulate an even earlier version of δ, then we cannot know that the order found by B was anything like D. Van de Sandt and Flusser by contrast suggest that it is equally possible that B omitted the block;[36] this would in turn imply that the block was established as a block prior to δ in TWT, and requires anyone wishing to argue that B rearranged TWT material found in an order proximate to that of D to explain the rearrangement as a whole, including the deliberate omission of this block. What is particularly significant is the observation that the *teknon* group of sayings have clear proximity to teachings which emerge in later Jewish literature.[37] As such we may see these particular warnings as deriving from a particular strand in the development of TWT. Their demonstrably distinct literary ancestry indicate that Kraft and Niederwimmer were right, and that, given that the material that B "omitted" forms a discrete section in the developed TWT, its absence in B is an indication that B had received the tradition at an earlier, and distinct, stage of development.

In conclusion, therefore, it is hard to justify seeing B as a rearrangement of D, and more probable that B reflects TWT in a different transmission altogether.

1.2.2.2 D as reordering of TWT preserved by B

That D is a re-ordering of B was extensively argued in the twentieth century, but these arguments largely derived from the rather eccentric view that D was a late fiction, intended to create a primitive past to the apostolic church. We will not consider these arguments, based as they are upon a view of D which is entirely discredited, but should give serious consideration to the argu-

---

36 Van de Sandt and Flusser, *Didache*, 73-74. In view of the linkage between these sayings and Jewish tradition observed by Kraft, *Apostolic fathers*, 146, it is more likely than not that this material was part of TWT before its Christian adoption. Kraft, however, believes that the material was joined to the tradition before the β branch diverged.
37 So van de Sandt, "James 4,1-4".

ments of Niederwimmer. Niederwimmer does not actually argue that D is directly based on B, but places them both in a single stream of tradition, and suggests that B represents a more primitive stratum.

He diagrammatizes his hypothesis thus:[38]

Diagram 4

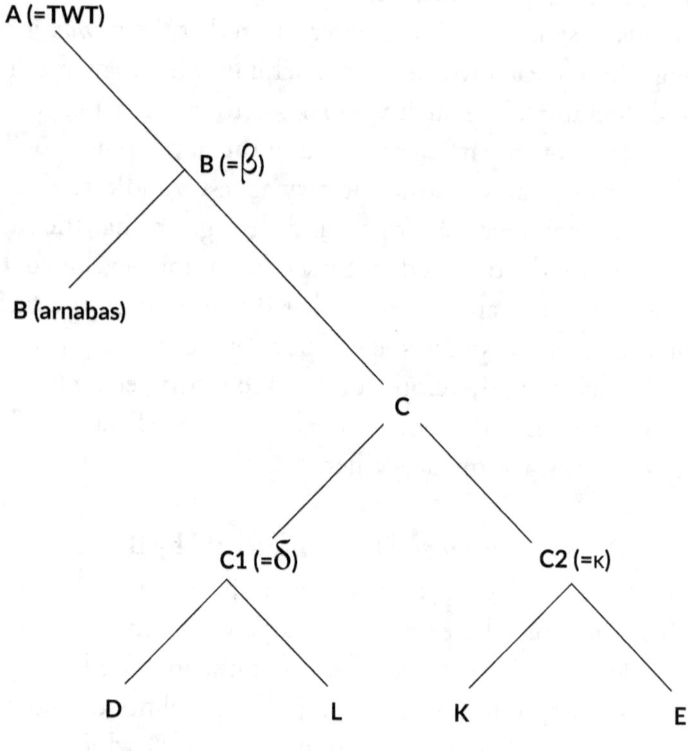

```
A (=TWT)
     \
      \
       B (=β)
      / \
     /   \
 B (arnabas)
           \
            C
           / \
          /   \
       C1 (=δ)   C2 (=κ)
        / \       / \
       D   L     K   E
```

At the earliest stage lies a loose collection of Jewish material. This material is lightly Christianized (β) and in this guise is a source of B. At this point the original eschatological conclusion is Christianized, and this Christianized eschatological conclusion

---

38 Diagram at Niederwimmer, *Didache*, 62.

appears in part in B21. He does suggest, however, that B uses this source very carelessly, and suggests that much of D had already attained a recognizable shape at this stage, which B disrupts. At the C stage the *teknon* sayings are added, as is the double-love commandment, which is absent in B and absent therefore in B's source (which we may label β). This version in turn forms the archetype for D and L, which drop the eschatological conclusion. C2, however, which is equivalent to our κ, retains it, for which reason it is found in K14.

There is much to commend Niederwimmer's reconstruction. He does not satisfactorily explain B's order, but this is not his concern, and neither is it ours. A minor criticism may, however, be levelled at Niederwimmer's treatment of the absence of the double-love commandment from B. Its form may suggest a Christianization of TWT, and so its absence in B may indeed point to a form of TWT closer to a Jewish original, as he suggests. Van de Sandt and Flusser, however, point out that the form of the commandment as found in D is not exactly synoptic, and is therefore not derived from the Gospels but from an independent tradition which, given that the linkage of love of God and neighbour is not exclusively Christian, might even be Jewish.[39] The absence of this commandment in B does not therefore necessarily mean that B is earlier, but is further evidence nonetheless for its independence.[40]

What is most critical however, for a study of K, is the fate of the eschatological conclusion; here we must part company entirely with Niederwimmer. Whereas Niederwimmer suggests that it was included at his C2 stage of development (roughly equivalent to κ) and was omitted by the C1 strand (roughly

---

39   Van de Sandt and Flusser, *Didache*, 73.
40   Butler, "The 'two ways' in the Didache", similarly suggests that TWT in B has undergone less Christianization than the version found in D, and therefore that B represents earlier tradition.

equivalent to δ), it cannot have been present in κ (=C2), because it is not in E. E, in common with δ, has the *Haustafel*, which K replaces with the eschatological conclusion, and so the *Haustafel* must have been present in κ, whereas the eschatological conclusion was not. Since the *Haustafel* is present in D in the same position as in κ/E whereas the eschatological conclusion is not, it is hardly likely that the conclusion was present in δ, for if it were we would have to assume that two redactors independently determined to omit identical material whilst otherwise following the same source closely. K must have the conclusion from elsewhere; the source of this we must determine at a later stage, but for the moment we must conclude that, as the *Haustafel* was present in κ, the eschatological conclusion was not, and since it was not in δ either, there is not the single stream of tradition which Niederwimmer perceives, but either that the eschatological conclusion dropped out early in the stream of tradition or that there are two streams. Otherwise, however, our conclusions concerning the relationship of K/E to D are in rough conformity with those of Niederwimmer. Niederwimmer's diagram is more complex than ours because he wishes to account for the presence of the eschatological conclusion in K whilst recognizing its relationship with D; when we realize that it had come to K from a separate source then the diagram can be simplified in the manner presented above. But since B contains the eschatological conclusion as well as the *Haustafel* it must be in a distinct strand. As such, β was not simply the TWT as received by δ, though it is fair to say that it is at least possible that δ has extensively reworked the tradition which may well have been closer to B (β) than to D in its original form.

1.2.2.3 D and B as independent variants of TWT

Since our concern is purely with K we need not be overlong detained on the details of the relationship of B and D; the study thus far has suggested that whereas they are each formed out of a loose compilation of positive and negative commands in a dualistic context which had existence in Judaism, they are not in a single stream of tradition but independent offshoots from TWT. We may accept this without commitment to any particular rationale for the difference in shape between B and δ.

However, the study has alerted us to the distinct use of TWT in B and D. Whereas D clearly employs TWT in catechesis, this is not the case in B. Niederwimmer therefore questions the common characterization of TWT as catechetical, suggesting instead (following Wengst), a school-setting.[41] This may be the setting for B, but B may, as Draper suggests, have altered the context of TWT through the inclusion of this traditional material into his discourse, and in particular by including it as an appendix. Niederwimmer's observation that ritual prescription is absent in the material, from which he concludes that it is unrelated to any liturgy of initiation, does nothing to support his argument, as, in keeping with the prescriptions of BT *Yebamoth* 47A–B, one would expect ritual prescription to *follow* the catechism, and therefore to have no place in the catechetical material itself. Rather, the independent forms of TWT in B and D imply that TWT need not be found within a catechetical frame. We may bear this in mind in examining K's use of the tradition. In particular we may be aware of the possibility that instruction continued after baptism; instruction in ritual is commonplace in later centuries, and, in the light of Jewish practice and in the light of D, which follows catechetical ethical instruction with instruction concerning the eucharist, this may be rooted in earlier practice. Thus if Hermas' *Mandates* are, as Henne has argued,[42] intended for a baptized audience, we may note that the first mandate begins with a basic article of faith, the oneness of God, which

---

41 Niederwimmer, *Didache*, 37–38.
42 Henne, *L'unité*.

one might expect in catechesis itself. In spite of its basic nature one may see this as part of post-baptismal paraenesis.

Such an insight, we may suggest, coheres with the most recent attempt to understand the appearance of TWT in B.[43] The case is made that the concluding chapters, summarizing the two ways, are more than simply an awkward appendix, and that TWT is part of the community's identity-formation. In particular it is suggested that this bolsters the author's identity as a figure of authority within the community. Certainly the case that the TWT suffuses the entire document is persuasive, and the suggestion that the Tradition contributes to the community's identity is attractive. Possibly, having dissuaded the community from the observance of the law, and in particular those elements of law-observance which serve as identity markers (such as the Sabbath and circumcision), the author has to employ the Two Ways as an identity marker setting out the positive directions which are to be followed in lieu of those which formerly took prominence and which mark out the Christian community as distinct. Such a use of TWT, moreover, takes it out of the catechetical ambit.

What is central to the case made here, most importantly, is the demonstration that the appearance of TWT within B is both literarily and socially independent of its appearance in D. As such we may see it circulating in distinct forms, and thus that it might exist in the K community in multiple forms and contexts.

1.2.3 The replacement of the Haustafel in K

In exploring the relationship between K and E it was observed above that the *Haustafel* which is replaced in K appears in E. From this, and from other considerations, it was deduced that K had employed an earlier redaction of the church-order which we have labelled κ. It is probably not possible to go beyond stating

---

43 Smith, "Epistle of Barnabas".

that the *Haustafel* was omitted in order to make room for the eschatological conclusion. However, it will be suggested below that K has so adopted the TWT that its provisions are directions aimed at clergy rather than catechumens. K's clergy, moreover, with the exception of the deacons, are celibate ascetics, as will be shown in more detail below, and so directions for the ordering of clergy families and households are largely redundant! Harnack, moreover, notes that the omission of the *Haustafel* material is implicitly recognized by the redactor who, in c15, has Peter state that the Scriptures are sufficient to teach of other directions.[44]

An account of the absence of the *Haustafel* in K alternative to suggestions that it was replaced is offered by Hennecke.[45] According to Hennecke, K is derived from a variant of TWT, identical to that from which B derived, the major reworking being on the part of B. Here is a simplified version of his diagram:

Diagram 5

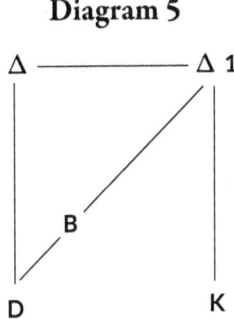

What K and B have in common, apart from some stray traditions, is an eschatological conclusion and an epistolary opening. Hennecke would seem to see Δ1 as a version of TWT with such an opening and conclusion. Thus he would not say that K has replaced the *Haustafel*, but rather that the *Haustafel* was never in the TWT received by K. We argue at 2.2 below that the opening

---

44 Harnack, *Lehre*, 211 n. 35.
45 Hennecke, "Grundschrift", 58–72.

is taken from elsewhere in the tradition, and so that this cannot be a defining element in TWT as received by K. More significantly Hennecke does not deal with E. It is the presence of the *Haustafel* there which is the clue to the existence of κ, and which tends to discount his hypothesis. However, there is some merit in his suggestion that there was a version of TWT which had an eschatological conclusion, and that this is reflected more closely in K than in B.

1.2.4 The additional material in K

In discussing the relationship between K and the other manifestations of the TWT it was determined that K is dependent on δ, whereas B is independently derived from TWT. The following stemma thus results:

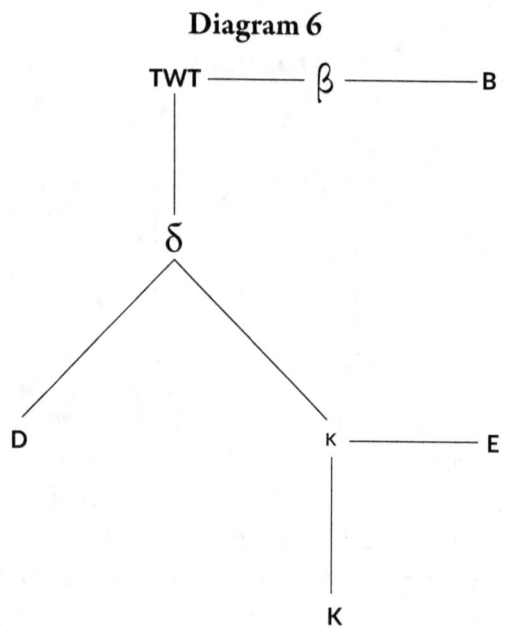

Diagram 6

However, there is a confusion in this simple picture. Namely, although K is dependent on the same branch of tradition as D, there are several agreements of B and K against D, as well as material which uniquely appears in K. We deal first with the material which is parallel between K and B.

1.2.4.1 K material with B parallels

In discussing the parallels between K and B a particular issue is whether K is directly and literarily dependent on B. This was the conclusion reached by Krawutzcky and Harnack, subsequently followed by Barnard.[46] The pattern of relationships expressed in the diagram at 1.2.4 above is essentially the same as that of Harnack,[47] and it is the need to explain these B parallels which led to Harnack's assumption that K had employed B. Before discussing the implications of these parallels, however, we need to examine them. They are as follows:

1. The opening greeting in K, which is similar to that in B, but has no parallel in D. We shall examine this point at section 2 of this introduction, where it will be argued that the greeting, together with the apostle list, comes from a different source altogether, and not from B.
2. In the statement of the love commandment K diverges from the version of D, the K version being comparable to the different version in B.
3. At K12 the commandment to treasure one's teacher is expanded in a manner with proximity to a similar statement at B.19.9.
4. As has already been noted, there is a significant difference between K and D in the conclusion, for whereas D has a *Haustafel*, K has an eschatological conclusion with similarities with B. Again, this is shown at Appendix 2.

---

46   Barnard, "Dead Sea scrolls", 102–103.
47   Thus note the diagram at *Apostellehre*, 32. The main difference (apart from the fact that we take no account of L here) is that Harnack does not reckon with the existence of κ as a first edition of TWT as found in K.

We deal with these latter three in turn, reserving discussion of the first parallel, which is not part of the two-ways material.

1.2.4.1.1 The commandment to love God
The different versions of this commandment are as follow:

D: πρῶτον ἀγαπήσεις τὸν θεὸν τὸν ποιήσαντά σε

K: πρῶτον ἀγαπήσεις τὸν θεὸν τὸν ποιήσαντά σε ἐξ ὅλης τῆς καρδίας σου καὶ δοξάσεις τὸν λυτρωσάμενόν σε ἐκ θανάτου·

B: ἀγαπήσεις τὸν ποιήσαντά σε, φοβηθήσῃ τόν σε πλάσαντα, δοξάσεις τόν σε λυτρωσάμενον ἐκ θανάτου·

Whereas D simply contains the command to love God the creator, this is expanded in K to love for creator and redeemer. The parallel with B is not exact, as B has a triple version, as well as minor divergences such as the position of the pronoun σέ, which tend to discount reliance upon B unless no other explanation is feasible. It should, moreover, be noted here that κ follows neither D nor B, in that the statement that love should be wholehearted is added to the love-commandment in K and E alike, conforming the saying better to Scripture. Given that they are present in each of these witnesses we must assume that they were present in κ, their common archetype, and that κ therefore is following a tradition independent of B. However, the critical words, καὶ δοξάσεις τὸν λυτρωσάμενόν σε ἐκ θανάτου are not present in E. E is certainly an abbreviation of κ, as may be seen where K and D are in parallel and E does not follow them, and so it is quite possible that they were in κ, and that E has let them drop. However, we do not know this, and must keep an open mind whether they derive from κ or K.

Although K and B are close, this parallel is simply one example of a host of such formulae. One may note, in particular, Hermas *Mand.* 1.1: πρῶτον πάντων πίστευσον ὅτι εἷς ἐστὶν ὁ θεὸς ὁ τὰ πάντα κτίσας καὶ καταρτίσας καὶ ποιήσας ἐκ τοῦ μὴ ὄντος εἰς τὸ εἶναι... πίστευσον οὖν αὐτῷ καὶ φοβήθητι αὐτόν... This is a particularly significant parallel because of its proximity to B, though not to D or K. Yet because the Mandate does not appear in a context of TWT there is no suggestion of any literary relationship between Hermas and B. This is recognized by Dibelius as a statement of traditional material of Jewish origin,[48] and, we may suggest, following Henne, is from the context of post-baptismal paraenesis. This is adduced not simply to illustrate the wide distribution of this material and the multiple forms which it could take—though this is itself significant, as such a wide distribution implies that B is not necessarily the source for the material here —, but also because this is further illustration of a background in Jewish paraenesis and Christian catechesis. Nonetheless, what is unique in K and B is the instruction to glorify Christ as the one who ransomed the hearer. Prostmeier suggests that the triple formula is a production of B, on the grounds that B is fond of such formulae,[49] but this could be a more widespread addition to the standard formula on the basis of the employment in catechesis or post-baptismal paraenesis. Thus Prostmeier notes that the reference in B is baptismal. Since the formula is found in this context, it is entirely feasible that the same tradition reached K (or possibly κ) independently. Whilst this cannot be proved, given the wide divergence between K and B, it is no less likely than dependence on B.

What is notable about the formula is that it seems to express a functional binitarianism of God the Father and Christ the redeemer. This is not a theological binitarianism—though the unreflective christological monotheism of, in particular, Melito, comes close to this—, but a traditional statement reminiscent of other passages which seem to reflect traditional credal formulae

---

48 Dibelius, *Hirt*, 497.
49 Prostmeier, *Barnabasbrief*, 537.

such as 1 Cor. 8:6 and 1 Tim. 2:5-6.[50] Thus given the extensive use of formulae like this it seems more probable that the tradition, rather than literary dependence upon B, is the source of this particular parallel, and, moreover, that the source of this tradition is catechetical or post-baptismal instruction.

1.2.4.1.2 Loving one's teacher as the apple of an eye

The different versions of this commandment are as follow:

D: τέκνον μου, τοῦ λαλοῦντός σοι τὸν λόγον τοῦ θεοῦ	K: τέκνον, τὸν λαλοῦντά σοι τὸν λόγον τοῦ θεοῦ καὶ παραίτιόν σοι γινόμενον τῆς ζωῆς καὶ δόντα σοι τὴν ἐν κυρίῳ σφραγῖδα ἀγαπήσεις ὡς κόρην ὀφθαλμοῦ σου,	B: ἀγαπήσεις ὡς κόρην τοῦ ὀφθαλμοῦ σου πάντα τὸν λαλοῦντά σοι τὸν λόγον κυρίου.
μνησθήσῃ νυκτὸς καὶ ἡμέρας	μνησθήσῃ αὐτοῦ νύκτα καὶ ἡμέραν,	μνησθήσῃ ἡμέραν κρίσεως νυκτὸς καὶ ἡμέρας,

---

50 See the discussion in Kelly, *Early Christian creeds*, 19–22.

Firstly, however, it must be noted that, whereas there is a clear parallel between B and K, the parallel is also a parallel between B and E:

B:
ἀγαπήσεις ὡς κόρην τοῦ ὀφθαλμοῦ σου πάντα τὸν λαλοῦντά σοι τὸν λόγον κυρίου. μνησθήσῃ ἡμέραν κρίσεως νυκτὸς και ἡμέρας,

καὶ ἐκζητήσεις καθ' ἑκάστην ἡμέραν τὰ πρόσωπα τῶν ἁγίων, ἢ διὰ λόγου κοπιῶν καὶ πορευόμενος εἰς τὸ παρακαλέσαι καὶ μελετῶν εἰς τὸ σῶσαι ψυχὴν τῷ λόγῳ...

E: τὸν λαλοῦντά σοι τὸν λόγον τοῦ θεοῦ καὶ παραίτιόν σοι γινόμενον τῆς ζωῆς καὶ δόντα σοι τὴν ἐν κυρίῳ σφραγῖδα ἀγαπήσεις αὐτὸν ὡς κόρην ὀφθαλμοῦ σου, μνησθήσῃ αὐτοῦ νυκτὸς καὶ ἡμέρας, τιμήσεις δὲ αὐτὸν ὡς κύριον, ὅθεν γὰρ Ἰησοῦς Χριστὸς λαλεῖται, ἐκεῖ κύριος ἐστιν.
ἐκζητήσεις δὲ αὐτὸν καὶ τοὺς λοιποὺς ἁγίους, ἵνα ἐπαναπαυσθῇς τοῖς λόγοις αὐτῶν...

Since the material appears in E as well as K we may deduce that the material appeared in κ. Proponents of a dependence upon B must therefore also argue that κ, as well as K, had knowledge of B and that both employed it in different ways! The appearance of this parallel in κ, which is in turn literarily dependent upon δ (since it is an expansion of δ material), therefore indicates that this parallel at least derives from the tradition and not from the use of any literary source. The assumption that the one who teaches is the same who baptizes the candidate is yet another indication that the locus for the transmission of the material is catechetical, and that it is catechetical speaks further against B as a source. A final indication of catechetical origin is the saying that sanctification accrues to the one who adheres to the saints. This appears at 1 Clem. 46.2, cited as Scripture. Obviously κ is not the source, but it likewise unnecessary to assume that κ derived it from 1 Clement, as otherwise there is no particular parallel.[51] Most probably it is a saying transmitted as part of catechesis or in more advanced school settings.

Also speaking to the catechetical origin of the saying is the debt to Proverbs 7:2. Here the teachings, rather than the teacher, are to be valued, but a transference of honour from teachings to teacher may readily come about in a catechetical context. What is most interesting, and indicative that this clause is the product of a relatively early stage in the Christian tradition, is the assumption that the teacher is also the baptizer. In the early third century we find that baptism is normally performed by the bishop, regardless of who had prepared the candidate. In an earlier period we must assume that this was not the case, but that independent teachers baptized their own candidates as they saw fit, and constructed the sort of patronal relationship which is envisaged and described here. Thus this B parallel is, once again, not derived from B, but from independent tradition which is of a similar date to B.

Finally we may note that there are echoes of this passage in the Syrian *Didascalia*. Of the support of the bishop the didascalist writes: "He it is who ministers the word to you and is your mediator, your teacher, and, after God, is your father who has regenerated you through the water. He is your chief, he is your master, he your powerful king."[52] And a little later, in stating that none should insult the bishop, he describes him as the one "through whom you have learned the word and come to know God, and through whom you have been made known to God, through whom you were sealed, and through whom you have become sons of light."[53] Connolly notes the parallels with K,[54] but we may suggest that if the didascalist has received this from a written source

---

51 Cf. Funk, *Doctrina*, 57. There are some possible parallels with 1 Clement further below in K, but these are not from κ material.
52 *Didascalia* 2.26.4.
53 *Didascalia* 2.32.3.
54 Connolly, *Didascalia apostolorum*, 87, 93.

then that source is catechetical. Given, however, that a few lines before the earlier citation there is an echo of D it seems likely that elements from the tradition are being freely employed.

1.2.4.1.3 The eschatological conclusion

We have already suggested that κ had the same *Haustafel* as D, and that K had altered the conclusion by omitting the *Haustafel* and replacing it with an eschatological conclusion. We have also noted that the same eschatological conclusion is present in part in B. A synoptic table of the eschatological conclusions is found in Appendix 2. There are several possible explanations of this phenomenon.

1.2.4.1.3.1 K revised in the light of B

One possible understanding of the relationship is that of Harnack, followed by Funk, that K also knew B, and revised the Two Ways section, taken from δ, in the light of B.[55] This would give a stemma thus:

Diagram 7

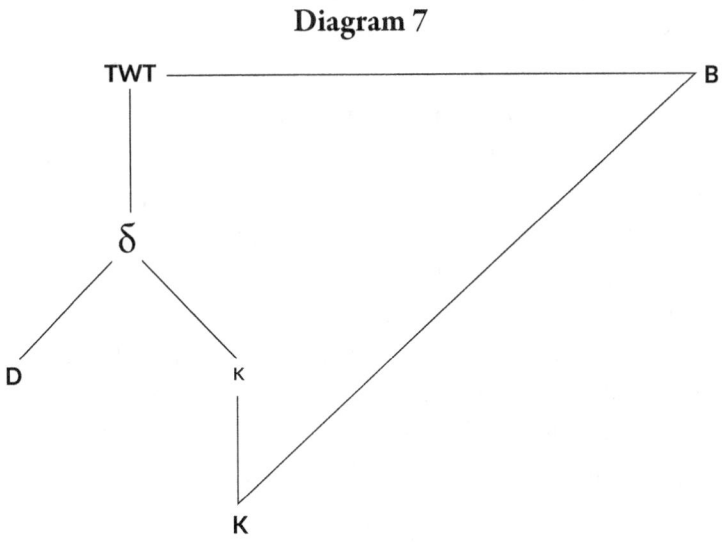

55 *Lehre*, 211; Funk, *Doctrina*, 58-59.

Although this is possible, there are two objections.

i) It is strange that K should follow δ so closely, and yet then undertake the complex literary task of comparing the text to another document in order to include a few stray points not picked up in the main source, whilst omitting the *Haustafel*.
ii) It is particularly strange that a redactor employing B should not include the material which is found in B (as in L) stating that angels are set over the two ways. As we shall see below, K has a cosmologically dualist view, and so it is particularly odd that material consonant with this outlook should be omitted.

1.2.4.1.3.2 The eschatological conclusion as inherent in TWT

The position that the eschatological material was in the TWT as received by K through κ is that adopted by Niederwimmer. We have already criticized this view at 1.2.2.2 above and need not repeat the critique here. This does not, however, mean that versions of TWT might not circulate with eschatological conclusions.

1.2.4.1.3.3 K as having a source independent of B

The possibility should be considered that K was aware of this material from a source other than B, whether oral or written. Whereas the *literary* relationship of K to D is that of joint dependence on δ, and whereas B represents an independent branch of the tradition, there may be elements of free-floating tradition besides which were known independently to B and K alike, or else K was aware of the literary source employed by B.

A related position is espoused by van de Sandt and Flusser and by Hennecke[56] namely that B and K draw upon the same lit-

---

56 Hennecke, "Grundschrift", 65; van de Sandt and Flusser, *Didache* 75.

erary source. For Hennecke this is true of the whole of TWT. Whereas this is possible, one would anticipate that the statement that angelic beings are set over the two ways is part of the Jewish original, as indeed van de Sandt and Flusser argue, and so part of the common source of B and K. Again, it is hard to explain this omission were this the sole source. Nonetheless it would be possible were we to suggest that K, in revising κ, was aware of the material independently of κ, and that K conformed this material to the apostolic shape given by κ, only preferring his own version of the material when it did not co-incide with the source before him. The other areas of common material between K and B have been identified as catechetical, and whereas there is nothing in the eschatological material which is self-evidently of a catechetical origin, there is likewise nothing which is inconsistent with such an origin. In this instance it is possible to see why the angelic powers over the two ways do not appear in K, namely because they were not present in κ, which at this point is close to D/δ, and that the reworking required would be too extensive.

Hennecke, in suggesting that the same literary source is employed, further suggests that K is closer to the origin than B, on the grounds of B's repetitions (of ἐρωτῶ and συναπολεῖται) and on the grounds that the introduction is more expansive.[57] Certainly this points to B's reworking of his source, and moreover indicates that K's fidelity to what the two have in common is greater. In turning to the parallels between B and K in the eschatological section we may observe that they are not all that extensive. On the basis of his use of κ, we may note that K is generally a conservative redactor of the TWT material, but the looseness of the parallels with B might be explained along the lines suggested by Hennecke that K has indeed used this source conservatively, whereas all the reworking is on the part of B.

---

57 Hennecke, "Grundschrift", 65.

What K and B hold in common is that each is an eschatological warning in conclusion to two-ways material, which indicates, if K is not dependent on B, that both knew a version of TWT which concluded with an eschatological warning. Such is far from impossible, as the version of the Qumran *Community Rule*, to which B is particularly close, has precisely such a conclusion. Whether the source was oral or literary may remain an open question. We may also note in this respect the conclusion of L: "If you act thus habitually and daily you shall be close to the living God. But if you do not do it you shall be far from the truth. Keep all this in your mind and do not be deceived with regard to your hope, but you shall come to the crown through these sacred struggles."[58]

That the TWT might originate in an apocalyptic framework is also a consideration which might shed light here. Draper, we noted above, suggested that B had removed TWT from the catechetical setting in which it is found in D,[59] but is it not also possible that D, perhaps on the basis of the covenantal content of the TWT,[60] found it appropriate to employ it as the basis of catechesis; in other words that B had not removed the tradition from a catechetical setting, but rather that D had put it there. We may also note, by contrast to L, to B, and to the version of TWT found in 1QS 3.13–4.26 (the *Community rule*), the absence of any reference to angels watching over the ways. As such, we must countenance the possibility that δ, followed by κ, had "de-eschatologized" the tradition.[61] Is this light we might suggest that K, aware of a TWT in which apocalyptic elements were more prom-

---

58 *Doctrina apostolorum* 6.2–3.
59 Draper, "Barnabas and the riddle of the Didache", discussed in 1.2.2.1 above.
60 On the covenantal origin of TWT see my *On the two Ways*, 13–19.
61 This is part of the argument of Wilhite, *"One of life and one of death"* that the D recension of TWT lacks many of the apocalyptic features present in other versions of the tradition. Wilhite concludes that this is a deliberate strategy on the part of D. A similar suggestion is made by van de Sandt and Flusser, *Didache* 62–3, 119.

inent, a tradition proximate to β, in re-employing the tradition as a basic rule for ascetics, also restored its eschatological direction. There are two small points moreover, albeit points at which the text of K is not absolutely secure, that also indicate a certain degree of tradition in common between B and K, and which indicate that, whether β was oral or written, K is citing from memory. Both occur in K13.

D: συγκοινωνήσεις δὲ πάντα τῷ ἀδελφῷ σου καὶ οὐκ ἐρεῖς ἴδια εἶναι· εἰ γὰρ ἐν τῷ ἀθανάτῳ κοινωνοί ἐστε, πόσῳ μᾶλλον ἐν τοῖς θνητοῖς;

E: συγμοινωνήσεις δὲ πάντα τοῖς ἀδελφοῖς σου καὶ οὐκ ἐρεῖς ἴδια εἶναι· εἰ γὰρ ἐν τῷ θανάτῳ κοινωνοί ἐστε, πόσῳ μᾶλλον ἐν τοῖς θνητοῖς;

K: κοινωνήσεις δὲ ἀπάντων τῷ ἀδελφῷ σου καὶ οὐκ ἐρεῖς ἴδια εἶναι· εἰ γὰρ ἐν τῷ ἀθανάτῳ κοινωνοί ἐστε, πόσῳ μᾶλλον ἐν τοῖς φθαρτοῖς;

B: κοινωνήσεις ἐν πᾶσιν τῷ πλησίον σου καὶ οὐκ ἐρεῖς ἴδια εἶναι· εἰ γὰρ ἐν τῷ ἀφθάρτῳ κοινωνοί ἐστε, πόσῳ μᾶλλον ἐν τοῖς φθαρτοῖς;

The extent to which E conforms to D at these points indicate that this was the reading of κ, which K has recast, and has thus brought into closer conformity with B. Otherwise we would have to imagine that E had independently recast the sayings and co-incidentally produced the same reading as D. But the conformity with B in the recasting by K is likewise unlikely to be co-incidental. An indication that the recasting is not made directly from a written source is the lack of balance in the last clause in K, in which ἀθανάτῳ is contrasted to φθαρτοῖς, rather than the θνητοῖς which we might otherwise expect. Had K been using a written source close to B, however, then one would expect that the earlier ἀθανάτῳ would have been replaced with ἀφθάρτῳ, in accordance with B. This not only indicates that β is oral, but the very proximity of K and B at this point, as contrasted to D and E, indicates K's access to a stream of tradition distinct from κ.

1.2.5 Some conclusions on the relationship between B, D and K

The stemma resulting from the conclusions reached above is:

Diagram 8

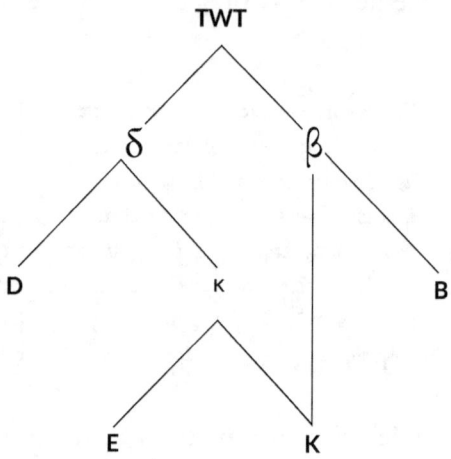

The significance of this lies not simply in ironing out the literary relationships between the various documents, but gives us the following information regarding the redactors of κ and K:

1) κ was in the δ stream of tradition.
2) K had a copy of κ.
3) Because K was aware of a version of TWT proximate to that deriving from the Essenes with an eschatological conclusion (β), K either functioned in the same area of tradition as β, or, if β is a document, had a copy of β.

The dating of δ is largely dependent on the dating of D, which used δ as a source; however, a dating at the turn of the second century is entirely reasonable. Its geographical location is similarly dependent on a positioning of D; however the consensus is that D is Syrian, and this would be consistent with the probability that TWT originated in Palestine. Thus Syria or Palestine is the original locus of δ, which was in turn employed by κ. The dating of β is similarly dependent on the dating of B. However, a time early in the second century would again not be ridiculous. As to the geographical location of this material, there is less certainty. The consensus is that B is Alexandrian. This has been ably defended by Carleton Paget,[62] but this does not mean that the sources employed are all from this milieu. In particular it is possible that β had come to Alexandria from elsewhere, in that the TWT material is found as an appendix to the body of B. Thus the question remains open, but since the use of B was a central plank in Harnack's argument for an Alexandrian origin to K this is significant nonetheless, as Syria or Palestine are more probable loci than Alexandria for κ and K alike.

1.3 Two-ways material in K which is not found elsewhere

Three salient features were identified above as emerging from a first glance at a synoptic arrangement of the two-ways tradition. There is also a fourth, not mentioned above, which is the inclusion in K of material which is without parallel in the other versions. Since we have determined that K is not the earliest exemplar of the two-ways tradition we may safely determine that these are either growths within the tradition or redactional additions. We should therefore determine their purpose and place within the redactional history of K.

---

62 Carleton Paget, *Barnabas*, 30–42.

1.3.1 Gendered demons

The first is the ethical expansion, which states that anger is a male demon and lust a female demon, which conspire to lead people to their destruction.

There is much here which breathes the atmosphere of early Judaism and its ethical discourse. Thus *Testament of Reuben* speaks of seven spirits which conspire against people and lead them to destruction[63] and *Testament of Dan* speaks specifically of the spirit of anger which co-operates with Satan.[64] The gendering of these demons is also consonant with early Judaism. *The Testament of Solomon*, with its complex demonology, alludes to the existence of female demons,[65] and 4Q560, an incantation against demons, whilst fragmentary, seems to envisage male and female demons which attack men and women in divergent ways. We may also be reminded of the syzygies of the pseudo-Clementine literature, again deriving from Jewish Christianity within Syria, and deriving from a context in which there is conflict with gnosticism.[66] The statement at K8.2 regarding the entry of a demon into the soul is also very proximate to the discussion of a similar phenomenon at Clem. *Hom.* 9.9. The closest parallel, however, is found in Clement of Alexandria. He is discussing a statement, possibly found within a gnostic work, in which Christ refers to a time when "you have trampled on the garment of shame, and when the two become one and the male with the female is neither male nor female." Clement attributes this statement to the *Gospel of the Egyptians*, but goes on to comment: "He (Cassianus, whose theories Clement is opposing) seems to me to fail to recognize that by the male impulse is meant wrath and by the female lust."[67] The manner in which this is stated

---

63 Test. Reuben 3.
64 Test. Dan 2-3.
65 Test Solomon 1.7; 4.1.
66 The significance of this conflict with gnosticism will emerge in 3.4.2 below.
67 Clement Strom. 3.91.

sounds as though it is considered common knowledge, and part of the catechetical tradition; elsewhere Clement makes passing reference to lust as female.[68]

Thus although the appearance of gendered demons at this point is a literary addition in the redaction of TWT the appearance of the statement in a catechetical context and as the basis of ethical exhortation is an indication that the redactor who added this material is close to the root of the tradition, and expands it here in a manner not alien to the milieu in which the tradition grew up and was fostered. Whereas it is possible that this is a free-floating piece of tradition which has survived and has been attached to the TWT by K, the very fact that that the tradition has been passed on through ethical paraenesis, and is found still in that context, indicates that the redactor understood the material with which he was dealing, and that the circle in which the tradition was passed on was a circle derived from the same early Jewish group in which the TWT was originated.

As such it is impossible to determine whether this was κ or K, and whether this was therefore a natural growth within the tradition or a deliberate redactional expansion. There is, however, one small indication that the expansion is the work of K. *Ev Phil.* 61a states that "among the forms of the unclean spirit there are male and female." On the basis that male spirits attack women, and female spirits attack men, it explains the apotropaic power of the rite of the bridechamber. This Gospel is a compilation of other material, but it is notable that Mary Magdalene has a prominence among the disciples. We note below that one of K's sources is likewise a Gospel in which an (unidentified) Mary is prominent, and we must ask whether K is privy to a similar selection of sources. This, however, is far from being a safe argument, as the tradition of *Ev. Phil.* may likewise be derived from the Jewish tra-

---

68 Clement *Strom.* 3.63.

dition. Nonetheless, since K, like Clement, is, as we suggest below, operating in an ambit in which Christian gnosticism is prominent, it is also possible that he is heir to the same tradition of interpretation, which is both shared and disputed between Christians of gnostic and anti-gnostic bent.

1.3.2 The support of teachers

In 1.2.4.1.2 above it was observed that the instruction that a teacher should be honoured was derived from the tradition and not from B. The direction continues:

> You shall honour him as much as you are able from your sweat and from the labour of your hands. If the Lord through him has made you worthy to be given spiritual food and drink and eternal life, much the more should you bring him corruptible and temporary food. "For the workman is worthy of his hire" and "You shall not muzzle a threshing ox" and "Nobody plants a vine and does not eat the fruit of it."

This is therefore a continuation of the direction that the teacher should be honoured, which was part of κ. Whether this is likewise part of κ or an expansion of K alone is hard to determine. However, if, as we intend to argue below, the qualifications of TWT are being read by K as no longer catechetical but as preliminary to the selection of clergy, then this is far from being an appropriate expansion, and may well be part of the original.

There is more that points in the direction of the earlier redactional level, in the significance of the patronal relationship here established. Paul implies that a particular relationship might come about between baptized and baptizer.[69] Theissen suggests that this relationship issued in hospitality offered to the baptiz-

---

[69] 1 Cor 1:12-17.

er,[70] who at this time would be an itinerant apostle, which in turn might be a means by which the baptized gained status in the community. The baptized thus becomes a patron of the baptizer. Although hospitality would no longer be necessary if the baptizer was no longer itinerant, it remains a possibility that those baptized might offer patronage to those who baptized them as a means of gaining status within the Christian community. This casts light on Ignatius' instruction that no baptism or *agapē* take place without the consent of the bishop.[71] As I have argued elsewhere,[72] the reason for this prohibition is that these two events are rituals which construct patronage, an *agapē* through the sharing of food, which may be construed as a patronal act, and baptism as the means by which the newly baptized might become a patron (or client) of the baptizer. Ignatius thus seizes upon them as events which are not to take place without the bishop's consent, since by this means the bishop would be able to control patronage networks. There is, however, no trace of such a relationship in a later period. Baptism is certainly tied up to patronage in third-century Africa, but in this event the baptizer, who is normally the bishop, becomes the patron, rather than the client. We must also note that these directions continue to tie TWT to pre-baptismal catechesis rather than to any other locus of instruction. We must therefore conclude that this is a natural growth within TWT, and is more probably from the κ redaction than from K, even though we may yet be open about the date of K.

1.4 Conclusions on the TWT in K

There is some evidence that K has reworked the TWT as found in κ, κ in turn being a derivation of δ distinct from D. The date of the reworking is uncertain, as is the location. The source, how-

---

70 Theissen, *Social setting*, 54–56.
71 *Smyrn.* 8.2.
72 Stewart-Sykes, *Life of Polycarp*, 70.

ever, is ancient. The other stream of tradition which may be recognized in the material is likewise ancient. Finally there are some independent streams redacted by K, but likewise showing signs of antiquity. Fundamentally the K version of TWT reflects second-century traditions. We may therefore go on to examine the other sources to determine whether they likewise are sources of antiquity.

2. The epistolary opening and apostle list
2.1 The apostle list

We have already observed that whereas twelve apostles appear in the prescript to K, only eleven speak. We therefore agreed with Schermann that the list implied by E is more original and that the presence of Jude the son of James was a rationalizing addition, though without accepting his hypothesis that K was directly derived from E. Part of the reason for not accepting his hypothesis was that without the fiction of an apostolic gathering the presence of the apostles and the attribution of speeches to them made no sense. The apostles and their presence are intimately bound up to the material which is found in their mouths in this recension.

To turn to the list of eleven certain peculiarities are obvious, namely the duplication of Peter and Kephas and the duplication of Nathanael and Bartholomew. Although, according to Harnack and Schermann,[73] the duplication of Peter and Kephas points to an Alexandrian origin, as the same peculiarity is found in Clement,[74] this argument is far from secure as Clement was not a native Alexandrian, nor did he spend his entire career in Alexandria. Rather, as Schmidt suggests, the list is far closer to

---

73 Harnack, *Lehre*, 217 n; Schermann, *Elfapostelmoral*, 22; Baumstark, "Alte und neue Spuren", 237.
74 Cited by Eusebius *HE* 1.12.

that of *Epistula apostolorum* 2,⁷⁵ and may indeed be derived from this document. Both are lists of eleven and both locate the gathering of the disciples after the resurrection.⁷⁶ The main difference between the two lists is that Matthew is moved higher up the list in κ.⁷⁷ We may accept Harnack's suggestion here that the redactor wishes to bring to prominence those apostles who had produced Gospels but should observe that the basis of the list, including the presence of John at the head, is best ascribed either to *Epistula apostolorum* or to a common source.⁷⁸

In answering the question whether K is directly dependent on *Epistula apostolorum* or whether the apostle lists derive from a common source we should note that not only do the documents share a list of apostles and a fictive setting but that their basic literary form is likewise the same. As we shall observe below, κ, like *Epistula apostolorum*, is a *Sendschreibe*. On the basis of this concatenation of similarities Schmidt suggests that the relationship is one of direct literary dependence. For Schmidt the relationship has to be dependence on the part of K on *Epistula apostolorum*, on the assumption that K is later than *Epistula apostolorum*.⁷⁹ Since we are dealing with an earlier redaction which was employed by K it is theoretically possible that the direct relationship works the other way, and that *Epistula apostolorum* has derived its list from κ. However, the editorial hand of κ is nonetheless clear in the movement of Matthew and since it is more

---

75   Schmidt, *Gespräche Jesu*, 242–243.
76   Giet, "Didache", 223–236, also contains some discussion of the apostle list in E and K.
77   This movement of Matthew's name may be deduced as the work of κ rather than of K because of the prominent position (second after John) of Matthew's speech in E and K alike.
78   It is taken as axiomatic that the list is derived from a source and is not the independent composition of κ because of the improbability that *Epistula apostolorum* and κ would produce two lists with the same peculiarities unless these lists were founded in some tradition (contra Funk, *Doctrina*, 50–51, who cannot see why the list should not have been the author's composition.)
79   Schmidt, *Gespräche Jesu*, 245.

likely that Matthew would be moved up the list than down priority has to be given to *Epistula apostolorum*. Nonetheless, there is not enough here to claim direct dependence, for Schmidt was assuming that K was an Egyptian work of the fourth century, whereas if κ is earlier then it may still be in direct contact with the same tradition that produced the apostle list of *Epistula apostolorum*.

Whether the redactor of κ was in possession of *Epistula apostolorum* or whether the two simply draw on a common tradition, in either event κ derives from a very similar circle. Although an Egyptian provenance has often been suggested for *Epistula apostolorum* an Asian provenance is far more likely.[80] Even so, if the apostle list of is a direct derivation from *Epistula apostolorum* it may be suggested that the provenance of the *Epistula* does not affect greatly the discussion of the origin of κ, as once produced it is quite easy for *Epistula apostolorum* to travel, but we may note that the Gospel of the Ebionites similarly adds Matthew to an essentially Johannine list of apostles, no doubt because of the attribution of a Gospel to Matthew and since this is an Asian document of the second century, the suspicion, though not proof, that κ is likewise Asian, is raised.[81] Thus far we have suggested that κ was in a circle of Syrian influence on the basis of the version of TWT which it employed; but TWT might likewise be a mobile tradition. The apostle list belongs with the TWT material, as it is to the apostles which are listed that TWT is attributed, but the combination may be secondary. But since the apostle list and the TWT were both combined in κ (we may deduce that κ was prefaced by some kind of list, since otherwise its apostolic attribution would have no meaning or context) it seems more likely that the combination was made at the source

---

80 So Stewart-Sykes, "Asian origin" and Hill, "*Epistula apostolorum*".
81 Maclean, *Ancient church orders*, 68, similarly suggests an Asian origin for K on the basis of the pre-eminence of John in the list of apostles.

of both elements, rather than that each should independently travel to some other part of the Christian world there to be joined. Thus we are pointed, once again, in the direction of Asia, possibly to the regions bordering Syria, such as Cilicia, though no region within Asia can be ruled out.

2.2 The epistolary opening

If the context and the apostle list are derived from the same circle as *Epistula apostolorum*, an important consequence derives from this. For whereas Harnack, Funk and Goodspeed[82] determined that the epistolary greeting, χαίρετε, and the address to sons and daughters, were derived from B, and Hennecke that it derived from Δ1 (which is equivalent to our β)[83] we may now, in keeping with the argument above that there was no direct literary relationship between κ and B, see that this greeting is likewise derived from the context. *Epistula apostolorum* is intended as a *Sendschreibe* from the apostles to the church across the world,[84] as, it would appear, was κ. Such a form was known in second century Asia,[85] and thus this may be taken as further evidence that κ is likewise to be attributed to that century. Although *Epistula apostolorum* is not unique in this form it shares with κ a fictive setting not of secret teaching before the resurrection, nor of prophetic revelation, but of apostolic directions given after the resurrection.[86] Again this does not oblige us to accept literary dependence, but certainly points to the same context.

However, before reaching any final conclusions on the open-

---

82 Goodspeed, "Barnabas", 232, Funk, *Doctrina*, 50.
83 Hennecke, "Grundschrift", 65–66.
84 So Hennecke, "Grundschrift", 66, correctly notes, though ascribing this to β on the basis that B is likewise a *Sendschreibe* with the same greeting.
85 So, apart from *Epistula apostolorum* itself, and possibly some exemplars in the New Testament, note the activity of Themiso in sending a general epistle, according to Apollonius at Eusebius *HE* 5.18.5, μιμούμενος τὸν ἀπόστολον. For discussion see Stewart-Sykes, "Asian origin", 425–426.
86 Schmidt, *Gespräche Jesu*, 244–245.

ing, we need to determine how much of the opening of the extant K is κ and what is to be attributed to the K redaction. At a literary level it may be observed that the greater part of K1 is redundant. The redundant passage is bracketed in the excerpt below:

> Greetings, sons and daughters, in the name of the Lord Jesus Christ. John and Matthew and Peter and Andrew and Philip and Simon and James and Nathanael and Thomas and Kephas and Bartholomew and Jude the son of James.
>
> In accordance with the command of Our Lord Jesus Christ the Saviour we gathered ourselves together, as he laid down: [Before you determine the eparchies, calculate the numbers of the places, the rewards of bishops, the seats of presbyters, the assistance offered by deacons, the understanding of readers, the blamelessness of widows and whatever is necessary for the foundation of the church, so that knowing the type of those things which are heavenly, they should guard themselves against every fault, seeing that, in the great day of judgement, they should give an account of those who heard and did not keep. And he ordered us to send these words out to the whole inhabited world.]
>
> It seemed to us, [therefore,] that we should command you as an admonition of brotherhood and an exhortation, so that you might be mindful through the writing of what the Lord revealed to each of us in accordance with the will of God through the Holy Spirit.

If this literary instinct is correct, we may secondly note that the description of the contents which is bracketed is not what follows immediately. K2, however, with its description of admonition and exhortation, may readily be applied to TWT. If this is the case then it is entirely possible that this is derived from κ, and accompanied the original apostle list and the TWT.

What then of the greater part of K1 bracketed above? K has joined this to κ in order to bolster the apostolic sanction to the church-order which follows TWT, and thus supplied the apostolic attribution to the sections of the church order. Possibly redactional are the addition of the final statement that the Lord had ordered the apostles to publish the order to the whole earth,[87] and the οὖν at the beginning of the next clause, in order to smooth the transition between the two sources. However, we must ask whether this whole section is not a composition on the part of K, intended to fit the church-order material into a single frame with κ, or whether it derives from the church order itself.

In the first edition of this work I argued that this passage was not the production of K, but was derived from the church order material itself. The reason for this attribution was that the church-order in its final state is concerned to align the service of presbyters and laypersons on earth with that of angels in heaven, which is precisely what K1 states is the intention of the directions which are to be given. I am now less convinced that this is the case. The attempt to align the order of the church on earth with the angelic hierarchy is found in the discussion of laity and of presbyters. However, it is not found in the discussion of the bishop, the deacons, or the readers. It is possible that the order concerned itself initially with presbyters and laics only, but against that is the appearance of material in K16, regarding bishops, which a close relationship to material in the *Didascalia apostolorum* 2.1.3–5. We will explore this further below, but the fact that the original order appears, on the basis of the common occurrence of this material in two church-orders, to have included the bishop, and yet did this without aligning the bishop's role to the heavenly hierarchy, is an indication that the heavenly hierarchy is not embedded in the original church order, but is from the hand of a later redactor.

A positive indication that the alignment of the orders of presbyters and laics to the heavenly hierarchy is the work of K, rather than deriving from a source, or even an intervening redactor, is

---

87 A similar suggestion is made by Duchesne, Untitled review, 362–363.

the common ground between this insight and *Testamentum Domini*. *Testamentum Domini* is a pseudonymous document claiming apostolic sanction, indeed claiming to have been revealed by Christ after the resurrection, with a substantial amount of church order material, but also primarily concerned that the earthly church should mirror the heavenly.[88] The link between the church on earth and that in heaven is made explicit near the beginning of the church order material as Jesus says to the disciples: "Truly I say to you, whoever knows the force of this commandment and of this testament and performs those things that are written therein shall be like to the angels who praise my Father and shall be sanctified to God."[89] Of the presbyter it is said "He should not neglect his own prayers, for he is the figure of the archangels."[90] In the dialogue surrounding the appearance of Jesus, which provides the springboard for the church order material, the women present, Martha, Mary, and Salome, ask regarding their duties and are told: "I desire that you should continue in intercession, that you should serve my gospel at all times, that you should show forth in yourselves a type of holiness for the salvation of those who patiently trust in me and that in all things you should be a likeness of the kingdom of the heavens."[91] This, incidentally, describes the duties and life of the widows of the *Testamentum*, a matter to which we will return. Finally we may observe that this theme of the mirroring of earth and heaven also emerges in the episcopal ordination prayer.[92] Although K and *Testamentum Domini* are not the only documents to link earthly and heavenly worship, indeed, this is an extension of a long tradition, it will be suggested below that they are distinct in that they particularly make the link between ascetic prayer and worship,

---

88 For treatment beyond the citations here note Sperry-White, "Imagery".
89 *Testamentum Domini* 1.17.
90 *Testamentum Domini* 1.31.
91 *Testamentum Domini* 1.16.
92 *Testamentum Domini* 1.21.

particularly that of those denoted as presbyters, and that of the angels. This is particularly notable because, although *Testamentum Domini* has often been ascribed a later date, and a Syrian provenance, recent discussion has suggested a fourth-century Cappadocian provenance,[93] precisely as we shall argue should be ascribed to K. As such we may be alert to their close relationship, and may consider that this aspect of the introduction of K is the work of the K redactor, undertaken in Cappadocia. The argument will be continued below, but for the moment we may suggest that K1 is the work of the redactor who joined κ to the church order material.

However, the church-order, with which K concludes, is certainly derived in part from a separate source, and so before finally determining the extent of K's redactional work, and thus to dating K as it has been received, we need to examine the extent of this source. Nonetheless, before moving to that section, we may remind ourselves of the suggestion that κ is Asian, or from an adjacent area, and that it is a product of the second century. We may also suggest here, on the basis of the linkage with *Testamentum Domini*, that K's introduction and reworking of κ would likewise seem to be derived from an Asian context.

2.3 Conclusions on the opening of K

Although both B and *Epistula apostolorum* have been suggested as sources for the opening of K, it is more likely that this is an independent product. The apostle list derives from the same Asian circle as *Epistula apostolorum,* and the epistolary greeting is part of κ, who had combined the TWT material with the apostle list. Another redactor, however, has supplied the greater part of K1.

The other significant point which is to be gathered from the introduction is that κ had the recognizable genre of a *Sendschreibe*.

---

93   White, *Daily Prayer* and, with additional argumentation, Stewart, *Testament.*

As a means of propagating prophetic literature this was known in second-century Asia. The dialogic form is secondary, but, as in *Epistula apostolorum*, may find its place within a *Sendschreibe*. The classification of K as a church-order thus blinds us to its true genre. The church-order content is secondary, as the *Sendschreibe* originally extended only to TWT, but the inclusion of this material by K has thus altered the work overall.

It is to this church order that our attention may now be turned.

3. The sources and redaction of the church-order of K

3.1 Harnack's two ancient sources

Once again we may begin with Harnack, who distinguished two ancient sources lying behind the church-order. First is that now found in K16–21, which he named κατάστασις τοῦ κλήρου, the second that beginning in K22, which he termed κατάστασις τῆς ἐκκλησιάς. In what follows we retain Harnack's name for the first hypothetical source, abbreviating it, for convenience, to κκ.

The reason for Harnack's division of the church order material in K is that K22 is a doublet of K20, and, we may note, in different grammatical form.[94] Having legislated for the appointment of deacons, and gone on to discuss widows, the subject then turns back to the duties of deacons. Harnack thus suggested that K22, together with what follows, was excerpted from a different source than K16–21. The first source, Harnack considered, could hardly be later than the first third of the third century,[95] the second he placed earlier, in the second century.[96] We will examine the dating of K's sources below but for the moment may note, with Harnack, that the doublet is clumsy as well as repetitive, and

---

94 *Lehre*, 213-214.
95 *Lehre*, 212.
96 *Lehre*, 214.

is indicative therefore of some redactional activity. This, however, is not the only peculiarity about the chapters. When John suggests that two presbyters should be appointed, he is contradicted by the other apostles, who demand three; again, this appears to be a redactional intervention.[97] Beyond this the discussion of the qualifications for a presbyter is not only more extensive than might be expected, but stands in tension to the statement about bishops in that whereas married bishops might seem to be allowed, though unmarried bishops are preferred, presbyters are simply to have had no congress with women. However, before tracing all the peculiarities of the church order we should examine Harnack's discussion of his two sources in more detail.

As we have seen, fundamental for Harnack's hypothesis is the doublet at K20 and K22, which led to his suggestion that K22, together with what follows, is the tail-end of a separate church-order which had already dealt with bishops and deacons, and now goes on to laymen at K23. However, it is to be noted that K23 compares the place of a layman with the conduct of an angel, which is the same imagery employed of the presbyters at K18. We may at this point refer to the conclusion above that K1 was the work of the K redactor, noting that it is from this hand that the statement regarding the mirroring of worship in earth and heaven is derived, and thus suggest that K23, employing the same imagery, is from that same hand.[98]

Thus rather than reflecting the juncture of two distinct church-orders it is possible that K22, like K23, is an interpolation from another source or a redactional composition which, rather than signifying the juncture of a second source, simply disrupts the flow. The subject immediately preceding is the charita-

---

97 The justification for this redactional intervention is discussed at 3.7.2 below. As it is it seems, as Faivre, "Apostolicité", 42, remarks, artificial and superficial.
98 It should be noted that this is a reversal of the position taken in the first edition of this work, in which K23 was assigned to κκ.

ble work of widows and what follows in K22 is a suggestion that the deacons should be engaged in this charitable work. Is it possible that a redactor who knew not of the work of widows, or who wished to downgrade this order, has supplemented what he found with a statement regarding the work of deacons as being that which, in essence, had been ascribed to widows? To an extent this decision is based on a decision about the redactional levels in the conclusion of the document, where the ministry of women is restricted to caring for indigent women. If this is part of a source then the source is surely different from that dictating the appointment of widows, whereas if this is a redactional composition then it too may be intended to downgrade the ministry of women in the church. It is clearly not from the same source as K16, as here it is assumed that deacons may aspire to the episcopate whereas, as will be shown below, the *episkopos* of κκ is elected from the number of the presbyters. The manner in which the social work of deacons mirrors that ascribed to widows is striking, and is likewise noticed by Funk, who suggests, however, that this is a single source dealing generally with diaconal works of charity.[99] He thus denies Harnack's two source theory on the grounds that K22 is speaking of a different aspect of a deacon's duties than K20. It remains nonetheless odd that the description of the duties should be split, and so although we may agree that the connection between K21 and K22 is the issue of social work, K22 does not continue K21 but contradicts it, a reading which gains strength from the discussion of women's ministry which follows.

We may enquire at a later stage whether this is a source or a redactional composition as we have yet to reach this stage in the argument. However, for the present we may set aside Harnack's two sources in favour of a hypothesis of the redactional interpolation of K22 into K's source, and the assignment of K23 to the

---

99 Funk, *Doctrina*, LIV–LV.

same redactor (or source) as K1. We may, nonetheless, recognize that a source lay behind much of K16–21.

3.2 Bartlet's hypothesis of a double revision

Harnack was not alone in discerning ancient sources behind the latter part of K. A series of interpolations in an ancient source is suggested by Bartlet. He suggests an original work from early in the third century, a revision at the end of the third century and a further revision in the fourth century. The original and the first revision he places in Cilicia or Cappadocia, and the final revision in Egypt. This second revision is presumably the work of the redactor who put the document into its final shape, and corresponds to our K.[100]

Bartlet's detailed argument, alas, can not be found. His publication on the subject was posthumously edited from among his notes by Cadoux, who reports the existence of 21 sheets of unrevised work dealing with the sources which were not publishable.[101] What survives are some examples illustrating this analysis. We can only guess at the arguments which he employed to support the analysis he offered. We cite each of these examples in full using Bartlet's English version rather than that published here. The punctuation, however, is slightly altered and, rather than using Bartlet's system of brackets, his first revision is shown in boldface and his second revision is italicized and boldfaced.

> Peter said, "If there exist a paucity of men, and there be not yet to hand a full complement of those able to vote about a bishop—less (that is) than twelve men, let them write to the neighbouring church(es), where it chances to be planted, in order that thence may come three chosen men and test carefully him that is worthy—if any one has a fair

---

100 Bartlet, *Church-life*, 99–105.
101 So C.J. Cadoux at Bartlet, *Church-life*, 103. The papers appear to have perished, as they are not among Cadoux's archive.

repute with the heathen, **if he is free from sin, a friend of the poor, self-controlled, not a drunkard, not a fornicator, not over-reaching or abusive, or a respecter of persons, and such-like.** *It is a fair thing indeed that he be without wife: but otherwise, having had (but) one wife, cultured, able to interpret the scriptures; but if unlettered, let him be of a meek disposition, and let him abound in love towards all*; lest perchance a bishop becomes convicted by popular opinion of any fault."

Whereas we can see why Bartlet chose to connect the final clause to the statement about good repute among the heathen, therefore attributing the intervening matter to secondary redaction, there is no reason why the final clause should not follow on from the qualification list. In that case the point is made that the qualifications should exist, and that for this reason the bishop might not be blamed in popular opinion. It is indeed possible that this last section has regard solely to the bishop's meekness, which is being seen as a consolation should he be unable to read the Scriptures, and is therefore an interpolation. With regard to the possibility that the qualification list itself has been subject to interpolation, we must immediately be suspicious of the statement that the bishop is better unmarried, and that otherwise he should be (or have been) once-married. That a bishop should be once-married is a qualification found in the Pastoral Epistles, and may be an ancient direction, but in its current context qualifies the statement that the bishop should be unmarried. It may, indeed, not even mean that. The statement ἀπὸ μιᾶς γυναικός is odd. Heid indeed takes it to mean "free of one wife," that is to say that the bishop should ideally never have been married, but otherwise may be widowed, and only once.[102] To say that he should have survived a single wife is almost otiose after the statement that it is better that he be ἀγύναιος. This may lead to the suspicion that κκ

---

102 Heid, *Celibacy*, 105–106.

simply read that he should be μιᾶς γυναικός (so 1 Tim. 3:2; Titus 1:6), but this has been rewritten, through the suggestion that he might be ἀγύναιος and through the addition of ἀπό.

It is unusual, though not unthinkable, that an early source should opt for an unmarried bishop,[103] but the manner in which the demonstrably more primitive qualification in this instance is the second option, and has probably been subject to editing, gives grounds for suspicion. Likewise odd is the conjunction of the requirement that he should be educated with the recognition that he might be illiterate. We turn to this point further at 3.7.3 below, but for the moment suggest that as the role of the bishop became more of an intellectual role as the second century progressed, and as the expectation grew that the bishop should not simply be a patron but should also have competence in teaching and preaching, the requirement that he should have some education is more likely to be later than earlier, and that a latter point in the redactional history of the passage is likely to be the point at which such a requirement was inserted, whereas the provision for an unlettered bishop is more probably original.

Taking these points into consideration the following possible redactional interpolations are shown in bold, with a conjectural adjustment, to be explained below,[104] in italics.

> ἐὰν ὀλιγανδρία ὑπάρχῃ καὶ μήπου πλῆθος τυγχάνῃ τῶν δυναμένων ψηφίσασθαι περὶ ἐπισκόπου ἐντὸς δεκαδύο ἀνδρῶν, εἰς τὰς πλησίον ἐκκλησίας, ὅπου τυγχάνει πεπηγυῖα, γραφέτωσαν, ὅπως ἐκεῖθεν ἐκλεκτοὶ τρεῖς ἄνδρες παραγενόμενοι δοκιμῇ δοκιμάσαντες τὸν ἄξιον ὄντα, εἴ τις φήμην καλὴν ἔχει ἀπὸ τῶν ἐθνῶν, εἰ ἀναμάρτητος ὑπάρχει, εἰ φιλόπτωχος, εἰ σώφρων, μὴ μέθυσος, μὴ πόρνος, μὴ πλεονέκτης ἢ λοίδορος ἢ προσωπολήπτης καὶ τὰ τούτοις ὅμοια. **καλὸν μὲν εἶναι ἀγύναιος, εἰ δὲ μή, ἀπὸ μιᾶς γυναικός.**

103 For Connolly, "Use of the *Didache*", 155, the very provision indicates a date later than the *Didascalia*; see, however, 5.2 below.
104 The conjecture will be explained and discussed at 3.7.3. below.

παιδείας μέτοχος, δυνάμενος τὰς γραφὰς ἑρμενεύειν εἰ δ᾽ ἢ ἀγράμματος· πραΰς ὑπάρχων καὶ τῇ ἀγάπῃ εἰς πάντας περισσευέτω, μήποτε περί τινος ἐλεγχθεὶς ἐπίσκοπος ἀπὸ τῶν πολλῶν γενηθείη.

Next Bartlet dealt with the saying ascribed to John regarding the appointment of presbyters:

> John said, "The appointed bishop **knowing the devotion and love for God of those about him** shall appoint whomsoever he shall have tested, as presbyters, two in number". *All replied to this and said, "Not two but three."* "The presbyters, then, must be men already of long time in the world, *in some fashion abstaining from sexual intercourse,* generous towards the brotherhood, not respecting a man's person, *fellow-initiates of the bishop and supporters of his, assembling the congregation together, zealous for the pastor."*

What is obscured by Bartlet's treatment here is that all around this there is the discussion of the manner in which the presbyters, around the bishop, represent the twenty-four elders of the Apocalypse.[105] The discussion of the elders at the right and the left is interrupted by the statement of qualifications. Without these interruptions the passage makes complete sense:

> For there are twenty-four presbyters, twelve on the right and twelve on the left. For those on the right receive the phials from the archangels and bear them to the master, and those on the left have authority over the company of angels. The presbyters on the right are to assist those who oversee the altar, so that they may distribute the gifts of honour and receive them as necessary. The presbyters on the left are to assist the congregation, so that it may be peaceful and without disturbance, once it has been instructed in all submission...

105 Rev. 4:4.

There are thus grounds for seeing not only the statements which are here italicized as secondary (as they certainly are), but the whole statement of qualifications as secondary. Harnack, moreover, notes that such a treatment of the qualifications of presbyters who are not, also, in some sense bishops, is unique before the fourth century, though he leaves it intact in his original source.[106] Finally we may note that the demand for celibacy is imposed apparently more strictly upon presbyters than upon the bishop, which again indicates that this is not part of the original, but may be the work of the redactor who inserted the words καλὸν μὲν εἶναι ἀγύναιος, εἰ δὲ μή, ἀπὸ in the section concerning the bishop. Thus, on the grounds of the manner in which the flow of the passage is interrupted, on the grounds that this is unique as a treatment of the qualifications of presbyters, and on the grounds of the contradiction with the earlier statement concerning the bishop, we may consider the entire passage regarding the qualifications of presbyters suspect. It is true that those parts which Bartlet attributes to the original are qualifications found in more ancient contexts than the fourth century, to which he wishes to assign K, but there is no reason why a later redactor might not imitate earlier statements of qualification. Certainly we may agree with Bartlet, as with Harnack, that the statement "All replied to this and said, 'Not two but three'" is the work of K. The way is prepared for this in K3.[107] But not this alone, but the whole of the list of qualifications for a presbyter, must be assigned to K, on the basis that the discussion is interrupted, and on the basis that K is imagining presbyters who have a more distinct status than that intended in the original.

κκ is close to the Pastoral Epistles in listing qualifications for other offices, but a sign that there is nothing here of κκ is the absence of any parallel.

---

106 Harnack, *Sources*, 11 n.9.
107 See 3.7.2 below for a rationale for this intervention.

> James said, "Let a reader be appointed, after first having been carefully tested, **not a tongue-wagger, not a drunkard nor yet a jester, seemly in bearing, persuasive, of good sense, first to hasten to the gatherings on the Lord's Day,** easy to hear, good at exposition **knowing that he is performing the office of an Evangelist,** *For he who fills the ears of one who does not understand shall be accounted as written down before God.*"

Whereas we have suggested that Bartlet was not radical enough in his excisions in the discussion of the presbyters, in the absence of his argument it is hard to see why anything here should not be assigned to the original source. Harnack is content to attribute the whole to the source, suggesting only that K may have struck εἰς at the beginning.[108] Since the office of reader is first otherwise found at the beginning of the third century this raises the question of the date and origin of this office and the source which enshrines the appointment, but we shall turn to this at 3.7.3 below. However, although there is no obvious reason why any part of this should be suspect, we may agree that the final phrase, the statement "whoever fills the ears..." is secondary to the rest. The reason for this is the manner in which the wording is echoed at K.29: "Whoever does a noble deed..." We shall return to this statement at 3.5 below.

> Kephas said, "Let widows be appointed, three in number- two of them persevering in prayer for all those in trial and with a view to revelations touching whatsoever is needful, and one attending upon those tried by sicknesses. **Let her be fit for ministering, sober, reporting to the presbyters what things are requisite, not a lover of filthy lucre, not addicted to much wine, so that she may be able to be soberly fit for night-services and for any other sort of good deeds she may desire to do. For these things are the Lord's chief good treasures.**"

---

108 *Sources*, 15.

Here the point which gives rise to suspicion is that the list of qualifications for the one widow who is to care for the sick and needy is rather extensive, whereas no qualification is given for the other two, and the obvious qualifications which one might expect, namely age and length of widowhood, are not mentioned. It will be noted below that K wishes to restrict the ministry of women to service of this nature, and it may well be that it is the hand of K, rather than an intervening redactor, as Bartlet suggests, who has extended the qualifications for social care. Nonetheless we may agree with him that the source has been extended somewhat at this point. In particular the final statement, "For these things are the Lord's chief good treasures" has an echo, we may note, in the wording, once again, of K29: thus we may compare ὁ ποιῶν ἔργον καλὸν ἑαυτῷ θησαυρὸν περιποιεῖται ὁ γὰρ θησαυρίζων in K29... to ταῦτα πρῶτα κυρίου θησαυρίσματά εἰσιν ἀγαθά here. Again, we return to this point at 3.5 below.

Thus, although as living literature it is quite likely that the church-order source which came to K had grown, there is no obvious reason why the fundamental inconsistencies which may be observed are not the result of K's own work. As we go on to examine the remainder of the document, this must be our working hypothesis. This does not exclude the possibility that κκ was itself the product of redactional expansion, indeed it would be surprising if it had not undergone redactional expansion, but is hard to see how such expansion might be identified, and we must suspect that this expansion had taken place before coming into the hand of K, from whose work derive the particular contradictions and tensions which we have noted. Bartlet does not discuss the first paragraph dealing with deacons which, we suggest below, carries some expansion within κκ, but in general there is not the evidence which would enable us to trace the multiple strata in a document whose very existence is hypothetical without any basis on which to identify the redactor and *his* interests, the basis on which it is possible to identify the work of K.

3.3 Interim conclusion

Whereas Harnack suggested that there were two sources to the church order found in K, and Bartlet suggested extensive interpolation by two redactors, we have found one ancient source, which may have undergone some development, and which has been interpolated extensively, probably by a single redactor. There is also the possibility of a second source. There is no reason to think that the final redactor of the ancient source is other than the K redactor who joined κκ to κ. We have yet, however, to deal with the conclusion of the document.

3.4 K24–28

In seeking to determine the sources lying behind these chapters and their redactional history we may begin with three observations which give some clue to the background of the discussion.

3.4.1 Jesus as teacher

Firstly we may concur with the observation of Harnack that at K22 and K26 Jesus is termed "the teacher."[109] This implies that both are from the same hand. However, this citation from "the teacher" is at the conclusion of the passage, and on this basis may be an expansion. However, even if an expansion of a prior text then such expansion may be laid at the door of K, since we have determined that, whether from a source or a redactional construction, the appearance of this chapter is the work of K. It thus follows that the introduction of K26 at least is also K's construction. In this light we may recollect the observation in 1.1 above that K had strengthened the TWT tradition regarding the manner in which the teacher should be viewed, as "the Lord", rather than as a master, and may thus see the basis for such a characterization of the teacher.

---

109 Harnack, *Lehre*, 215.

3.4.2 The presence of Mary and Martha

Secondly we may agree with Harnack that Mary and Martha are not actually present in the fictive scene, and that their statements are not part of the dialogue for, as he notes, the apostles alone are gathered;[110] rather the names as they appear are in reported speech. The prose is thus not particularly elegant, but if the two were taken as present this would stand in tension to the list of apostles at K1. This exchange is thus taken from a source, and it is entirely possible that in the source John, Martha and Mary were all present and that the passage as presently found in K stood as dialogue, and has been lifted with no editing, but that the two women are not present in the envisaged dialogue of K.[111]

The particular source of this dialogical exchange, however, is lost to us. Harnack suggests that it is the *Gospel of the Egyptians* on the grounds that there seems to have been much here about the interrelationship between male and female,[112] though he notes that in the *Gospel of the Egyptians* the talk is of the negation of maleness and femaleness rather than, as would appear to be the case in the saying that the weak is saved through the strong, the subjugation of the female to the male. Harnack also noted the appearance of Mary in *Pistis Sophia* and *Acta Philippi*, in the latter of which Martha also appears. Since Harnack wrote, *The Gospel of Thomas*, which states that the female must become male,[113] has been discovered, as have other works which afford a prominence to Magdalene among the disciples, namely the *Gospel of Philip, Epistula apostolorum, Gospel of Mary* and *Dialogue of the Saviour*. Although the agrapha reported in K26

---

110 Harnack, *Sources*, 25 n. Cf. Faivre, "Apostolicité", passim, who assumes that Mary and Martha are present, make up the number 12 and are included in the opening address to sons and daughters (which is not at all to the apostles, but is epistolary.)
111 Cf. Ernst, *Martha*, 243 n. 27, 248-249.
112 Harnack, *Sources*, 26.
113 *Ev. Thom.* 114.

do not appear in these, the scope of the possible origin of this exchange is broadened considerably (though it is not certain that the Mary here is indeed Mary Magdalene);[114] interestingly, however, all of these are products of the second century.

Also significant in terms of an investigation for the provenance of this position is the pairing of Mary with Martha. The two are paired in *Epistula apostolorum* as going to the tomb, as also in the *Book of the resurrection of Bartholomew the apostle*,[115] in the Hippolytean *In Cant.* 25.2, and, as already observed, in *Acta Philippi*. We may also note that the gnostic *Apocalypsis Jacobi* links Martha and Mary together. This text, like other gnostic texts, is concerned to reveal the negation of femininity though absorption into the male. By contrast, *Epistula apostolorum* may be seen as an anti-gnostic text (though the section concerning Mary and Martha at the tomb is not particularly concerned with gnosticism), and the Hippolytean commentary is particularly concerned to deny the gnostic tenet of the absorption of the female by suggesting instead that women are restored to their original state in Eve.[116] Not only, therefore, does the presence of Mary indicate that the source employed at K26 derives from the second-century debate with gnosticism but the pairing with Martha likewise indicates a second century and Asian provenance which engages with the gnostics. For as Harnack had noted, the emphasis here is on the subordination of the female rather than, as in gnostic literature, the transcending of gender, but nonetheless it is possible to see this source as part of the same discussion, as a response to gnostic speculation about the disap-

---

114 Her appearance alongside Martha would indicate that Mary of Bethany is intended. Bovon, "Mary Magdalene", 82, n. 33, however, suggests that the two are conflated by the redactor of the *Acta*.
115 An observation first made by Baumstark, "Alte und neue Spuren"; Baumstark also observes the link with K, but is thereby led to give an Egyptian provenance to the tradition.
116 Note the discussions of Cerrato, *Hippolytus*, 194–198, and Smith, *Mystery*, 106–132.

pearance of gender. We may also note the particular significance of the material which is held in common with *Epistula apostolorum* since, as has already been established,[117] the apostle lists in K(κ) and *Epistula apostolorum* are linked. Given that this latter section is the work of K, we may thus observe that K is not so far removed from the context which engendered his sources.

We have already noted that κ, like *Epistula apostolorum*, was simultaneously a *Sendschreibe* and a dialogue. Whereas this section is the work of K, who continued the dialogical form adopted by κ, nonetheless we have noted that this section has likewise been excerpted from a dialogue, thus leading to a dialogue within a dialogue. The dialogue here would appear to be a revelation dialogue. This was a form much employed by gnostic groups, in particular to publish revelation given by the Lord.[118] It is the same form which *Epistula apostolorum* employs, and indeed Hermas' revelations are often reported as dialogues, which leads one to suggest that this was the recognized form of publishing new revelation, as the dialogue reflected at a literary level the discussion which might take place when early Christian prophets delivered their material.[119] Thus although the revelation dialogue is not necessarily or originally gnostic—indeed Rudolph notes that Christian dialogues preceded the gnostic dialogues and that the extant dialogues reflect a specifically Christian gnostic milieu[120] —, it is in gnostic circles that the form continues to live and flourish. Indeed, of the possible sources mentioned above, several are revelation dialogues with gnostic tendencies. Once again a context engendered by debate and involvement with gnosticism would seem to be the context of this exchange, since the literary

---

117 At 2.1. above.
118 For a discussion, and form-critical analysis, of the Gnostic revelation dialogue, see Rudolph, "Gnostische Dialog", 85–107.
119 Cf. Rudolph, "Gnostische Dialog", 104, who suggests an origin in the schools, and Koester, "Überlieferung und Geschichte", 1475.
120 Rudolph, "Gnostische Dialog", 104–105.

tool employed to further the debate is typically gnostic. This, however, is the work of K; κ, although attributed to apostles, has no dialogic elements. Finally significant for locating the traditions employed by K is the tension between Mary and Peter; a similar tension is to be found in *The Gospel of Thomas*, the *Gospel of Mary* and *Pistis Sophia*.[121] As noted below,[122] the names of apostles might be used as ciphers in polemical writings marking differences between early Christian groups, and Peter is found as the particular representative of "orthodox" thinking. Although Mary is ultimately claimed here as a similarly orthodox voice, the source would imply that originally a certain tension lay between them, which is again indicative that the use and engagement with this source indicates an engagement with heterodox groups who exalted the position of Mary above that of Peter. In time the name of Mary is substituted with that of Peter, or that of the Mother of the Lord, in order precisely to remove focus from Mary Magdalene. As Brock suggests, this derives from the implicit threat posed because of her prominence in certain gnostic groups.[123] K's source is faced by the same threat, and K employs this to counter a threat which is close to home, but employs a different strategy as well as, as Ernst notes,[124] considerable effort, to counter it.

3.4.3 The offering of the Body and Blood

Thirdly we must observe the odd description of the eucharist as the offering of the Body and Blood. As Connolly puts it: "Can any parallel be brought from an ante-Nicene document to this absolute use of the 'oblation of the Body and the Blood?'"[125] Such is difficult, though ante-Nicene uses of the language of offering

---

121 See, with full references, Brock, "Peter, Paul and Mary", 180.
122 4.2.
123 Brock, "What's in a name", 112.
124 Ernst, *Martha*, 250–251.
125 Connolly, "Use of the Didache", 156.

and descriptions of the eucharist as the Body (or blood) of the Lord are not hard to find. However, Cyprian comes close to a doctrine as expressed here[126] and, more relevantly for K, the Syrian *Didascalia* come close in charging that the likeness of the royal body of Christ is to be offered.[127] An absolute statement like that here is more typical of the mediaeval west than of any patristic author, but if it should be considered a shorthand then the shorthand is as likely to come from early in the third century as from the fourth. Thus we may note the use of Firmilian[128] who refers to the eucharist quite simply as the offering of a sacrifice. This final usage is of particular interest as it derives from Cappadocia, which is the locale to which Bartlet sought to ascribe K, and to which we have ascribed *Testamentum Domini*, and because the context is that of a woman who celebrated the eucharist. It is indeed possible that this passage lay behind Bartlet's suggestion of Cappadocia.

3.4.4 The redaction of K24–28

We may conclude that whereas K employs sources in this section, and in particular alludes to a dialogic Gospel involving Mary and Martha, as well as deriving the *agraphon* concerning women sitting from a source, K24–28 as a whole is his own construction. The sources are all from the second century, and there is nothing in his language which prevents a similar date being ascribed to his redactional activity here. We must therefore ask whether it is possible to construct a *Sitz im Leben* for the discussion within that period.

These chapters are concerned with one issue, namely the impropriety that women should have any liturgical role in the eucharistic celebration, and that their ministry should be

---

126 See the discussion in Hanson, *Eucharistic offering*, 17–19.
127 *Didascalia* 6.22.2.
128 At Cyprian *Ep.* 75.10.5.

restricted to care for women in need. The fact that the subject of the eucharist is introduced by Peter as soon as Andrew mentions ministry for the women is indicative that this is what really is at issue. The whole point of the discussion is to subordinate women's ministry, and in particular to legislate against women's participation in the celebration of the eucharist. We have already suggested that K introduced K22 as a qualification of what is said about the ministry of widows, and may suggest that this is part of an overall strategy to minimize the significance of women's ministry. It is the manner in which this description of deacons' duties mirrors that of the earlier description of the work of one of the widows which leads to the suggestion that the chapter is a redactional composition, and indeed leads to the suspicion that the entire exchange of K24–28 is K's production in pursuit of the same objective. At a literary level it is hard to see how K24–28 can exist as a coherent piece once the dialogic elements and the introduction to K26 is removed, and we may note that the majority of the material is a citation of diverse testimonia all intended to refute any claim of women to a liturgical ministry. Whereas K was not the originator of these sayings, as he is apparently quoting from some source or sources in these chapters, it would appear to have been K who strung them together in their current form, and derived them from a source which was likewise hostile to the liturgical ministry of women.

Rather than exercising a liturgical ministry, these women are to be concerned with social care. As such they are comparable to the deaconesses of the Syrian *Didascalia*. This proximity of role has led to the suggestion that the passage here is a polemic against deaconesses, but as Gryson rightly points out, the term is not employed here.[129] Either deaconesses were never known in the K

---

129 Gryson, *Ministry*, 48, in response to a suggestion by Daniélou, *Ministry*. It is notable, however, that the Latin and Sahidic versions introduce deaconesses here in their rendering of Andrew's statement.

community or, more probably, they had yet to emerge. The polemic, however, is not against deaconesses but against a liturgical ministry by women, and the answer that the women's role is that of social care is one which might in turn lead to the emergence of the deaconess order. Here the functions are to be exercised by widows but in the *Didascalia* the widows are reduced to being recipients of charity rather than those who exercise good works. We may suggest that even in a charitable role widows had become too powerful for the community of the *Didascalia*. Methuen thus suggests that the deaconess order is a creation of the didascalist circle as a means of bringing female ministers under episcopal control and as a means of emasculating a powerful order of widows.[130] The stage of development of K is that of widows functioning in the role which in time would be filled by deaconesses, and so K either precedes the *Didascalia* or derives from an entirely different circle—though one in which similar developments are occurring. We may, however, note that widows in the *Didascalia* are to pray for the sinner undergoing repentance,[131] as for others. Is this what is meant when it said that the visionary widows are to pray for those in trouble? An additional puzzle is posed by the *Testamentum Domini*, which envisages a role for widows and deaconesses alike. The order of deaconess, however, may have been a later importation into the community which produced *Testamentum Domini*, for which reason the deaconess is clearly subordinate to the widow.[132] Thus *Testamentum Domini* knows of powerful widows who have a liturgical role, standing behind the presbyters on one side of the bishop. Is this the tradition which has come to K, and which K is opposing? We may note in support of this suggestion, both the presence of

---

130 Methuen, "Widows", 201–202, building on earlier suggestions. Similarly Stewart-Sykes, *Didascalia apostolorum*, 63–69.
131 *Didascalia* 6.6.9.
132 *Testamentum Domini* 1.19; 1.23. See my "The deaconess in *Testamentum Domini*".

Mary with Martha (and Salome) in the setting of *Testamentum Domini*, where they are told that they are to serve the Gospel,[133] and the fact that *Testamentum* has elements of a revelation dialogue.

If the concern is with the liturgical role of women then this implies that some women at least had claimed a liturgical role. We have already mentioned the female prophet who caused such alarm to Firmilian. This incident may be dated to 235. But beyond noting the event we may suggest that this was no innovation, but rather an anachronism. The *Didache* recognizes that prophets might celebrate the eucharist,[134] and although nothing is said of their gender, the existence of female prophets is well attested in early Christianity.[135] Firmilian may be surprised at the normative nature of the rites which she employs,[136] but we should not be so. A female prophet baptizing and celebrating the eucharist is simply an example of liturgical archaism.[137]

Just as prophets might give thanks at the eucharist in the community of the Didache, and just as at Melito's functionally eucharistic paschal rite the Lord comes to be present through prophetic utterance as much as through sacramental media,[138] so prophecy is bound up to eucharist in the ritual of the Marcosians. The presence of women at the altar in Marcosian rites which, whatever their divergence from the emerging normative eucharist, continued nonetheless to have many similarities, may likewise be seen not as an innovation but as an archaism.[139] Having noted the prominence of women prophets in early Christianity

---

133 *Testamentum Domini* 1.16.
134 Didache 10.7. See also the discussion of Trevett, *Montanism*, 188–189.
135 Thus note, for instance, Ammia (*HE* 5.17.3-4), the daughters of Philip (*HE* 5.17.3; 5.24.2), and the female prophetic activity described in the *Acta Pauli*.
136 Firmilian in Cyprian *Ep.* 75.10.5.
137 For a further discussion of liturgical archaism in separated Christian groups see my discussion of Marcionite liturgy in "Bread, fish, water and wine".
138 So Stewart-Sykes, *Lamb's High Feast*, 13–14 and 201 with reference to *Peri Pascha* 103.
139 See the discussion of A. & C. Faivre, "La place".

we may suggest that the continuance of female prophecy in heterodox sects in a later period is a further example of the preservation of practices obsolete in the *Grosskirche* among heterodox and separated communities. It is to be noted that two of the widows of κκ are to have revelations. Indeed the very qualification of widowhood as the basis for prophecy may be significant, since the original Montanist female prophets separated from their husbands at the time of prophesying.[140] Although it is possible that women continued to prophesy in orthodox circles even into the fourth century,[141] the expectation that a church which may not muster twelve males capable of offering patronage would nonetheless be able to support two (female) prophets indicates that this is indeed an ancient source. Thus it is entirely reasonable to suggest that women had exercised a liturgical role in the K community, and possible that they continued to do so.

However, it is fair to say that female presidency at the eucharistic celebration was not known except among sectarian groups by the third century. Although Jensen argues that the anonymous woman prophet of Cappadocia was a catholic Christian, suggesting that there is no strong indication that she was a Montanist,[142] Trevett cites a number of indications that she is indeed of the new prophecy,[143] such as her ecstatic mode of delivery, the geographical setting, and her statement that she had come from "Jerusalem", which may be read as a reference to the characterization of certain Phrygian villages as Jerusalem.[144] In Firmilian's perception, at least, she was Montanist. We may reckon with the possibility that the gap between the time of the prophet and that of Firmilian meant that the liturgical role of women had dimin-

140 So Apollonius at HE 5.18.3.
141 So Trevett, "'Angelic visitations'".
142 Jensen, *God's self-confident daughters*, 185–186.
143 Trevett, "Spiritual authority", 48–50 in particular but also *passim*.
144 So Apollonius at Eusebius 5.18.2 For discussion see Powell, "Tertullianists and Cataphrygians", 44, and Tabbernee, "Revelation 21".

ished and this event therefore was all the more shocking to a bishop in the middle of the third century, but even if this is the case it indicates that by the middle of the third century women did not celebrate the eucharist in catholic communities. Along similar lines Jensen suggests that the ban on female presbyters in the eleventh canon of the canons of Laodicea indicates that the presbyteral activity of women was known into that period,[145] but there is no necessity that these presbyters were liturgical presbyters.[146] It is as likely that this title is honorific or indicates a patronal role. Jensen's assertion is based on an assumption that the social leader of a community is also the liturgical leader.[147] We may re-iterate, therefore, the statement that female eucharistic presidency was unknown in Asian (specifically Cappadocian) catholic communities in the third century.

Nonetheless, widows have a place in the sanctuary at the celebration of the eucharist in *Testamentum Domini*,[148] which may imply a memory of a more prominent role in proceedings, and indicates that in this community at least women continued to have a role alongside the male *klēros*. A similar situation may be envisaged by the redactor of *Acta Philippi* 8.2, who describes Mary as preparing the bread and salt for the breaking of bread, and Martha as administering (eucharistic gifts?) to the people.[149] The pairing of Martha and Mary here is surely significant, as this seems directly to speak to the situation envisaged by K, to the extent that we may suggest that K is a direct response to the liturgical role of women presupposed by *Acta Philippi*.[150] Thus the subjugation of women, justified by the agraphon concerning the

---

145 Jensen, *God's self-confident daughters*, 185.
146 The same objection may be levelled at the discussion of Torjeson, *When women were priests*, 14–38, who, in citing evidence for women's liturgical leadership, cites evidence for women having presbyteral titles in catholic communities.
147 Such an assumption is laid to rest in my *Original bishops*, 144–185.
148 *Testamentum Domini* 1.19; 1.23.
149 A connection first observed by Zahn, *Forschungen*, 24, n. 3.
150 Such is indeed suggested by Bovon, "Mary Magdalene", 83.

salvation of the weak through the strong, is here particularly liturgical. The context of the dialogue may originally have related to speculation regarding maleness and femaleness, but K is solely concerned with women's ministry.

It is thus a similar context to that described by *Acta Philippi* and *Testamentum Domini* which is addressed by K. In particular we may observe what John says in response to Andrew: "when the teacher requested the bread and the cup and blessed them... he did not permit the women to stand alongside us." Ernst reasonably asks what is meant by συστῆναι ἡμῖν. "Are Martha and Mary excluded from standing in a leadership function (either assisting or presiding) at the eucharist, or are they excluded from standing with the congregation...?"[151] She concludes that some kind of assistant role is in question.[152] It is in the light of *Testamentum Domini*, and in particular the linkage already noted between K and the *Testamentum* that we may understand more precisely what "assistantship" is at stake, namely that the widows might stand with the presbyters.

We have to ask why this female ministry, which is rooted in tradition and which occurs elsewhere, should cause such alarm to K. Possibly there was a memory of more ancient practice in the community, possibly women had demanded a role, or possibly the struggle is a literary struggle aimed either against Montanists, who had female officers, or against the gnostic groups who produced the Magdalene literature and who perhaps continued to involve women in the eucharistic celebration alongside men—though possibly innovating in the manner in which their participation was interpreted. Further evidence for such a reading may be provided by the scene in the *Gospel of Judas* where Jesus laughs,

---

151 Ernst, *Martha*, 236.
152 Ernst, *Martha*, 240–241.

sardonically, at the disciples celebrating the eucharist.[153] We may, perhaps, interpret Mary's laughter in the same light, namely as indicating a certain superiority to the eucharistic activity. Possibly K is alarmed by a practice similar to that described in *Testamentum Domini*, obtaining in the community, or a community close to it geographically and ideationally, on the grounds that it is suspiciously close to gnostic practice?

A literary struggle is possible; given the tools employed the struggle is more probably with gnostic groups than with Montanists, though the latter possibility cannot be ruled out altogether as the new prophets seem to have read a variety of material including, it has been argued, literature from Nag Hammadi.[154] As to internal pressures which involvement with Christian gnostic or Montanist groups might have brought about we can know nothing certain. However, as we have noted, *Testamentum Domini* would seem to describe the very situation which K is seeking to prohibit, and *Acta Philippi* similarly seems to presuppose such an arrangement, which in turn implies either that there was pressure from the widows to maintain a role within the celebrations of the community or else that K is alarmed by the situation which obtains and, rather than recognizing that this is ancient tradition, believes this to be a gnostic innovation, so using gnostic tools (the dialogue) and anti-gnostic tools (apostolicity) to oppose it.[155] The K community is one distinct from that of the *Didascalia*, and so knows no deaconess order, but seeks to exercise control over women through a similar strategy, namely by demoting their role to a social role and by denying them any liturgical function. But it is close, ideationally and, on the basis of

---

153 *Ev. Jud.* 34. Similarly Ernst, *Martha*, 242, suggests a derisory and superior laughter, though without reference to the Gospel of Judas.
154 So Denzey, "What did the Montanists read". Hippolytus *Haer.* 8.19 refers to the large number of writings valued by the new prophecy.
155 Similarly Ernst, *Martha*, 234-241. See also Kateusz, *Mary*, 144-147, though this treatment is rather less nuanced.

the argument so far, geographically, to the Cappadocian *Testamentum Domini* community, where the widows stand with the presbyters. This is the meaning of συστῆναι ἡμῖν. In response Kephas, apparently quoting, states that "women should not pray upright but seated on the ground." This prevents the women standing with the presbyters.[156]

It is an odd statement nonetheless, given the ample evidence of women praying in a standing position.[157] I suggest that it has been removed from a distinct context to be employed here to prevent women, particularly widows, standing with the presbyters. Its original context may be illuminated by the *Quaestiones Bartholomaei* 2.1–14, where Mary is gathered with the disciples. When they come to pray, she says: "Let us stand up in prayer." However when the apostles stand behind Mary she suggests that Peter should not stand behind her but before, and quotes 1 Cor. 11:3 as from the Lord: "The head of the man is Christ, but the head of the woman is the man." Eventually they prevail upon her and she stands, spreads out her hands and prays. Thus a standing position is established, but there is debate concerning the propriety of women leading prayer. It seems that Mary is only permitted to lead prayer on this occasion on the basis of her particular significance as the one who bore Jesus, which is the subject which the apostles wish to discuss.

After they prayer she says: "Let us sit down on the ground. Come, Peter, chief of the apostles, sit on my right hand and put your left hand under my shoulder. And you, Andrew, do the same on my left hand. And you, chaste John, hold my breast. And you, Bartholomew, place your knees on my shoulders and press close my back so that, when I begin to speak, my limbs are not loosed." Thus she sits, as Peter in K states that women should. It seems that this is related to prophecy. Are the apostles perhaps holding

---

156 So Martimort, *Deaconesses*, 130, n. 169.
157 As noted by Harnack, *Sources*, 27 n. 13.

her down lest the mantic manifestations of a prophet under ecstasy become too extreme? It would thus be possible that the agraphon cited by K originally related not to the prayer of women but to their prophesying, insisting that women should prophesy seated. The holding of the arms is interesting, as the same is found in Hermas *Vis.* 1.3.4 where the old lady (who, incidentally, is likewise seated, a posture arguably derived from the circles of magic and ritual)[158] is carried away being held by the arms when she has finished her revelation.

The fact that this illuminating parallel is to be found in *Quaestiones Bartholomaei* is significant since, as Brock observes, this text is intended to exalt Peter's authority as a cipher for "apostolic" orthodoxy over female disciples in much the way that K does.[159]

The versions are clearly puzzled by the statement. Syriac completely alters the direction, stating instead that women should approach the sacrifice with heads covered. Sahidic makes the statement the opposite of that here. In both cases there seems to be some attempt to correct and update the statement, though Maclean, partly on the basis that a similar direction to that found in the Syriac is found in *Constitutiones apostolorum* 2.47 and elsewhere in the church order literature, reckons the Syriac reading original.[160] However, the very existence of these parallels indicates an attempt to correct the text and Maclean's suggestion of an erroneous reading, as noted in the textual commentary, does not explain the extensive departure from the Greek and Latin versions.

Because the whole focus of K in the end is a vision of church-order which relegates the role of women to social care, nothing is said of the widows who are to pray and prophesy whereas extensive qualifications are added to the discussion of

---

158 On which see Peterson, "Beiträge".
159 Brock, "What's in a name", 121–123.
160 *Ancient church orders*, 27–28.

the widow who is to engage in good works. In time even this would become controversial, but for the time being K is sufficiently motivated to redact an ancient church-order in order to clarify that women have no part in it. They are not to stand with the presbyters, as do the widows of *Testamentum Domini*.

3.5 The redaction of K22 and K29

We have suggested above, in 3.1, that K22 is inserted by K, either deriving this from a source, or constructing it redactionally. We argued that since the deacon might become the bishop it was certainly not derived from κκ. We also noted at 3.4.1 that the use of the term "teacher", to refer to Jesus, was an indication of K's hand in K22.

We have also, in 3.2, observed verbal linkage between the conclusion of K19 (on the reader), K21 (on widows), and K29, a concluding saying regarding sharing. We may note now that there is also a verbal linkage with K22. We thus discuss these linkages before reaching a conclusion regarding the provenance of K22 and conclusions regarding the redaction of K29.

The linkages are as follow:

First, in K19 we hear that ὁ γὰρ ἐμπιπλῶν ὦτα μὴ νοοῦντος ἔγγραφος λογισθήσεται παρὰ τῷ θεῷ. This has close verbal association with the second part of K29: ὁ γὰρ θησαυρίζων ἐν τῇ βασιλείᾳ ἔγγραφος ἐργάτης λογισθήσεται παρὰ τῷ θεῷ. Next, in K21, we hear that ταῦτα πρῶτα κυρίου θησαυρίσματά εἰσιν ἀγαθά, and we noted above the verbal link with the first part of K29: ὁ ποιῶν ἔργον καλὸν ἑαυτῷ θησαυρὸν περιποιεῖται.

Moreover the network of verbal similarities in K29 does not end here, as we may also compare διάκονοι ἐργάται τῶν καλῶν ἔργων in K22 to both parts of K29. As such we might even see this as the proper conclusion to K22, separated by other K material.

However, the verbal parallels, scattered across the second part of the document, together with the intrusive nature of K22 itself, lead to another suggestion, namely that these sayings are derived from a *gnomologion*, linked together, as these collections often were, by linkwords and catchwords.[161] The statement ὁ ποιῶν ἔργον καλὸν... ἐργάτης λογισθήσεται, actually two *gnomai* linked by the common use of θησαυρόν and θησαυρίζων, thus, I suggest, provides the basis on which K22 was composed, rather than being its conclusion. K provides this statement, to emphasize the scope of the male diaconate, and then returns to the *gnomē*, after discussing the lack of liturgical roles for women, in order, once again, to point up the charitable role of widows as opposed to any liturgical role.

3.5.1 Redaction and sources in K19, 21–22, 26–27, 29

Thus we suggest that K22 is redactional composition, rather than a distinct source. Nonetheless there are sources underlying much of K's expansion of κκ; a *gnomologion* provided K29, but also the conclusions to K19 and K21, as well as providing the basis on which K22 was composed. Although K26 is from a distinct source, of the nature of a Gospel, K27 may be from the same *gnomologion*, although in the absence of any catchword this is impossible to prove.

3.6 The conclusion to K

As has been noted, K was produced through the adjuncture of church order material with a document of TWT; an opening was provided and fitted into an epistolary setting in order to produce that which is now extant. We may also suggest that he provides K30 as a conclusion.

Since the injunction that nothing should be added or subtracted from the content of teaching is part of TWT in D, E and K and thus, we may surmise, in δ and κ likewise, it seems most probable that the source of this statement at K30 is κ. Although

---

161 So Wilson, *Mysteries*, 39–41.

K has already redacted this material at K14, the conclusion to κ provides a conclusion for his entire work.

The prior part of the chapter, however, goes beyond staking an apostolic claim and states that the content is commanded by the Lord. There is a superficial similarity with B4.9, and thus it is possible that the material may be attributed to β, but the similarity is superficial only, for whereas the point of B4.9 is to deny authority of the rabbinic type as part of the appeal to the listener, here an even higher authority is claimed.[162] Since K has used a number of agrapha attributed to Jesus earlier in his redactional construction, and is concerned to root his apostolic order in the teachings of Jesus, we may surmise that this is his redactional conclusion, reworked from one of his fundamental sources.

3.7 The ancient church order lying behind K

We thus conclude that K's major source was a church-order consisting of K16–21 (less interpolations), which we have termed κκ. Quite possibly there was more, but even though, as we suggest below, the *Didascalia* employed this church order as one of its own sources, and may therefore preserve more of this source, it cannot readily be recognized in the context of the *Didascalia* except where there is a parallel also extant in K. It was suggested in the first edition that part of K1 and K23 were also derived from this source, though further reflection, particularly in the light of *Testamentum Domini*, has suggested that these sections should be seen as redactional constructions from K.

At this stage we may examine this source, insofar as it may be reconstructed, in an attempt to determine its age, provenance, and significance.

---

162 Schermann, *Elfapostelmoral*, 88, likewise denies a connection.

3.7.1 κκ as a qualification list

Fundamental to κκ is a statement of the qualifications suitable for each office. Inevitably this leads us to compare the catalogues to those of the Pastoral Epistles for the same offices. Some examination of these qualification lists was undertaken at 3.2. above, but there is more to say.

It may indeed be noted that a number of comparable qualifications may be found both in K and in the Pastoral Epistles. Thus the *episkopos* of K is to be of good repute (φήμην καλὴν ἔχει ἀπὸ τῶν ἐθνῶν, cf. 1 Tim. 3:7, μαρτυρίαν καλὴν ἔχειν ἀπὸ τῶν ἔξωθεν), temperate (σώφρων, cf. 1 Tim. 3:2, Titus 1:8, σώφρονα), not a drunkard (μὴ μέθυσος, cf. 1 Tim. 3:3 and Titus 1:7, μὴ πάροινον), not grasping (μὴ πλεονέκτης, cf. μὴ αἰσχροκερδῆ Titus 1:7). Similarly deacons are to be μονόγαμοι (cf. 1 Tim. 3:12, μιᾶς γυναικὸς ἄνδρες), raising their children well (τεκνοτρόφοι, cf. 1 Tim. 3:12, τέκνων καλῶς προϊστάμενοι), temperate (σώφρονες, again cf. 1 Tim. 3:2, σώφρονα, Titus 1:8), kindly (ἐπιεικεῖς cf. 1 Tim. 3:3, of an *episkopos*, ἀλλὰ ἐπιεικῆ)... not irascible (μὴ ὀργίλοι, cf. Titus 1:7, μὴ ὀργίλον).

But for all the similarity between the lists we may observe, as is evident from the paragraph above, that different vocabulary is used for the same qualities. This makes a direct literary relationship highly unlikely, though an indirect relationship, perhaps a mutual dependence on an early Christian associational *lex*, is plausible.[163]

Historically the catalogues of the Pastoral Epistles have been compared to similar qualification lists in the ancient world, principally that of Onosander for a general, but also to those of Lucian (for a dancer) and Soranus (for a midwife.) To this Paschke has added the possibility that the *cura morum* of Roman censors might have had some influence.[164] The debate has centred

---

163 So Bartsch, *Anfänge*, 82–111, largely following Harnack, *Sources*.
164 For all this see Paschke, "Cura morum"; Goodrich, "Overseers".

around the question of whether these catalogues are simply standardized and have been borrowed by the author of the Pastorals, or whether they are specific to the offices to which the author is applying them. Given the ethical *koinē* of the Hellenistic world a degree of overlap is inevitable, and since, as I have argued elsewhere, the responsibilities of these officers, whilst changing, is growing out of an economic office, certain criteria such as ἀφιλάργυρον (which appears in Onosander and K, though not in the Pastoral Epistles) and not being bibulous (in the Pastoral Epistles and K, and in the *cura morum* presented by Dionysius Halicarnassus,[165] though not in the commonly cited classical lists) are to be expected. The most instructive approach to these catalogues is to discern what is not common ground, to allow us to see the specifics of the office.[166] Thus διδακτικόν, found in 1 Tim. 3:2, is an indication that the episcopate is becoming a scholasticized office. The same is true of the *episkopos* of K, with the direction that he should be competent to interpret the Scriptures. Unique to κκ is the demand of the bishop that he be προσωπολήπτης, and the comparable statement with regard to the deacons that μὴ πρόσωπον πλουσίου λαμβάνοντες. Although these do not appear in the Pastoral Epistles, or in the classical parallels, these demands are prominent in the *Didascalia*, as a means of ensuring that generous patrons do not receive preferential treatment, again indicating common economic ground in the office, and the possible use by the Didascalist's source of κκ.

The specifics of these catalogues may be kept in mind as the examination proceeds. However, what may be observed at this stage is the complete absence of parallel between the presbyteral qualification list in K, and the qualifications of ministers in the Pastoral Epistles, or indeed elsewhere, which tends to support the hypothesis suggested above that these are the work of K.

---

165 So Paschke "Cura morum", 114–115.
166 The approach of Goodrich, "Overseers".

3.7.2 The bishop and presbyters in κκ

The first thing which may be deduced about the episcopate is that, given that the quorum required is twelve, the bishop is head of a single congregation. Although this may indicate a rural position, if the order is ancient we may yet be in a context in which the monepiscopate as later understood had not yet emerged, namely that a bishop may head a single congregation rather than a group of congregations, and thus it is entirely possible that the congregation in question is urban.[167] It is also possible that the number twelve may make the congregation appear smaller than it was, in that the order not only excludes women but moreover does not state what qualified a man as an elector; we cannot simply assume that all men had a vote, for it is possible that householders or persons of property only were so competent. This position will be argued at greater length below, but for the moment we may observe that the *episkopos* is not a *monepiskopos* in the sense that he had charge of more than one congregation, but that he is what is frequently, though inaccurately, described as a presbyter-bishop. The assumption that monepiscopate, understood simply as a single bishop in a community, rather than a bishop set over multiple communities, had emerged from originally collective leadership has caused confusion here. Thus Lemoine suggests that Peter's discussion of *oligandria* concerns the election of *a* bishop, as opposed to *the* bishop, and suggests that the bishop here is hardly distinguished from a presbyter,[168] and Faivre alike suggests that presbyters might not be closely distinguished from the *episkopos*, as it is to the presbyters that a fundamentally disciplinary role is assigned, and on the grounds that K17 refers to presbyters assisting the bishops (plural) at the altar.[169] To take

---

167 On the distinction between *episkopos* and *monepiskopos* see my *Original bishops*, 3–5.
168 Lemoine, "Étude", 10.
169 Faivre, "Texte grec", 36.

these arguments in turn, we may first point out that the bishop is elected as a single bishop, and a definite article is unnecessary since it is clear that a single community is meant. The situation is thus probably as that envisaged by Ignatius, the *Didascalia*, and *Testamentum Domini*, namely that the *episkopos* is not *episkopos* set over several communities but is *episkopos* within one church. Secondly, although it is true that the presbyters and the bishop are συμμύσται τοῦ ἐπισκόπου καὶ συνεπιμάχοι, and even assuming that these qualifications are not, as suggested above, interpolated into κκ by K, this does not mean that they are at every level indistinguishable. Faivre points to a certain ambivalence within the *Didascalia* about who has disciplinary functions, but this does not impact on K. Finally the textual support for Faivre's argument has disappeared in view of the emendation to the text proposed below.[170] This said, there is a close relationship between *episkopos* and presbyters and a certain overlap of function.

A widespread hypothesis regarding the origins of the threefold order of bishop, presbyter, and deacon is that it emerged as a fusion (*Verschmelzung*) of two systems, the presbyteral and the episcopal-diaconal. This was given classic expression by Lietzmann,[171] but was commonly held in the late nineteenth century, and was held particularly by Harnack, who found support for this hypothesis in K, and particularly in the differing qualifications for presbyter and bishop. He thus suggested that this illu-

---

170 See the text and textual commentary ad loc.
171 Lietzmann, "Zur altchristlichen Verfassungsgeschichte".

minates the distinct origins of the two offices.¹⁷² However the inconsistencies he points out, such as the demand for celibacy and age of presbyters, neither of which is demanded of bishops, may be attributed to the K redaction, and so we cannot uphold the independent origin of these offices in the community of κκ on that basis. We may, however, deduce that by the time of K the presbyterate had been clericalized, since particular demands are made of the presbyters, whereas earlier the presbyters were simply senior male members of the community. We do not criticize Lietzmann's theory here, beyond suggesting that K does not lend the support to the theory of *Verschmelzung* that Harnack had thought it did.¹⁷³

Having cleared these standard hypotheses from the table, we may turn to explore what K has to say about the origins of church order with a new vision.

We may begin by returning to the question of whether the twelve electors are simply members of the congregation or those who exercised patronage within the church. This would mean that that the *oligandria* is not absolute but specifically a shortage of men who are competent to elect. Two points speak in favour of this interpretation. Firstly the election is said to take place ἐντὸς δεκαδύο ἀνδρῶν; although Harnack takes this phrase as qualifying the *oligandria* and meaning "less than twelve", the phrase is a long way from the mention of the shortage of men. It may perhaps, therefore, be taken with ψηφίσασθαι, and to be

---

172 Harnack, *Sources*, 28-35. It is clear from Nautin's papers that he too considered that the most ancient stratum of K revealed a two-fold order of bishop and deacons, and on these grounds suspected the word πρεσβυτέρους in K17, assigning the second part of this chapter, and the following chapter, to a distinct source, and suggesting that the appointment of deacons here described is picked up at K20 (hence his suggestion noted below that the three means the bishop and two deacons.) Whereas we have seen that there is much that is suspect in K18, this does not extend to the entire chapter, but solely to the statement of qualifications. Moreover, K20 does not easily follow on from K17a, even if πρεσβυτέρους is replaced by διακόνους.
173 For a critique of Lietzmann see my *Original bishops*, 309-315.

translated as "from among twelve". The twelve are thus candidates as well as electors. Secondly this avoids the oddity of having a community of twelve which nonetheless has a minimum of eight clerics![174]

That office and patronage were joined together in early Christian circles is widely recognized. In some instances this meant that the offices of *episkopos* and *diakonos* were held as *honores* by patrons, in a manner similar to the honouring of patrons by synagogues as *archisynagogos*. However, I have argued that in Asian communities, and communities of Asian origin in Rome, there is a distinct group of patrons within churches who labelled themselves as πρεσβύτεροι. We may find evidence of this group in the Pastoral Epistles, in *Traditio apostolica*, and in *Acta Petri*, as well, potentially, in the Ignatian correspondence. There is also evidence of a patronal group appointing officers in D and DA, though here the group does not appear to have been designated as πρεσβύτεροι.[175] We cannot say that these twelve were, or were not, designated presbyters,[176] but may accept that they functioned in the same way as those Asian groups who were so designated.

That the group of patrons was known as presbyters may gain support from what is said of the activity of these presbyters at the eucharist: "The presbyters on the right are to assist those who oversee the altar, so that they may distribute the gifts of honour and receive them as necessary. The presbyters on the left are to assist the congregation, so that it may be peaceful and without disturbance, once it has been instructed in all submission." Thus Harnack, like Faivre, points out that the duties of these presbyters are, in accordance with those of the bishop, disciplinary and economic. Some presbyters are to distribute the gifts at the altar,

---

174 So also Vilela, *Condition collégiale*,165–167.
175 On all this see *Original bishops*, 134–185.
176 Duchesne, Untitled review, 364, is the first to suggest that these twelve are presbyters; he would not, however, see them as patrons.

whereas others are to see good order. Of course this is bound up to the liturgy, but the distinction between liturgical action and economic action is a fine one. Two examples may suffice. Justin states that the offerings of the congregation made at the eucharist are received by deacons and then distributed among widows and orphans,[177] and the *Didascalia* closely connect offering for the support of the bishop and the poor to the eucharistic offering.[178] Harnack finds support in this for his hypothesis, derived from Hatch,[179] that the origins of the episcopate lay in an economic office. This view is not much found now, though I have argued for it at length elsewhere;[180] further argument is thus is beyond the scope of this introduction. Nonetheless the fact remains that these are the duties of the *episkopos* and of the presbyters in this community. By the time of K the eucharist is distinguished as an offering of the Body and Blood, but for κκ the issue is indeed that of good order at the distribution of gifts. The point is that this distribution is an act of patronage, and thus the presbyters are seen to be patrons in the same way that the electors are. This indicates that they are the same people.

As already noted, Faivre likewise observes the disciplinary role of the presbyters. He also notes that the provision for dealing with an insolent member is closely proximate to the Essene provisions of the Community Rule dealing with insolence.[181] Although this may perhaps point, once again, to an originally disciplinary aspect to the offices of the community of κκ, Faivre suggests a more direct connection to Essene practice, noting the similarity of the three chosen men and the twelve electors in the notice regarding the election of a bishop with the provision for

---

177 1 *Apol.* 67.6.
178 Note especially *Didascalia* 2.36.4.
179 Hatch, *Organization*.
180 In *Original bishops*, 55–119.
181 Faivre, "Texte grec", 36–37 with reference to 1QS 8.16–19.

twelve men and three priests in the *Community Rule*.[182] This section of the *Community Rule* is legislating for a minimal and foundational community; in this instance there is a definite linkage with the twelve of K, as in both instances we are concerned with a minimally competent group. K does not, however, concern itself with three priests; the three of the Community rule are, moreover, additional to the twelve, whereas in K they are a substitute. On the basis of the parallels with Essene documents, Faivre characterizes the community of κκ as Judaeo-Christian, as forming a community similar to the Essenes, and as located in Syria early in the second century. Even if the parallels are not quite so pressing as they appear to be at first sight, nonetheless the importance placed on the community of goods, which is overseen by the bishop and presbyters as well as the disciplinary functions assigned to the bishop in this context may be seen as proximate indeed to Essene practice, and so it is likewise possible that there is an organic link to the twelve who form the electoral college for the bishop and the twelve who are the minimal foundational community in the *Community rule*. Again, the number twelve may indicate a group of leading members of the community. One cannot avoid being reminded of the persistence of the twelve who form a sanhedrin in Acts,[183] of the system by which twelve presbyters would elect the Alexandrian patriarch from their number, of the statement in *Testamentum Domini* that a community should have twelve presbyters,[184] and of the ordination of twelve presbyters alongside a bishop in the pseudo-Clementines.[185]

On the basis that the twelve are actually presbyters, and

---

182 Faivre, "Texte grec", 37–39, with reference to 1QS 3.1–4.
183 A number which, given the possible Essene foundation of the Jerusalem Christian community, may even relate to its appearance in the *Community rule*.
184 *Testamentum Domini* 1.34.
185 *Rec.* 3.66 (Zacchaeus is ordained bishop alongside twelve presbyters and four deacons) and *Rec.* 6.15 (also *Hom.* 11.36) (Maro is ordained bishop alongside twelve presbyters, with deacons and the order of widows is established).

because the situation envisaged is that, perhaps in a foundational community, there are not twelve, then Duchesne,[186] followed by Vilela,[187] suggests that the three men who are to come from a neighbouring church are three bishops. However, the three selected are not said to be bishops, indeed they cannot all be bishops if they come from a single congregation. Nonetheless Harnack and Duchesne alike are certainly right in connecting this regulation to the standing rule that bishops should be consecrated by three external bishops.[188] In particular both point to the report of Cornelius' letter to Fabian of Antioch at *HE* 6.43.8–9, where Cornelius states that Novatian had obtained consecration. What is significant here is not simply that three are required for the consecration of a bishop, but that the three come to Rome in order to deal with issues which are disturbing the church. Thus we may note, again with Harnack, that 1 Clement 63 and 65 refer to the Roman church sending three persons to Corinth.[189]

This group of twelve thus represents a primitive community organization, coherent with the picture sketched elsewhere, but unfortunately adding little to our knowledge. The *episkopos* is probably elected from among their number, as the qualifications which are given similarly indicate a patronal ministry: even if those found elsewhere in qualification lists are excluded, the bishop is not to be προσωπολήπτης and is to be φιλόπτωχος—a qualification otherwise only appearing in *Testamentum* Domini.[190] This, taken with the evidence already adduced for an overlap between the functions of the *episkopos* and the presbyters, indicates that in κκ at least the *episkopos* is a member of the presby-

---

186 Duchesne, Untitled review, 364–365.
187 Vilela, *Condition collégiale*, 166.
188 Duchesne, Untitled review, 364–365; Harnack, *Sources*, 36–38. The rule that three bishops should ordain is subsequently confirmed by the 4th Canon of Nicaea.
189 Harnack, *Sources*, 36–38.
190 *Testamentum Domini* 1.20.

tery, and functions as their officer and leader. They participate in his economic ministry; thus the widows are to disclose information about women in need to the presbyters, and not, as might otherwise be expected, to the bishop. Presumably this enables them to ensure that these needy women receive fairly at the distribution of goods.

On this understanding we may return to what is said of the appointment of these presbyters:

> John said: The bishop who has been installed, knowing the care and the love of God of those who are with him, should install two presbyters of whom he approves. $_2$ All said in reply: Not two but three. For there are twenty-four presbyters, twelve on the right and twelve on the left. 17$_1$ John said: You have recalled this well, brothers.

I have suggested above that 17.2a ("all said in reply...") and 18.1a ("John said:...") is a redactional addition from K. The text continues:

> For those on the right receive the phials from the archangels and bear them to the master, and those on the left have authority over the company of angels.

There then follows the statement of qualification for a presbyter, already assigned, on the basis that the flow is interrupted, to K. The text continues:

> The presbyters on the right are to assist those who oversee the altar, so that they may distribute the gifts of honour and receive them as necessary. The presbyters on the left are to assist the congregation, so that it may be peaceful and without disturbance, once it has been instructed in all submission.

We may thus surmise, as long as a double-redaction in the K form is not suspected, that the material about presbyters at the altar came into the hand of K as part of κκ. We may also deduce that κκ legislated for the appointment of two presbyters, here following Krawutzcky and Harnack, who saw the two presbyters as bringing about a symmetry on either side of the bishop, reckoning that two was therefore the minimum number of presbyters.[191] Although Funk suggests that there would be an apparent contradiction between the existence of twelve presbyters in the account of election and the appointment of two (or three) below,[192] we may suggest in response that the provision for appointment is to be followed if there is no existing quorum. It may, however, on this understanding, be a redactional growth within the κκ tradition. A further possibility which should be considered is that there has been a textual corruption in κκ, before it reached the hands of K. Namely that rather than legislating for the appointment of two presbyters, it legislated the appointment of twelve, δεκαδύο, rather than two (δύο). Hilgenfeld, indeed, suggested such an emendation, namely: πρεσβυτέρους δεκαδύο. πάντες ἀντεῖπον· ὅτι οὐ δεκαδύο ἀλλὰ εἴκοσι καὶ τέσσαρες (κδ ´).[193] The second part of the emendation is unnecessary, and is hard to explain. The first part, namely the appointment of twelve, is conceivable as a textual corruption, explicable in turn if the community no longer mustered twelve presbyters, and would also make sense of John's speech as indicating that if there are twelve presbyters already (the quorum) the bishop should appoint a further twelve, to make up the number of twenty-four, of older men who might not necessarily be of the patronal class. Again we think of the occasions on which the number "twelve" is found, most particularly in the Essene communities (which may explain the persistence of the number in Acts),[194] and in the (contextually rel-

---

191 Krawutzcky, "Altkirchliche Unterrichtsbuch", 400; Harnack, *Sources*, 10.
192 Funk, *Doctrina*, 60.
193 Hilgenfeld, *Novum Testamentum*, 101–102.
194 That is to say, as suggested in *Original bishops*, 224–233, the "twelve" in Acts were not the apostles, but an Essene community gathered around James.

evant) *Testamentum Domini*.[195] But if δεκαδύο stood in κκ originally, it surely did not in the version transmitted to K. Thus he increases the number from two to three.

Although not strictly relevant to the form of κκ we may deal here, for convenience, with the question of why K increased the number of presbyters to be appointed to three, as this will be a matter of concern when we deal with the deacons in κκ. It is certainly odd, and disrupts the symmetrical arrangement that the distribution of gifts would seem to require.

In the first edition I essayed the suggestion that K thought that an appointment of two would not really be an appointment of two, because the election of a bishop from among the existing presbytery would actually only augment the presbytery by one—due to the loss of the bishop. I am less than sure that this is correct, not least because of the close relationship between bishop and presbytery, which implies that the bishop is still a member in any event. We may also note Harnack's suggestion that that the redactor cannot imagine that two presbyters would be sufficient,[196] but this is insufficient rationale for the intervention. My sole suggestion, derived from Funk,[197] is that given that the number three stood in the statement of appointment of deacons and widows, that K is ensuring that there are at least as many presbyters as there are widows (and deacons), not understanding that the twelve had all themselves originally been counted as presbyters. We have already seen the extent to which K is troubled by the widows, and so any basis on which to bolster any counterbalance to their influence might readily be ascribed to this redactor.

3.7.3 The reader
Our understanding of the role of the reader depends on the state-

---

195 *Testamentum Domini* 1.34.
196 Harnack, *Lehre*, 212.
197 Funk, *Doctrina*, 62.

ment about the unlettered bishop. As the text stands, the illiteracy of the bishop does not readily fit with the requirement that he be generous, and therefore looks like an interpolation. An emendation to the text may therefore be proposed: where the extant Greek manuscript reads δυνάμενος τὰς γραφὰς ἑρμενεύειν· εἰ δὲ ἀγράμματος, πραΰς ὑπάρχων I suggest that κκ read: δυνάμενος τὰς γραφὰς ἑρμενεύειν εἰ δ᾽ ἦ ἀγράμματος· πραΰς ὑπάρχων...

The reason for the emendation is that, although there is no reason why an early source might not legislate for an illiterate bishop, the connection to generosity is odd. The qualification for generosity is ancient, it is found in D, for instance, and relates to the ability of the bishop to supply financial support to the congregation but it in no way connects to literacy. Rather the comment about literacy connects to what went before, namely the requirement that the bishop should be able to interpret the Scriptures, and not what follows; thus the emendation to the text and repunctuation puts the matter of illiteracy alongside the requirement that the bishop be able to interpret the Scriptures. The point is that the bishop should be capable of interpretation, and that illiteracy is not a bar to that competence. Harnack cites several examples of illiterate bishops from the third century, and Funk two examples from the fifth![198] If the emendation is not accepted, then as an interpolation the statement "if he is unlettered" is unlikely to be the work of K, but must be assigned to some intermediate level in the growth and development of κκ, before it came to K, whereas the statement that he should have some education, provisionally ascribed to K above, must be original. If this is the case it is at this time likewise that the discussion of the reader, whose role in the reading and interpretation of Scripture appears to complement that of the bishop, came about. But the original probably belongs in κκ; the readership is comple-

---

198 Harnack, *Sources*, 10; Funk, *Doctrina*, 61.

mentary to the episcopate, however, because if the bishop cannot read then somebody has to read the Scripture for him in order that he may then interpret it. At this point, however, we should note again that the final comment of the chapter seems to fit the text as given in the manuscript. We have already suggested that this is K's interpolation, and may therefore suggest that K read the text as it stands in the manuscript. Either the corruption had already taken place, or possibly K simply misread what was in front of him. A deliberate alteration is, however, possible.

The position of reader thus comes about as somebody has to read the text so that a bishop who is unable to read can interpret it. Such a position could simply be a local arrangement on the basis of an illiterate bishop in the κκ community, but it is likely that an illiterate bishop was far from being an isolated phenomenon, and thus that readers may have been widespread. Given the uncertainty of the date of κκ, the first clear evidence of a reader is found in Tertullian's *De praescriptione haereticorum* 41, where he states that in heretical communities a person may one day be a reader, another a deacon. Since, however, he is referring to Marcionite communities, and Marcionites were liturgically conservative,[199] the office may already have been ancient in eastern communities. We are thus reminded of the blessing upon the reader of the Apocalypse[200] as indicating that readers held some kind of position from a relatively early period.

For Faivre the provision for an unlettered bishop is close in spirit to the simple priest of the Damascus document.[201] To follow through this analogy we may see the position of the reader as close in spirit to the learned levite, who is to advise the *mebaqqer* on matters of ritual law. However, it is more probable that the similar phenomena have come about not because of a direct his-

---

199 On Marcionite liturgical conservatism see my "Bread, fish, water and wine".
200 Rev. 1:3.
201 Faivre, "Texte grec", 39–40, with reference to CD 13.2–6.

torical connection but because the bishop, like the *mebaqqer*, is chosen on the fundamentally social grounds that he is a person in a position to offer patronage to the community, and on these grounds need not be literate.²⁰² Thus the provision for a lettered reader assisting an unlettered bishop may represent the social setting in which an unlettered master may be reliant upon literate slaves for aspects of management; the context for the operation of a reader in the eucharistic setting may derive from the employment of slaves to read to a company in domestic settings.

It is said that the reader is to be διηγητικός. The meaning of this word is not entirely clear. Obviously the reader is to read, and is to have a voice that is easy to hear, but it appears that something more is demanded.²⁰³ If the term refers to something beyond reading, we may note that according to Dionysius Thrax reading is to be followed by *exēgēsis*.²⁰⁴ But this is the procedure of clarifying difficulties, and is to be distinguished from *diēgēsis*, which is the construction of a narrative. If we were to suggest that the practice here is derived from the rhetorical, rather than the grammatical, curriculum, then the role of *diēgēsis* in a speech may give a clue to the significance of the term διηγητικός here. The progymnasmatic authors give directions on the construction of *diēgēmata*, and Quintilian recommends that instruction in narrative should be first of that given by a rhetor as it links in with direction already given under a *grammatikos*.²⁰⁵ The *narratio*, or *diēgēsis*, is part of any speech, according firstly to Aristotle, who is followed by all subsequent writers, and consists of the statement

---

202 Harris, *Ancient literacy*, 251–252, whilst suggesting that wealthy persons are more likely to be literate, nonetheless notes cases both fictional and historical of persons of wealth who were unlettered.
203 Cf. Funk, *Doctrina*, 65, who, rightly disagreeing with Harnack's suggestion that the term refers to an ability to interpret, takes it as indicating facility in reading, alongside εὐήκοος.
204 πρῶτον ἀνάγνωσις ἐντριβὴς κατὰ προσῳδίαν, δεύτερον ἐξήγησις κατὰ τοὺς ἐνυπάρχοντας ποιητικοὺς τρόπους... (*Ars Gramm.* 1).
205 Quintilian *Institutio oratoria* 2.4.1.

of facts preliminary to any proof to be gathered from it.[206] Thus we may suggest that the reader was to construct a narrative on the basis of the reading. The bishop, who was unable himself to read, might then *interpret* the scripture, drawing out the lesson for the hearers, thus fulfilling the rhetorical function of proof which, Aristotle suggests, might consist of amplification and of the provision of examples.[207] Thus *diēgēsis* is not interpretation[208] but rather a narrative preliminary to interpretation. The pattern which seems to be implied is rather like the "word of exhortation" identified in early Christian and Jewish literature by Wills, by which ethical lessons are drawn from an *exemplum* or *exempla*.[209] The *exempla* are scriptural, and the pattern may well follow on from a reading. We may thus suggest that the reader, apart from reading the Scripture, is to narrate the *exempla*, and that the bishop is then required to draw out the ethical lesson. As such we may compare the report of Justin at *I Apol*.1.67, where it is said that the προεστώς draws out the lessons of Scripture in a word of νουθεσία and πρόκλησις, παυσαμένου τοῦ ἀναγινώσκοντος.

The origins for such an arrangement may be catechetical. *Canones Hippolyti* 37, in common with κκ, seems to suppose that the reader should be first in the assembly. If, as I have argued elsewhere, the liturgy of the word was created by the adjuncture of catechumenal instruction in the morning with a morning eucharist (with associated psalmody) transferred from the evening,[210] the direction that the reader should be first in the assembly may be a reminiscence of this earlier practice. Thus we may note that Cyprian enrolls Optatus specifically among those readers who read on behalf of those presbyters who are teaching catechu-

---

206 Aristotle *Rhetorica* 3.13.1-3.
207 Aristotle *Rhetorica* 3.17.3-5.
208 Cf. Harnack, *Sources*, 16; Gamble, *Books and readers*, 223, for whom they are the same.
209 Wills, "Form".
210 "Domestic origin".

mens.²¹¹ The close association in eastern canonical material between readers and psalm-singers²¹² may likewise result from this juncture of practices, due to the close association of psalmody and reading in the earliest liturgy of the word. The close association between readers and exorcists in western material²¹³ may likewise indicate that the origin of the readership lay in catechesis, since the preparation of catechumens was the principal occupation of both.

Harnack traces the origins of the reader as distinct from other minor orders. Although we cannot altogether follow him in tracing the origins of the readership to the routinization and downgrading of charismatic offices such as that of the teacher and prophet,²¹⁴ and even less may follow him in tracing the minor orders more generally to the adoption of a pagan sacrificial system in third-century Rome, we may, however, agree generally that there is a tendency for functions to become offices, and for offices to be seen in the light of clerical orders. For this reason *Traditio apostolica* 11 is clear that a reader does not receive a laying on of hands; as such it is resisting the tendency to clericalize the reader. In time the reader became indeed a minor cleric, and the scope of the task diminished, but we may see in κκ the distinct role of the reader and gain some insight into the origins of the office.

Finally we may note with Harnack that, like κκ, the didascalist knows no other minor order but the reader.²¹⁵ For Harnack this was the most pressing parallel to the situation found in κκ. Although we argue below that κκ was a literary source employed by the didascalist, the context in which the provision for a reader is found is not paralleled in κκ, and therefore that the presence of a reader and of no other minor order in the *Didascalia* is not the

---

211 Cyprian *Ep.* 29.1.2.
212 On which see Harnack, *Sources*, 66.
213 See Harnack *Sources*, 57–58, though with a different explanation.
214 An approach followed by Gamble, *Books and readers*, 218–224.
215 Harnack, *Sources*, 70–72.

result of any literary relationship, but occurs because the situation is indeed the same, and had come about through the same process of development.

3.7.4 The deacons

We have suggested that the puzzle of duplication of discussions of deacons comes about because the K redaction, concerned to put the pastoral and social ministry of the church entirely into male hands, clarified that this was to be carried out by deacons, rather than by widows. We shall find further reasons for this additional paragraph below, but for the moment we clarify that the concern of this section is solely with K20, which is to be ascribed, *in nuce* at least, to κκ.

The extant text reads simply that deacons are to be appointed, and then adds: "Every matter of the Lord shall be established by three." Harnack suggests that the number three stood adjacent to deacons, and was deliberately omitted by K, in the same manner that K had increased the number of presbyters to three.[216] It is hard to see the logic of this. We may compare to this the suggestion of Nautin that "two" had stood here originally, and that the number three, in the statement that each matter of the Lord is established by three, referred to two deacons taken with the bishop.[217] Against this, at least as far as κκ is concerned, is the fact that whereas the presbyters and the bishop are in close relationship, this is not the case with regard to the deacons, although it is the case elsewhere in the church order tradition and beyond.

In accounting for the presence, or absence, of the number we may next observe the radical interpretation of the entire passage concerning presbyters and deacons proposed by Duchesne, followed by Vilela.[218] Rather than seeing, as Harnack did, two pres-

---

216 Harnack, *Lehre*, 212 n. 36.
217 A suggestion derived from Nautin's unpublished notes.
218 Duchesne, Untitled review, 366–367; Vilela, *Condition collegiale*, 167–171.

byters as symmetrical alongside the bishop at the altar, he suggests that the citation from Revelation regarding the twenty-four at the altar relates to the number three. The function of keeping order in the congregation, he suggests, which is that of the presbyters on the left of the bishop, is more properly that of deacons; thus there are three on either side, forming a presbytery, of whom the three on the right are presbyters, and the three on the left deacons. There is no theoretical objection to seeing deacons as among the presbytery,[219] if presbyters are seen as a patronal class, and the deacons as members of that class holding office. We may build on this by suggesting that if K saw the deacons as numbered among the presbytery, this explains the substitution of three for two at K17.2. The redactor realized that symmetry was required, but counted the deacons as part of the presbytery, and thus made provision for the appointment of three presbyters at this point in order to balance the three deacons.[220]

However, although K20.3 indicates that one of the diaconal functions was to keep order, it also implies that another task is to obtain gifts for distribution, which seems to fit with the presbyters on the right. In other words, the function of these deacons is almost entirely parallel to those of the presbyters, and not simply those ranked on the left. It is indeed notable that the functions ascribed to the presbyters are exercised elsewhere in the church order tradition by deacons. We may thus compare what the *Didascalia* has to say:

> The presbyters are to be seated in the eastern part of the house with the bishops, and then the laymen, and then the women, so that when you stand up to pray the leaders should stand first, and then the laymen and subsequently the women. For it is required that your prayers should be

---

219 Powell, "Ordo Presbyterii", 306–307, suggests that presbyters may hold office in some contexts as deacon or bishop.
220 So Funk, *Doctrina*, 62.

> directed towards the east, as you know what is written: "Give glory to God who rides upon the heavens of heaven, towards the east." One of the deacons should continue to stand by the offerings of the eucharist; another should stand outside the door observing those who come in. And afterwards, when you are offering, they should minister together in the church. And if anyone is found sitting in a place which is not his the deacon within should warn him and make him stand up and seat him in the place which is his own, as is right.[221]

Not only is this indicative of a literary relationship, as suggested below, but it may be observed that here deacons are performing duties comparable to those of presbyters in K. It would seem that *Didascalia* knew an episcopal-diaconal church-order, as it has little to say about presbyters. Most significantly this disciplinary activity is placed explicitly at the eucharist. Although K does not make this explicit, that would seem to be the context of the activity here. However it is to be noted that the arguments would seem to be less about the distribution of sacred food but of food in general. We may imagine *sportulae* being prepared and distributed at the altar on the same occasion and in the same context that sacred food is distributed. Hence there is a need for jealousy and dispute to be policed—as any parish priest who has presided over the distribution of harvest offerings will know well. By the time, and in the community, of the construction of the *Didascalia* the distribution of offerings has been separated from the distribution of eucharistic food and so the disciplinary provisions are brought to apply to the matter of honour in seating, rather than honour in the receipt of foodstuffs.

Harnack is basically correct in reading κκ as referring to presbyters, and not deacons, around the bishop. As already argued κκ envisaged an even number of presbyters, and they perform the

---

221 *Didascalia* 2.57.5-7.

duties undertaken elsewhere by deacons. This reference to presbyters acting on the right and left of the bishop is not a disguised reference to deacons.

As such, the number of presbyters does not impact on the number of deacons to be appointed. There are, however, yet further possible explanations of the citation. Possibly it is a reference to the threefold order of the economic ministry, justifying the introduction of deacons into this community, rather than to the number of deacons. And possibly it is, as Harnack suggests,[222] the number required for witnesses when juridical matters are brought before the presbytery. As such it is possible that no number stood here. However, on balance, on the basis that three widows are to be appointed, and on the basis that K deliberately balanced the number of presbyters (as argued above) to match the number of widows, we may suggest that, even if κκ did not include a number, K might well have done. It is easy to see the absence of a number as an accident of textual transmission, and that γ´ had accidentally fallen out before γέγραπται.[223] However, as a final point, if κκ had a number it is, on the basis of *Testamentum Domini* 1.34, more likely to be seven, than any other number, especially since here three widows (as in κκ) are numbered with twelve presbyters (as possibly in κκ). It is the appearance of the citation "every matter of the Lord is determined by three" which dissuades me from actually making the emendation.

Whereas the issue of number is thus, possibly, solved, a new issue is brought up. If the liturgical functions generally carried out by deacons are carried out by presbyters in the κκ community, what did deacons do? The only possible answer, given that K20 states that deacons keep order, administer discipline, and elicit gifts, is that they do this outside the liturgy. Thus when we hear of the deacon in K that he is "carefully mindful of those who are con-

---

222 Harnack, *Sources*, 39.
223 So Hauler (apparatus reproduced in Tidner, *Didascaliae apostolorum*, 106.)

ducting themselves in a disorderly manner, warning some, encouraging others, threatening others," we may compare this to the role played by the deacon in the penitential process of *Testamentum Domini*, where the deacon instructs penitents outside the liturgical context,[224] and when we hear of the deacon soliciting contributions we may recollect the process by which the deacons of *Testamentum Domini* take account of the offerings and record the names of those on whose behalf the offerings are made.[225]

I have previously argued that deacons were a secondary addition to the church-order of the κκ community, resulting from the existence of deacons elsewhere and that this in turn explains the position of deacons after readers in the hierarchy of κκ.[226] I would not now continue to maintain many of the details of the argument, in the light of subsequent work on the development of office, but it is certainly plausible that a bishop with a small community might not need diaconal assistants. Earlier it was suggested that whereas κκ had probably undergone some growth, we were essentially limited by the evidence to studying the K redaction. K's hand has been clearly recognized in the second paragraph concerning the diaconate (K22), following on from the discussion of the caritative work of widows, and so we may be clear that the earlier discussion of deacons, concerning their appointment (K20) may represent a stage in the development of κκ. We cannot, however, be certain as to the time at which the addition took place.

3.7.5 The widows

We have already discussed the role of widows above, so here need note again simply that the provision for widows who, functionally, may practice visionary prophecy, indicates an early date for

---

224 *Testamentum Domini* 1.37.
225 *Testamentum Domini* 1.19.
226 "Deacons".

κκ. A widow might engage in caritative functions beyond, but this is not stressed by κκ, rather the emphasis on this aspect of a widow's duty is a primary concern of K as a means of diminishing their liturgical leadership.

3.7.6 The text of κκ

Harnack presented a reconstruction of the text of κκ.[227] In the first edition of this text I did the same, though the text was distinct from his. I stressed that it was highly conjectural, and representative not of the entirety of the document but only that preserved within K. Because the extent of K's interpolation is not altogether certain and, most particularly, it must be stressed that κκ is itself the product of redactional growth, probably within the second century, and may also have been subject to textual corruption before reaching the hands of its final redactor, I have determined not to print this text again. We may however summarize the main points of the argument, and the main questions relating to its reconstruction.

One question is that of whether part of of K1 should be incorporated, namely the statement that the apostles are to set "the numbers of the places, the dignities of bishops, the seats of presbyters, the assistance offered by deacons, the understanding of readers..." is part of κκ or not. It was determined above that this was K's redactional effort, on the grounds that the fundamental controlling imagery here, which is the alignment of the worship of the church on earth to that of the heavenly church, is not consistently followed in what is certainly κκ material, in particular not in the section regarding the bishop. Of all the conclusions reached herein, however, this is one of the less certain, given that such imagery appears in the treatment of presbyters, which is to be assigned to κκ with some certainty.

---

227 Harnack, *Sources*, 5–21.

We may also suggest that the notice of the election of a bishop in K16 has been abbreviated. We would anticipate a statement that a bishop should be elected, presumably couched in the passive, like the statements governing the appointment of readers, deacons and widows.[228] It is also possible that some of this material is preserved in the *Didascalia*; we have already suggested at 3.7 above that the *Didascalia* may preserve elements of κκ which have been omitted, and this may provide a *prima facie* example.

We have already discussed the points at which the notice of the appointment of a bishop in κκ has been interpolated by K. Also to note in this section is the question of the punctuation and reading of the statement regarding the bishops' literacy, or lack thereof, discussed at 3.7.3 above.

We have similarly discussed the notice regarding presbyters, suggesting that the reference to the apocalypse is original to κκ, but that it κκ's work has been extensively interpolated, probably by K. A particular issue here is that of whether κκ demanded δύο or δεκαδύο presbyters.

In discussion above it was concluded that the statements about the reader, the deacons, and the widows (K19–21) were substantially κκ, although there was some suspicion that the widows' qualification list had been extended.

A degree of uncertainty attaches to the statement about the layman, which is the result of the uncertainty regarding K1. This section, again, employs the imagery of angelic worship. It seems that if K1 is to be assigned to κκ, then so should K23; this is the position taken in the first edition. That it follows on from the second notice about deacons is not relevant, as this is certainly the work of K and so the interruption of the flow is hardly relevant. On the basis that K1 has been assigned to K, so K23 has

---

228 The statement concerning the appointment of presbyters is different because this concerns the appointment of presbyters by the bishop on his election.

been assigned to the same redactor, though this is, again, one of the less certain conclusions to be reached here.

3.7.7 The date and origin of κκ

Harnack dated κκ to the middle of the second century. In essence his logic was that the document demonstrated a stage of development at which institutionalization had begun but was not complete.[229] He is, however, open to the suggestion that development was not linear or uniform.

The following indications of date may be significant.

1. The eucharist still retains aspects of a *Sättigungsmahl*, as the fundamental concern of the text is the distribution of goods, rather than sacred food as such.
2. The presbyterate shows signs of being a patronal, rather than a ministerial, class.
3. There is no embarrassment about the prophetic activity of widows.

As such Harnack's dating of his source is probably accurate. We thus receive a valuable insight into the development of order in one particular congregation. Although Faivre's linkage with the practice of Essene communities was considered uncertain though not impossible, a date as suggested here does not detract from his hypothesis of an Essene foundation to the community of κκ. There is nothing in the text which gives a clear indication of provenance, but since we have already suggested that κ derived from Asia or Syria, and since a Cappadocian provenance has already been suggested for K, to receive further argument below, this would seem the most probable location for the growth of κκ as well.

---

229 Harnack, *Sources*, 52–53. Harnack employs other arguments, few of which would now be followed.

4 The extent of K's editorial work

On the basis of the foregoing discussions we may now turn again to the question of the extent of K's editing. According to Harnack K's work was as follows:

a. Paragraphs 1–3 complete.
b. The assignment of single groups of sentences to the several apostles.
c. Unimportant additions in 4–15.
d. Small but important cancellings and an addition in paragraphs 16–23.
e. A certain degree of editorial work in 24–30, the extent of which is hard to ascertain.[230]

We may examine each of these in turn.

4.1 K1–3

Harnack was undoubtedly led to assign the whole of K1–3 to K on the basis of his belief that the opening greeting was derived from B and on the assumption that E, containing the list of apostles, was secondary to K. However, having recognized the existence of κ, and having cause to doubt the use of B, we may now scrutinize this critically. If the apostle list is derived from the same context as *Epistula apostolorum*, as suggested above, then the sole involvement of K is the addition of a twelfth apostle, Judas the son of James, where previously eleven had stood in κ.

It was noted above that K2 linked closely to what followed, and for this reason the greater part of K1 was bracketed. However, a close relationship between this bracketed section and K18 and K23 was discerned, in that whereas the preface states that the earthly hierarchy is to correspond in some way with the celestial hierarchy, we find in the latter section of the document

---

230 Harnack, *Sources*, 2.

that presbyters are to represent the angels on the left and the right of the throne; thus the presence of presbyters on either side of the bishop represents on earth what was occurring in Heaven. Likewise it is said that the layperson imitates the angels in not going beyond what is proper. Thus we were left uncertain about whether K1 and K23 were from κκ or were the work of K. It is possible that this part of K1 is derived from the church order, and that K has combined the introductions of κκ and κ in just the same way that he has combined the two church-orders overall. Harnack remarks that the introduction, which he would assign to the final redactor, demonstrates a major divergence between K's interests and those of his sources.[231] But this is far from true as the two introductions fit the two sections admirably; the inconcinnity results from the clumsy juncture of the two.

In this context we must observe the employment of the word *eparchia*. Whereas in *Lehre* Harnack suggests that this enables us to fix the date of K at around 300, on the grounds that this term indicates the imperialization of the church, the term first being used in the canons of Nicaea,[232] he recognizes in *Sources* that the term does not necessarily fix the date as such.[233] Indeed Funk points out that provincial synods seem to have been known in Asia during the third century, and that Nicaea is regularizing what already occurred.[234] Beyond this Clark notes the extent to which provincial synods were a regular feature of church life in the areas around Cappadocia and Antioch.[235] Thus although Lemoine opines that there is a weight of technical vocabulary employed here which means that the earliest date of this section

---

231 Harnack, *Lehre*, 218.
232 *Lehre*, 218.
233 Harnack, *Sources*, 4–5.
234 Funk, *Doctrina*, LV; he cites Firmilian at Cyprian *Ep.* 74.4.
235 Clark, *Letters of Cyprian* 4, 254–255, on Cyprian *Ep.* 74.4, pointing out numerous incidences.

must be 220, and more probably 300,²³⁶ it is hard to see the basis for such an assertion. The reference is to the division of the mission field of the world among the apostles; before they do this they have to determine the manner in which each church is to be organized. This is a legend known in the third century.²³⁷

Finally we should note that K3 is obviously a redactional construction,²³⁸ preparing the way for the later qualification of the number of presbyters and for the dialogue which follows on Andrew's suggestion that ministries be established for the women, the very point which K is most concerned to contradict.

4.2 The assignment to apostles

Here, again in contradistinction to Harnack, we may suggest, again due to the existence of κ, that the assignment to the apostles in the first part is not the work of K. The manner of the assignment is reminiscent, as Vilela points out, of the manner in which councils and synods are reported.²³⁹ There is nothing in this, however, which militates against the early date assigned to κ as, although unreported in detail, councils met in Asia to discuss Montanism in the time-frame envisaged for κ above.²⁴⁰

The assignment of speeches in the adaptation of the church-order section is, however, the work of K, undertaken in order to make the second part of the document consonant with the first, but also succeeding in answering the prominence given to Mary in anti-apostolic gnostic writings through making the apostles (and Peter in particular) the arbiters of propriety, and through the use of an apocryphal work clearly deriving from the same context as, for instance, *Acta Philippi*. Parrott similarly

---

236 Lemoine, "Étude", 7.
237 *Acta Thomae* 1; something of this sort is attributed to Origen by Eusebius at *HE* 3.1.
238 So Harnack, *Lehre*, 212.
239 Vilela, *Condition collegiale*, 165.
240 So the anonymous anti-Montanist cited at Eusebius *HE* 5.16.10.

notes the possibility of polemic between Christians and gnostics over the names of apostles, suggesting that Peter, John and James generally represent the voice of orthodoxy, whereas the Philip circle is claimed as gnostic.[241] It would perhaps be mistaken to schematize the apostle lists overmuch, and there is no obvious logic in the assignment of speeches to disciples in the church-order section of K, but it is nonetheless fair to note the prominence of Peter here, and that Peter, John and James are the first three to speak, alongside the claiming of Mary (?Magdalene) in her absence as an orthodox voice. Faivre similarly notes that in the *Gospel of Mary* it is Andrew who introduces the subject of women (as in K) and Peter (again, as in K) who denies Mary's input (though unsuccessfully in the event.)[242] Again, although there is not the evidence to posit a close relationship between the two there is certainly some engagement with the polemic which Parrott identifies.

4.3 K's engagement in TWT

We have observed above the extent of K's interpolation into TWT. It was hard to determine in some instances what was interpolated and what lay in κ, for the interests of the two are arguably close. What is most important is the substitution of an eschatological conclusion for the *Haustafel* found in κ. The motivation for this is not obvious; the conclusion, moreover, is not a composition of K but probably stood in the version of TWT with which he was familiar.

Thus we may note that in the two ways section of the work, the hand of K appears, but reveals little about himself or his interests. An Asian provenance is likely, and a date earlier than the fourth century is possible, but there is little here to guide us.

---

241 Parrott, "Gnostic and orthodox disciples".
242 Faivre, "Apostolicité", 49.

4.4 K16–23

Far from supplying "small... cancellings" we have suggested that K has extensively reworked his source, and supplied K22 in order to minimize the social work of widows by contrast to that of deacons, and possibly K23, to create a division between the presbyters and the laymen. We may glean something of K from the manner in which he is involved in interpolating the sources before him.

Thus in the section concerning the qualifications for bishops he is concerned that the bishop should be unmarried or widowed, and that presbyters likewise should be abstinent. The extensive list of qualifications for presbyters, like the demand that they should be abstinent, is unique, as Harnack notes.[243] We may also suggest that K is concerned that the bishop should have competence in preaching, and be educated to a degree that enables him to do this. Finally we may gather that K is familiar with women undertaking social work in the community, and particularly among other women. What then can be deduced from this?

Whereas for Bartlet the demand for celibacy points towards a late date, it points equally well to encratite circles in the second century. However, given that presbyters have a more extensive qualification list than is usually presented, a later date is implied. The presbyters, who in the original form of κκ were patrons and older men, have evolved into something resembling an office. Thus the earlier part of the second century at least cannot be considered.

Although the demand for celibacy by presbyters may represent second-century encratite circles, there is perhaps more. In particular we may turn once again to *Testamentum Domini* for illumination.

Although *Testamentum Domini* incorporates *Traditio apos-*

---

243 Harnack, *Sources*, 11.

tolica, it also uses at least one other source, and a redactional hand is also apparent. Thus, in contrast to the Hippolytean source, it is noteworthy that the presbyters and bishop, as well as the widows, are said to be constant in prayer.

The prayer texts and provisions of *Testamentum Domini* have been subjected to a detailed study by White, who concludes that these texts derive from an ascetic community, in particular observing parallels from the (Cappadocian) ps.-Athanasian *De virginitate*, for instance between the *horaria* of the two documents.[244] We may also note, with White, that one of these additional sources is represented in the description of presbyters' duties, which forms a coherent literary unit.[245] The prayer texts for presbyters similarly show distinct concerns. Thus the presbyter is to pray "each at his own occasion," which, White suggests, means that each of the (twelve) presbyters is to pray at some hour of day or night so that prayer is continuous.[246]

What is particularly to be noted is that the duties of the presbyter, beyond the maintenance of the life of prayer and fasting, seem principally to be in the direction of ascetics. Thus White points out the extent to which the vocabulary of the section dealing with the work of presbyters (*Testamentum Domini* 1.31) mirrors that of Evagrius.[247] The presbyter is to examine those who hear the word for signs of *askēsis* and negative dispositions that, in Evagrian terms, are to stir up the passions. So much emphasis is placed on the prayer practice of the presbyter, who is not to leave off prayer for more than an hour, that White concludes that the presbyter in this circle is an older male ascetic, rather than an ordained liturgical officer. As such he sees the presbyter as more or less a male equivalent to the widows who have such promi-

---

244 White, *Daily Prayer*, 47, 80, 98, 127-129.
245 White *Daily Prayer*, 94.
246 White, *Daily Prayer*, 90.
247 White, *Daily prayer*, 92-98.

nence in the *Testamentum*.[248] The presbyters form a cadre of older men devoted to prayer.

We may thus observe what K has to say of the presbyter, namely that he is ἤδη κεχρονικότας ἐπὶ τῷ κόσμῳ.[249] The presbyter of K is an older man. Moreover, as already discussed, he is τρόπῳ τινὶ ἀπεχομένους τῆς πρὸς γυναῖκας συνελεύσεως,[250] something which indicates an ascetic direction to the presbyter. *Testamentum Domini* has formed the historic office of patron-presbyters into an ascetic group. We have already suggested that κκ envisages the presbyters as a group of patrons. We may now suggest that K, like *Testamentum Domini*, has transformed this group into an ascetic kernel to the local church. As such, we may see K, and what it says about ministry, in the light of the longer, and more detailed, *Testamentum Domini*.

Thus the bishop's office in *Testamentum Domini* is likewise asceticized. All that is said of the bishop's duties pertains to his life of prayer (being constantly by the altar) and fasting.[251] As such, Heid's reading of the section regarding the preference for an unmarried bishop, namely that although this is preferred he should otherwise be in a continent marriage, may be put aside.[252]

It is the close relationship between bishop and presbyters as ascetics, moreover, that explains much else in the presbyteral qualification list which, in our discussion of the presbyters and their numbers above was, we suggested, inserted into κκ by K. That a presbyter should be a συνεπίμαχος arguably applies to the spiritual struggle, and that he is a συμμύστης again implies a common spiritual teaching.[253]

We may also allow *Testamentum Domini* to cast light on K23.

---

248 White, *Daily prayer*, 92–94.
249 K16.1.
250 K16.2.
251 *Testamentum Domini* 1.22.
252 Heid, *Celibacy*, 107.
253 See the notes the translation ad loc.

As already shown, the idea that the earthly church might mirror the heavenly church is not unique to K and *Testamentum Domini*, but these two documents appear to have developed the idea in a particular and distinct direction by making a distinction between presbyters, as a class of ascetics, and the non-ascetic congregation. It is on this basis that we may conclude that K23, which incorporates laypeople into the angelic hierarchy, but in a different class, is a product of the K redaction, rather than a source. If K23 is redactional, then the conclusion reached above that the greater part of K1 is from the K redaction is to be maintained.

Finally we may return to K22, in which the deacon's ministry is described. Here, once again, we see that the role is fundamentally economic, as was, historically, that of the bishop. The deacon is to ensure that the poor are provisioned and the wealthy assist with the provisioning. This may imply that the deacon was, as elsewhere, simply the bishop's agent, but here he appears to have taken over the task entirely. The addition of the chapter may have been brought about in order to limit the activity of female ministers, but it is also possible that the deacon is becoming more active as the bishop becomes more centred on prayer, like the bishop of the *Testamentum Domini* "constant by the altar."[254]

4.5 K24–30

Whereas we have suggested that part of K30 derives from κ, and is a doublet of the conclusion to the TWT in K14, the rest of this part of K is, we have suggested, a construction of K, formed from various sources, principally to polemicize against the ministry of women.

---

254 *Testamentum Domini* 1.22. *Testamentum Domini* 1.34–37 has an extensive list of deacons' duties, which implies that by this stage of development in the ascetic community the deacon has taken on the entire pastoral role.

4.6 Conclusions on K's editorial work and his sources

We may thus gather together what we have learnt. K took hold of a version of the TWT in which the material was attributed to apostles, and joined it to an ancient church-order, combining the two prefaces, in order that the whole might have the appearance of a church-order of apostolic origin. It is not clear what the function of TWT is in the church-order as a whole, but the adoption of κ was essential to construct the apostolic fiction. It is possible that TWT functions in K as a rehearsal of the qualifications of those who are to hold office. It is interesting that in the fourth century the material which was originally directed at catechumens comes to be directed towards clergy; thus canon 46 of the Council of Laodicea directs that "they who are of the priesthood, or of the clergy, shall not be magicians, enchanters, mathematicians, or astrologers; nor shall they make what are called amulets, which are chains for their own souls. And those who wear such, we command to be cast out of the Church." It is thus possible that K had read the material in the same light as the council, for which reason, despite the promise of hearing two ways in K4.1, only the way of life is described. Similarly, Faivre notes the extent to which the qualifications laid down for the deacon in the latter part of K mirror the moral qualities besought in the Two Ways section,[255] and we may note that the same transference of qualities from catechumens to clergy has occurred in the *Didascalia*; "Let him not be double-minded or double-tongued", states the didascalist of the qualifications of the bishop, and in discussing the meekness of a young bishop seems to echo D3.7–8,[256] the point being that this TWT material is found in the *Didascalia* among the qualifications for the episcopate. All this is in accordance with Bradshaw's suggestion that the earlier of the church-order materials deal with the ethical conduct of the Christian, whereas

---

255 Faivre, "Documentation canonico-liturgique", 291–292.
256 *Didascalia* 2.6.1; 2.1.5.

the later orders tend to concentrate more and more upon the clergy. Bradshaw picks on *Traditio apostolica* as responsible for this development.²⁵⁷ We may suggest in turn that the redactor of *Traditio apostolica* found material regarding ordinations already present,²⁵⁸ but K has done what Bradshaw suggests was done by the redactor of *Traditio apostolica* by joining together two particular kinds of document, namely κ, concerned with moral qualities, and κκ which, as a document concerning the organization of a church under clergy, might circulate quite independently of an order for Christian conduct. Nonetheless, as a result of these movements, church orders develop as Bradshaw describes.

κ was thus joined to the ancient church order which we have termed κκ, and this ancient church order was further interpolated, in part to conform it the better to the church order known to the author, to regulate the ministry of deacons, to asceticize the presbyters and the bishop, but fundamentally to legislate against a liturgical role for women within this ascetic community.

4.7 The date and provenance of K

Throughout the work we have found hints of K's date and provenance. All the sources employed are of the second century, and are either Syrian or Asian. The language points to the early part of the third century. We may, therefore, examine the basis on which Harnack established the consensus that K derives from the fourth century, or the latter part of the third.

4.7.1 Harnack's dating of K

Harnack dated K to the fourth century on five bases,²⁵⁹ none of which, on examination, convince. We examine each briefly

---

257 Bradshaw, *Search*, 95.
258 So my "Ordination prayers", a revision of my earlier position that these prayers were entirely redactional.
259 Harnack, *Sources*, 5.

in turn, in some cases simply summarizing conclusions already reached in this introduction.

4.7.1.1 The division of the regulations among the apostles

Whereas Harnack considered this the work of K, this we have seen to be the work principally of κ, a source which we may reasonably assign to the second century. The division of the church order material among the apostles, however, is K's work.

4.7.1.2 The clerical degrees are formed according to the type of heavenly things

Again, for Harnack, the idea that the ranks of clergy were modelled on heavenly orders indicated a later date for K. However, far from necessitating a later date, this is ideationally close to Ignatius, who sees the bishop as a type of God the Father, and the presbyters around like the angels around the throne.[260] Similarly Clement sees the position of those who are subservient in the church as like that of the angels gathered around the throne of God.[261] The image of the bishop with presbyters is perhaps also taken up in the Apocalypse, which represents the angels around the throne, and so the comment that the presbyters represent the angels at the left and right is a commentary on *Revelation* which is close to the fount of the image.

4.7.1.3 The appointment of the presbyters

The presupposition that the bishop alone appoints the presbyters is, for Harnack, indicative that the date is late. This, along with the extensive qualifications set out for presbyters, is the most

---

260 Ignatius *Trall.* 3.1. NB also Clement of Alexandria *Strom.* 4.8, where the earthly church is seen as an image of that in heaven.
261 1 *Clem.* 34.1–6. One may also note that Clement of Alexandria (*Strom.* 4.8) also considered that the earthly church was a type of the heavenly, though not in this case with regard to clerical degrees.

marked indication of a later, rather than an earlier date. However, we do not know what systems were in use in which places for the appointment of presbyters such that we can claim that an episcopal prerogative in the appointment necessarily points to a later date. In the third century it is reported that Boukolos appointed Polycarp as presbyter, apparently without consultation.[262] The source of this report is Smyrna, a city in which it would seem that the presbytery remained powerful. We may also note the strong ascetic bent in *Vita Polycarpi,* illustrating the ideal represented by K. Thus neither K's provision for the episcopal appointment of presbyters, nor indeed the ascetic ideal he presents, precludes a date in the third century.

4.7.1.4 The offering of the Body and Blood

We have already examined the expression concerning the offering of the Body and Blood, used at K25, at 3.4.3 above, where it was observed that not only Harnack, but Connolly and Bartlet likewise, considered this a mark of a late date. However, although this usage is strange, we have already noted that this could be the usage of the third century.

4.7.1.5 The nature of the use of D

For Harnack, K's omission of the second half of D is indicative of date. This argument, however, even if it had weight, would hardly apply since K made no direct use of D, but, as argued above, employed a distinct version of TWT.

4.7.2 Conclusions on the date of K

None of the arguments for redaction in the late third or fourth century have been found valid. On this basis, in the first edition of this work I concluded that the work should be dated much

---

262 *VitPol* 17.

earlier in the third century than previously had been thought.

Apart from the failure of previous arguments, and the early date of the identifiable sources (any and all of which might have derived from the second century), this suggestion was made on the basis that the major motive for the production of K was to present apostolic opposition to the ministry of women, and contrasts this "apostolic" practice to that of gnostic groups. On this basis the gnostic groups must still have been active and in contact with members of K's community, which would place K earlier in the third century. Harnack, moreover, believed that K22–29 had been derived from a distinct source. He recognizes that the engagement with apocryphal literature and the very fact that the liturgical role of women was discussed indicates a degree of antiquity for this section.[263] Since it was determined that this was a construction of K, I was led to attribute the same antiquity to the K redaction. The sources employed by K seem all to have derived from the second century.

Thus all the positive indications, such as the engagement with Christian gnosticism and the second-century origin of the sources employed by K, pointed to the latter part of the second century or the earlier part of the third. I felt Faivre's suggestion of 135–180 might be a little early, given the development of the presbyterate into an independent office,[264] and so suggested the earlier years of the third century.

However, the re-examination here of K's polemic against the ministry of women, particularly in the light of *Testamentum Domini*, indicates that although the sources employed were forged in the anti-gnostic struggle, they have been re-employed in a different context. They are concerned with a liturgical practice directly comparable to that of the community of *Testamentum*

---

263 Harnack, *Lehre*, 215.
264 See 3.7.2 above. Faivre's estimate is based on the hypothesis that episcopate and presbyterate were not distinguished in the earliest period.

Domini, where the widows stand with the presbyters. In an examination of the "heretics" of the *Acta Philippi*, Peterson observes the manner in which the legislation of the Council of Gangra opposes tendencies found within these *Acta*. He also notes the linkage between Mary and Martha's eucharistic activities in the *Acta*, and the discussion of female ministry in K.[265] *Testamentum Domini*, as has already been argued, derives from the middle of the fourth century, although it incorporates earlier sources. The synod of Gangra met in the mid-fourth century.[266]

Thus in *Testamentum Domini* we see a further developed form of the church order found in K. K precedes *Testamentum Domini* and Gangra, but perhaps not significantly so. The critical question is that of when asceticism took root in Anatolia, such that an ascetic community like K might be found. Conventionally the development of asceticism is dated to the period after persecution,[267] though there is evidence of ascetic groupings in Asia (quite apart from Egypt) prior to this date. We meet a cadre of dedicated virgins under a πρεσβυτέρα in the account of the martyrdom of Theodotus,[268] in the reign of Maximinus Daia. Thus, on the basis that K precedes *Testamentum Domini*, but belongs in the same context, a date for K in the first third of the fourth century would seem reasonable.

4.7.3 The provenance of K

Harnack argued for an Egyptian provenance on the grounds that the four of the five sources employed, which he believed to be D, B, the apostle list, κκ and his *katastasis tēs ekklēsias* (which employed, he thought, the *Gospel of the Egyptians*) were derived

---

265 Peterson, "Häretiker".
266 The date is conventionally given as 340, though Barnes, "Date", has argued for 355.
267 Thus, e.g., Frazee, "Anatolian Asceticism", 16.
268 *Passio Theodoti* 13 (Ed. di Cavalieri).

from Egypt.²⁶⁹ However, D is no longer generally believed to be Egyptian, we have shown that the apostle list is derived from an Asian source, have suggested that B was not a source for K, and noted that the use of the *Gospel of the Egyptians* is at best uncertain, and that in any case his second source did not exist, but the material to which he assigns it is the work of K. In our separate examination of K's sources we have found none which is Egyptian; as far as can be seen, all are Asian or, more precisely, Cappadocian. More precisely within Egypt Harnack suggests the regions of Arsinoe, where chiliasm was present. Although κκ, if not K itself, may derive from a rural district, where there may not be twelve competent to elect a bishop, this is not necessarily the case, as much depends on the interpretation of the twelve, and although a region in which chiliasm was prominent would certainly be anti-gnostic, we may note the absence of any bishop from Dionysius' report of his visit to this district.²⁷⁰ Hennecke thus suggests that the discussion of the presbyters is relatively early, and that only subsequently did these presbyters come under episcopal control, something of which is indicated by K16.²⁷¹ However, we have seen that, on the contrary, the discussion of presbyters is late but nonetheless that the episcopate has probably emerged from among the presbyters. Thus even if arguable the connection is tenuous.

All this results from the attempt to conform K to what is known of Egyptian practice. It would be better to abandon the idea of an Egyptian origin and to accept, on the basis of the sources employed, that it is most probable that K is a product of Asia or, if the report of Firmilian, and the parallels with *Testamentum Domini*, are to be given weight, specifically of Cappadocia or perhaps Phyrygia. The situation envisaged by K, however, seems less

---

269 Harnack, *Lehre*, 219.
270 At Eusebius *HE* 7.24.
271 Hennecke, "Zur apostolischen Kirchenordnung", 244–247.

to be the actual celebration of the eucharist by women as their presence in the sanctuary alongside a male bishop and presbyters at the celebration. This is a situation envisaged by *Testamentum Domini*. Since we have already observed the similarities between practices described in *Testamentum Domini* and those of Cappadocian ascetic communities, not least in the *horarium* proposed and in the prayer practices described[272] we are again pointed in the direction of Cappadocia.

5. K among the church orders

As a church order with apostolic attribution, found in all the major ancient collections of church orders, K is clearly identifiable as one of a group. Before concluding the introduction we may ask how it relates to the other church orders.

5.1 The apostolic attribution of K

We have already suggested that the attribution of individual elements of K to individual apostles derived from the use of this device in κ, which is then picked up and extended to the other church order material. κ was to be dated to some time in the second century and having employed a list of apostles broadly similar to that of *Epistula apostolorum* to attribute the TWT material to individual apostles might be considered to have arisen in a similar locale.

Unlike the *Constitutiones apostolorum* there is no elaborate fictionalization of the apostolic meeting,[273] but there is more here than the general apostolic attribution of D. It is perhaps close to the *Didascalia* which likewise anchors its setting in a meeting of the apostles (though not before the ascension as K, but as an

---

272 So Sperry-White, *Testamentum Domini*, 6–7, 31.
273 Faivre, "Apostolicité", 26–27.

extension of the later council in Jerusalem), though this setting is not revealed until towards the end of the document, with occasional speeches in the meantime being attributed either to a single apostle or explicitly to the apostles as a group. Faivre suggest the general principle that the more explicit and rational a reference to Scripture is the more likely it is to be part of a later apostolic fiction.[274] This may be illustrated from the K redaction when the (κκ) discussion of twenty-four elders before the thrones is attributed to John, author of the Apocalypse. There are other possible indications of this, such as the attribution of the discussion of an unlettered bishop to Peter, said at Acts 4:13 to be unlettered.[275] The greater part of K, however, is simply the repetition of traditional material largely derived from earlier documents and given light apostolic dress through the attribution of the material to individual apostles. Pseudepigraphy may thus be defended, as Faivre and Schöllgen in different ways suggest,[276] through noting that in large part the material is ancient and derived from tradition. Schöllgen also argues that one function of apostolic pseudepigraphy was to extend the scope of Scripture; insofar as κκ material mirrors the Pastoral Epistles, K, through extending the apostolic attribution to this material, may be seen as employing the apostolic device in a similar way. But insofar as the overall purpose of K is to create something new out of this traditional material the defence eventually fails. The all-male church-organisation which K defends is not actually apostolic! K stands between the general apostolic attribution of D and the detailed pseudepigraphy of *Constitutiones apostolorum*, but in the end leans more towards *Constitutiones apostolorum* than to D.

Given the gnostic use of the *Sendschreibe* it was suggested above that this form was adopted by *Epistula apostolorum* as a

---

274 Faivre, "Apostolicité", 28.
275 Faivre, "Apostolicité", 55.
276 Faivre, "Apostolicité"; Schöllgen, "Pseudapostolizität und Schriftgebrauch".

direct counter, and that κ was pursuing the same strategy, that is to say the true tradition was anchored in apostolic directions which might be traced back to Christ. It must, however, again be noted that there is a distinct difference between *Epistula apostolorum* and κ, in that there is no revealer figure as such in κ. In *Epistula apostolorum* and other revelation dialogues the revealer is supernatural, either Christ or some other supernatural revealer, whereas in κ the attribution is directly to the apostles. Thus Aland's suggestion that early pseudepigraphy might be associated with the practice of prophecy, in which an individual might speak in the person of a revealer figure,[277] does not really apply, as there is no evidence that prophecy was given in the person of departed individuals. Part of the reason for this is that there is no new revelation claimed in κ, but simply the repetition of what is already traditional material. As such we are nearer to the explanation of pseudonymity offered by Steimer, namely the maintenance of tradition, than that of Schöllgen, who insists that the continuation of Scripture has primacy.[278] Nonetheless the manner in which traditional material is repeated, as K shows us, can reveal redactional purpose quite beyond the maintenance of tradition.

In K it was argued that we find a deliberate answer to the gnostic use of individual apostle-traditions. Thus K is following the same strategy, namely the adoption of the same form as gnostic writings, as κ, and doing so for a comparable reason, namely in order to oppose catholic order to that perceived to be heterodox.

5.2 K and the Didascalia

One of the mysteries of the church orders continues to be the sources which each employed. The relationship of K and D has already been extensively discussed. Our conclusions were reached

---

277 Aland, "Problem".
278 See Schöllgen's response to Steimer, *Vertex traditionis*, "Der Abfassungszweck der frühchristlichen Kirchenordnungen", 55–77, especially 70–76.

in section 1 above that K employed a TWT type document, which we have termed κ, which was derived from the same source as the TWT in D (termed δ). Having observed the relationship between K and D one may enquire what relationship obtains between K and other church orders. We begin the examination with the *Didascalia*, which both contains some TWT material and material corresponding at points with the second half of K and which, as observed above, is similar in its approach to pseudonymous apostolic authorship.

With regard to TWT material Connolly persuasively argues that the didascalist knew and employed D as material with D parallels is found throughout the *Didascalia*, and the parallels are, moreover, found from material distributed throughout D.[279] Thus K, or κ, cannot be the source for this as the parallels extend to material not found in K, and, moreover, to material which was not part of δ. The didascalist thus had access to D.[280] It may be that this is the result of one of the later redactions of the *Didascalia*, material from D being incorporated at a later stage, whereas one of the sources of the *Didascalia* was an independent version of TWT, but nonetheless we may safely say that the TWT within the *Didascalia* is a branch of the tradition independent of κ.

However, this leaves those points in the *Didascalia* which are reminiscent of K and which are not related to TWT. Firstly, in dealing with bishops, the didascalist writes:

> If, however, the congregation in which the bishop is to be ordained is small, and nobody of age is found of whom testimony to his wisdom and suitability to stand in the episcopate might be given but, however, there is a youth, of whom those with him bear witness that he is worthy of the episcopate and who, in spite of his youth, shows evi-

---

279 Connolly, "Use of the Didache".
280 The situation is, however, confused by the redactional complexity of the *Didascalia*; it is possible, for instance, that some of the didascalist's sources were derived from δ, and that elsewhere D is the source.

dence of maturity in his meekness and good conduct, he should be tested and if he receives such testimony from all he should be made bishop in peace. For Solomon likewise was king over Israel at the age of twelve years, and Josiah reigned in righteousness at the age of eight years, and Joash likewise reigned when he was seven years old.

Therefore, even if he is young, however, let him be meek, fearful and peaceable, since the Lord God says through Isaiah: "On whom shall I look, except upon one who is meek, peaceable, and always trembling at my words." Likewise, in the Gospel, he speaks thus: "Blessed are the meek, for they shall inherit the earth."[281]

On this Connolly writes: "This and other passages leave little doubt in my mind that there has been contact between the *Apost. Ch. O.* and the *Didascalia*, and I have as little doubt that the borrowing was on the part of the first-mentioned."[282] Bartlet similarly advances the opinion that K had employed the *Didascalia*, though is inclined to think that the influence was at an early redactional stage.[283]

On the grounds that K prefers a celibate bishop and on the basis of the expression concerning the offering of the Body and Blood, both of which are discussed above, Connolly had concluded that the *Didascalia* preceded K. However we have determined in the discussion above that neither statement is inconceivable in a third-century context. However, quite apart from the fact that Connolly's arguments do not necessitate the conclusion that the *Didascalia* preceded K, and thus do not necessitate the conclusion that K must have borrowed from the *Didascalia*, and apart from the fact that we are dealing with sources here rather than the completed *Didascalia*, it is also conceivable that the passage cited above indicates that the didascalist

---

281 *Didascalia* 2.1.3–5.
282 Connolly, *Didascalia*, 31 n.
283 Bartlet, *Church-life*, 102. For Bartlet's redactional theory see 3.2 above.

was acquainted not with K but with κκ. Obviously it has been thoroughly rewritten here,[284] and shows the influence of D,[285] but we have to ask whether it is more likely that K (or rather κκ) should take something akin to the *Didascalia* and produce what is presently extant, or whether the influence is more probably the other way around. The *Didascalia* is concerned with the election of a youthful bishop, and the scriptural exempla are therefore directed at that problem, whereas κκ is concerned with the election of any bishop, being concerned that the election should be properly carried out when there is not a quorum. In a discussion of the qualities which are to be found in a bishop the general issue of a quorum is surely more likely to be discussed than the issue of a young bishop. Moreover, since κκ assumes that the presbyters provide the candidates and that these candidates form an electoral college, it is therefore less likely that a young bishop would be elected whereas the situation envisaged by the *Didascalia* is one in which all participate in the election. Neither system can be said to be earlier than the other, but they are different, and whichever, therefore, used the other as source would have to make the necessary alterations. If an electoral college system were being written into a source instead of a system of popular election then one would expect that it would be more explicit, whereas a popular election need not be described. Finally, when the passage turns to the qualifications of a bishop, the statement in κκ simply states that the bishop should be generous, even though he be unlettered. *Didascalia*, however, expands the statement with further TWT material, as noted above, but does this

---

284 In observing the rewriting we may note the statement that Solomon was twelve as a linkage to Genesis R 11, which makes the same statement.
285 We may particularly note that some material from TWT has been included. This TWT material is not from K since, as Connolly, "Use of the Didache", 150, points out, the phrase translated above as "always", διὰ παντός, (represented in the Latin version and in the parallel section of *Constitutiones apostolorum* though omitted from the Syriac version) is present in D but not in K.

again pursuing the question of the bishop's youth, rather than moving the subject on to the qualities expected of a bishop. Again, it seems less likely that the discussion extant in K would emerge from that of the *Didascalia*, with no sign of the question of a youthful bishop, than that the didascalist, in pursuit of a particular issue in that community, should recast directions for the election and particular qualities of the bishop. Finally we may compare K's conservative treatment of TWT received through κ to the free treatment which TWT, whether received through D or from an earlier part of the tradition, receives in the *Didascalia*. Elsewhere in the *Didascalia* where any source is extant, for instance in *Didascalia* 21, the source has received a free treatment and considerable expansion. Thus it is far less likely that K reworked the *Didascalia* than that the didascalist reworked κκ. This is the conclusion which was reached by Nautin, though the grounds of his conclusion are not clear.[286]

Faivre also notes several parallels between the judicial role of the bishop and presbyters, set out in the *Didascalia*, and that of the bishop and presbyters of K, one of which, the image of a gangrene spreading through the body, is particularly close.[287] Again, however, it is possible that this image is taken from κκ, since it derives from the discussion of the disciplinary role of presbyters. In my discussion of the sources and redaction of the *Didascalia* I suggest that κκ was one of the sources employed, entirely independently of its subsequent incorporation into K, and that when

---

[286] P. Nautin announced in *Annuaire de l'École pratique des hautes Études, Ve section: sciences religieuses* 90 (1981-1982), 335-339, that he had uncovered a common source to K and the *Didascalia*, corresponding roughly to what here has been termed κκ. No work on this was, however, published. I have examined Nautin's notes and, as noted above, Nautin believed that K employed a source consisting of K16-17a, 20-21. However, there are no notes connecting this to the *Didascalia*. He does note that both the *Didascalia* and K open with a gathering of apostles, but this scene within the *Didascalia* is the result of a secondary and late recension.

[287] Faivre, "Texte grec", 35, citing *Didascalia* 2.42.1, and 2.46.6, 2.47.1.

the *Didascalia* turns to the appointment of a bishop, and subsequently to the duties of deacons and the appointment of widows, it is following a source which has either developed or incorporated κκ.[288]

Finally Connolly notes that number of adjectives found as qualifications for various offices, namely εὔσκυλτοι, εὐήκοος and εὐμετάδοτος are to be found both in K and the *Didascalia*. He concludes that whereas "the *Apost. Ch. Order* is appreciably later than the *Didascalia*... there has been borrowing on one side of the other."[289] We may, however, suggest that the appearance of these adjectives in passages concerning the qualifications for ministries indicates not borrowing on the part of either finished church order, but a use by the didascalist, or rather one of his sources, of κκ.

Quite apart from these literary parallels, however, we have already found certain similarities between K and the *Didascalia*. It was argued above that a common catechetical tradition underlay certain statements in K and the *Didascalia* concerning the bishop, and both confront the issue of women's ministry—though in different ways. Both, moreover, are concerned with the role of the bishop in the distribution of the community's goods as well as in discipline. We need not, however, seek a common literary stratum to explain all of this. The one point concerning discipline where there is the possibility of a literary relationship does not concern the bishop but the role of deacons, who at this point in the *Didascalia* are performing a role analogous to that performed by presbyters in K.[290] What is pertinent is not the possibility of a literary source but our argument that K derives from a fourth-century Cappadocian context. It is hardly co-incidental that a similar date, albeit a Syrian locale, is to be ascribed to the *Didascalia* for, quite apart from any literary relationship, the two share a common

---

288 Didascalia apostolorum, 11-14.
289 Connolly, Didascalia, lxxxv.
290 Didascalia 2.57.5-7; cf. to this K18.3.

thought-world.²⁹¹ In constructing their apostolic fictions, therefore, the two readily draw upon the same traditional material.

5.3 K and Testamentum Domini

As has already been observed, the *Testamentum Domini* envisages the church as the centre of an ascetic community in the same way as K. The seventh canon of Gangra states that ascetics are not to help themselves to the offerings of the church, and overall seems to envisage any ascetics as part of the localized Christian community. The extremes criticized in this council, for instance the refusal of some Christians to countenance married clergy,²⁹² seem to reflect experience of a community much like that of K, and of *Testamentum Domini*. Thus it is no co-incidence that we have understood K's characterization of Martha and Mary, and the discussion of female participation in the eucharist, in the light of the *Acta Philippi*. These all appear to derive from the same context.

Thus our examination of the presbyters of K has been illuminated by the detailed discussion of presbyters in *Testamentum Domini*. In both they have proved to be older male ascetics. In both, moreover, there is a close relationship between these ascetic presbyters and their ascetic bishop. We may also observe that K and *Testamentum Domini* have in common the idea that the church mirrors the life of heaven. This is found in K2, which may be the work of K, but also, in the statements regarding the presbyters and the laity. This is an indication that there were really two classes in this community, each of which in its own way mirrored the heavenly realm, namely presbyters (ascetics) and laypeople.

---

291 On the dating of the *Didascalia* see my *Didascalia apostolorum*, 49–55. Apart from the final dates of redaction of K and the *Didascalia*, the principal sources of the *Didascalia*, in particular that concerning the office of the bishop, and the appointment of ministers, are to be dated to the same period essayed here for the sources of K.

292 Canon 4.

There is also some evidence of a literary relationship: in listing the qualifications for the bishop, which are largely traditional and probably derive from a source akin to κκ, or that of the Pastoral Epistles, we read: "It is good if he is without wife, but should at least be the husband of one wife, so that he may sympathize with the weakness of the widows."[293] The reflection here of K's καλὸν μὲν εἶναι ἀγύναιος, εἰ δὲ μή, ἀπὸ μιᾶς γυναικός is almost palpable, and suggests either that *Testamentum Domini* is aware of K, or else that they have drawn on the same ascetic rule.

Either is possible, in particular since *Testamentum Domini* is either Cappadocian or from a neighbouring area such as Phrygia. This was argued for *Testamentum Domini* originally by Cooper,[294] and the suggestion was revived by White.[295] Finally I have lent support to this with further argument.[296]

Not all of these arguments apply to K, but some do, namely that the ascetic life described has a striking similarity to the Pseudo-Athanasian and Cappadocian *De virginitate,* that the issues over the ministry of women, and widows in particular, seem to be those legislated at the Council of Laodicea, that the continued practice of visionary prophecy by widows is at home in a Cappadocian or Phrygian setting, and that the development of a cadre of presbyters is understandable as a development from groups of patron-presbyters found in Asian communities in the first two centuries. This, together with the network of connections in turn between K, *Testamentum Domini, Acta Philippi,* and the Council of Gangra, including what has been identified as the opposition of K to some aspects of female ministry in a community very like *Testamentum Domini,* seems to present conclusive evidence that the most closely related of the church orders

---

293 *Testamentum Domini* 1.20.
294 Cooper and Maclean, *Testament,* 41-45.
295 White, *Daily prayer,* 160-162.
296 In *The Testament of the Lord,* 52-61.

are K and, especially once *Traditio apostolica* material is removed, *Testamentum Domini*.

6 Conclusion

In this introduction we set out to revisit Harnack's conclusions on the date and provenance of K, and as part of this to determine the sources employed both for their own sake and in order to uncover K's redactional purpose through understanding the manner in which the sources were used.

We have argued, broadly in line with Harnack, that two main sources were employed, a document of the two-ways type (κ) and a church order (κκ). Both appear to be documents of the second century, both of an Asian or Syrian provenance. κ had employed a tradition concerning the names of the apostles deriving from this context and of this date, which is brought into K. In distinction to Harnack, however, we have suggested that there was no other church-order source, though it is possible that some of the material employed towards the end of the document was gathered from other written sources.

In terms of redactional history I have sought to show that there is no evidence for intervening levels of redaction, but that it is entirely reasonable to see the sources being put into their current shape by a single redactor. The final chapters would seem to indicate that fundamental to the redactor's purpose was the exclusion of women from a liturgical role, and the promotion in lieu thereof of a caritative role, particularly among women. The nature of ministry and qualifications for ministry are established, using traditional material, prior to the clarification that women are excluded from any liturgical role or any form of leadership.

The nature of the redactional purpose and the date of the sources employed would tend to point to a slightly earlier date than that assigned to K by Harnack; a fourth-century date has been maintained, though on completely different grounds. Yet more certainly we may suggest that an Egyptian provenance is most unlikely, but that an Asian provenance, more specifically a Cappadocian or Phrygian provenance, is most probable.

That K has been seriously and unduly neglected is beyond doubt. The purpose of this introduction has been to suggest that the document is of the greatest interest both in the sources it employs and in the use to which it puts them.

Text, textual commentary, and translation

The following abbreviations are employed in the textual commentary:

A	Athous, Koutloumousiou 39 f. 79va, l. 16–79vb, l. 3: Ed. David Lincicum, "An Excerpt from the Apostolic Church Order (CPG 1739)," *Sacris Eruditi* 57 (2018), 439–444.
Ar.	Arabic version: Ed. G. Horner, *The statutes of the apostles or canones ecclesiastici* (London: Williams and Norgate, 1904), 89–95. This version is not much used as it is dependent upon S.
Arendzen	J.P. Arendzen, "An entire Syriac text of the 'Apostolic Church Order'," *JTS* 3 (1901), 59–80.
D	The Didache: Ed. W. Rordorf and A. Tuilier, *La doctrine des douze apôtres* (Paris: Cerf, 1998), 140–199.
E	Epitome of the canons of the apostles: Ed. Theodor Schermann, *Eine Elfapostelmoral oder die X-Rezension der "beiden Wege"* (Munich: Lentner, 1903), 16–18.
Eth.	Ethiopic version: Ed. G. Horner, *The statutes of the apostles or canones ecclesiastici* (London: Williams and Norgate, 1904), 1–10. This version is not much used as it is dependent upon S.
Funk:	F.X. Funk, *Doctrina duodecim apostolorum* (Tübingen: Laupp, 1887), 50–73.
Harnack	Adolf Harnack, *Die Lehre der zwölf Apostel nebst Untersuchungen zur ältesten Geschichte der Kirchenverfassung und des Kirchenrechts* (TU2.1; Leipzig: Hinrichs, 1886).

Harnack, Sources	Adolf Harnack, *The sources of the apostolic canons* (ETr; London: Norgate, 1895).
Hauler	First edition of the Latin version. Hauler's apparatus is reproduced by Tidner (see Lat. below).
Hennecke	E. Hennecke, "Zur apostolischen Kirchenordnung," *ZNW* 20 (1921), 241–248.
Hilgenfeld:	A. Hilgenfeld, *Novum Testamentum extra canonem receptum* 4 (Leipzig: Weigel, 1864), 95–106.
L	*Doctrina apostolorum*: Ed. W. Rordorf and A. Tuilier, *La doctrine des douze apôtres* (Paris: Cerf, 1998), 207–210.
Lagarde	P. Lagarde, *Reliquiae iuris ecclesiastici antiquissimae* (Leipzig: Teubner, 1856), 74–79.
Lat.	Latin version: Ed. Erik Tidner, *Didascaliae apostolorum, canonum ecclesiasticorum, traditionis apostolicae versiones Latinae* (TU 75; Berlin: Akademie, 1963).
Mosq.	Codex Mosquensis 125: Ed. O. Gebhardt et al., *Patrum apostolicorum opera* 1.2 (Leipzig: Hinrichs, 1878), XXIX–XXXI.
Pitra	J.B. Pitra, *Iuris ecclesiastici Graecorum historia et monumenta* I (Rome: Collegium Urbani, 1864), 77–88.
S	Sahidic version: Ed. P. Lagarde, *Aegyptiaca* (Göttingen: Hoyer, 1883), 238–248.
Schermann	Theodor Schermann, *Die allgemeine Kirchenordnung, frühchristliche Liturgien und kirchliche Überlieferung* I (Paderborn: Schöningh, 1914), 12–34.
Syr.	Syriac version: Ed. Arendzen (q.v.)
V	Codex Vindob. gr. hist. 7. This fourteenth century MS is the basis for all editions.
Wilamowitz Moellendorff	U. von Wilamowitz Moellendorff, "In libellum ΠΕΡΙ ΥΨΠΟΥΣ coniectanea," *Hermes* 10 (1876), 334–346, in note on 341–342.

αἱ διαταγαὶ αἱ διὰ Κλήμεντος καὶ κανόνες τῶν
ἁγίων ἀποστόλων[1]

---

1 Rufinus, *Expositio symboli* 36 in discussing canonical and non-canonical books, refers to a work which was called *Duae uiae, uel Iudicium secundum Petrum*. Hilgenfeld and Funk each suggest that this was K. Although we may suggest that the title best fits κ, we cannot be sure that this work was still circulating in the fifth century. The title given is that of V, though the first part is surely secondary, resulting from inclusion in a canonical collection. Arendzen suggests that the simple title given in Syriac, ܡܠܦܢܘܬܐ ܕܬܪܥܣܪ ܫܠܝܚܐ (=διδαχή [or διδασκαλία] τῶν δωδεκα ἀποστόλων) is most original. Note, however, should be taken of the title in A and E, ἐκ τῶν διατάξεων τῶν ἁγίων ἀποστόλων. Although these both derive from κ rather than K, αἱ διατάξεις τῶν ἀποστόλων might also be an early title. We must recollect that titles in the ancient world were not unique identifiers but a guide to contents.

The directions through Clement and the canons of the holy apostles

1

χαίρετε υἱοὶ καὶ θυγατέρες ἐν ὀνόματι κυρίου Ἰησοῦ Χριστοῦ. Ἰωάννης καὶ Ματθαῖος καὶ Πέτρος καὶ Ἀνδρέας καὶ Φίλιππος καὶ Σίμων καὶ Ἰάκωβος καὶ Ναθαναὴλ καὶ Θωμᾶς καὶ Κηφᾶς καὶ Βαρθολομαῖος καὶ Ἰούδας Ἰακώβου.

κατὰ κέλευσιν κυρίου ἡμῶν Ἰησοῦ Χριστοῦ τοῦ σωτῆρος συναθροισθέντων ἡμῶν καθὼς διέταξεν ἡμῖν·[2] Πρὸ τοῦ μέλλησαι κληροῦσθαι τὰς ἐπαρχίας,[3] καταλογίσασθε[4] τόπων ἀριθμούς, ἐπισκόπων ἀξίας, πρεσβυτέρων ἕδρας, διακόνων παρεδρείας, ἀναγνωστῶν νουνεχίας, χηρῶν ἀνεγκλησίας[5] καὶ ὅσα δέοι πρὸς θεμελίωσιν ἐκκλησίας, ἵνα τύπον τῶν ἐπουρανίων εἰδότες φυλάσσωνται ἀπὸ παντὸς ἀστοχήματος, εἰδότες, ὅτι λόγων ὑφέξουσιν ἐν τῇ μεγάλῃ ἡμέρᾳ τῆς κρίσεως, περὶ ὧν ἀκούσαντες οὐκ ἐφύλαξαν. καὶ ἐκέλευσεν ἡμᾶς ἐκπέμψασθαι τοὺς λόγους εἰς ὅλην τὴν οἰκουμένην.

2

ἔδοξεν οὖν[6] ἡμῖν πρὸς ὑπόμνησιν τῆς ἀδελφότητος καὶ νουθεσίαν ἑκάστῳ ὡς ὁ κύριος ἐπεκάλυψε κατὰ τὸ θέλημα τοῦ θεοῦ διὰ πνεύματος ἁγίου μνησθεῖσι λόγου ἐντείλασθαι ὑμῖν.

---

2 ἡμῖν is added following Syr. and S (Eth.).
3 ἐπαρχίας: ὑπαρχίας may be preferred on the basis of the Syriac transliteration, but this is unnecessary. V has ἐπ' ἀρχείας.
4 Πρὸ τοῦ μέλλησαι κληροῦσθαι τὰς ἐπαρχίας, καταλογίσασθε ... Cf. eds. who punctuate ... πρὸ τοῦ. Μέλλετε κληροῦσθαι τὰς ἐπαρχίας, καταλογίσασθαι ... The punctuation and text here is adopted following the suggestion of Arendzen that the reading underlying the Syriac text is preferable. There is some support for this in S and, moreover, it should be noted that V reads μέλλεται. If πρὸ τοῦ is taken with διέταξεν the text is difficult; πρὸ τοῦ might be emended to πρότερον, but this seems somewhat radical.
5 ἀνεγκλησίας: V has ἀνεκκλησίας. Pitra suggested παρακλήσεις, but Lagarde's conjecture, printed here, won editorial acceptance.
6 οὖν: Lagarde suggested that this word be deleted. I believe that it was provided by K, to link to the κκ material previously cited. See the introduction, 2.2.

1

Greetings, sons and daughters, in the name of the Lord Jesus Christ. John, and Matthew, and Peter, and Andrew, and Philip, and Simon, and James, and Nathanael, and Thomas, and Kephas, and Bartholomew, and Jude the son of James.

In accordance with the command of Our Lord Jesus Christ the Saviour we gathered ourselves together, as he laid down for us: "Before you determine the eparchies,[7] you are to calculate the numbers of the places,[8] the dignities of bishops, the seats of presbyters, the assistance offered by deacons, the understanding of readers, the blamelessness of widows and whatever is necessary for the foundation of the church, so that knowing the type of those things which are heavenly,[9] they should guard themselves against every fault, seeing that, in the great day of judgement, they should give an account of those who heard and did not keep." And he ordered us to send these words out to the whole inhabited world.

2

It seemed to us, therefore, that we should command you as an admonition of brotherhood and an exhortation, so that you might be mindful through the account of what the Lord revealed to each of us in accordance with the will of God through the Holy Spirit.

---

7 Or, if the emendation proposed in the text is not accepted: ... as he laid down before. "You are to determine the eparchies..."
8 This is to be taken as the number of episcopal seats, which are to be established before any provincial arrangements are made.
9 See the introduction, 4.7.1.2, on the idea that the earthly church should typify that in heaven.

3

Ἰωάννης εἶπεν· Ἄνδρες ἀδελφοί, εἰδότες, ὅτι λόγον ὑφέξομεν περὶ τῶν διατεταγμένων ἡμῖν, εἷς[10] ἑνὸς πρόσωπον μὴ λαμβάνωμεν,[11] ἀλλ' ἐάν τις δοκῇ τι ἀσύμφορον λέγειν,[12] ἀντιλεγέσθω αὐτῷ. ἔδοξε δὲ πᾶσι πρῶτον Ἰωάννην εἰπεῖν.

4

₁Ἰωάννης εἶπεν· Ὁδοὶ δύο εἰσί, μία τῆς ζωῆς καὶ μία τοῦ θανάτου, διαφορὰ δὲ πολλὴ μεταξὺ τῶν δύο ὁδῶν. ₂ἡ μὲν γὰρ ὁδὸς τῆς ζωῆς[13] ἐστιν αὕτη· πρῶτον ἀγαπήσεις τὸν θεὸν τὸν ποιήσαντά σε ἐξ ὅλης τῆς καρδίας σου[14] καὶ δοξάσεις τὸν λυτρωσάμενόν σε ἐκ θανάτου, ἥτις ἐστὶν ἐντολὴ πρώτη. ₃δευτέρα δέ·[15] ἀγαπήσεις τὸν πλησίον σου ὡς ἑαυτόν, ἥτις ἐστὶν ἐντολὴ δευτέρα, ἐν οἷς ὅλος ὁ νόμος κρέμαται καὶ προφῆται.

10 εἷς: V, whereas a later corrector to V writes εἰς.
11 λαμβάνωμεν: so V, followed by Lagarde, Hilgenfeld and Harnack. Schermann prints λαμβάνομεν; Wilamowitz Moellendorff suggests λάβωμεν.
12 ἐάν τις δοκῇ τι ἀσύμφορον λέγειν: so Harnack and Funk following Syr., S(Eth.); Cf. V and Schermann: ἐάν τις δοκῇ συμφέρον ἀντιλέγειν.
13 ἡ μὲν γὰρ ὁδὸς τῆς ζωῆς V and Funk; since D reads ἡ μὲν οὖν ὁδὸς τῆς ζωῆς, and E reads ἡ οὖν τῆς ζωῆς Schermann is led to suggest ἡ μὲν οὖν τῆς ζωῆς, and Harnack ἡ μὲν οὖν ὁδὸς τῆς ζωῆς. Mosq. reads simply: ἡ μὲν τῆς ζωῆς, and A ἡ μὲν τῆς ζωῆς ὁδός. Decisive is the agreement with V and A of Syr., ܪܘܚܐ ܕܝܢ ܕܚܝܐ, and S (Ar., Eth), ⲧⲉϩⲓⲏ ⲙⲉⲛ ⲙ̄ⲡⲱⲛϩ. It seems to me that Harnack and Schermann are unduly influenced in their inclusion of οὖν by D and E; this may have been the reading of κ, but K is clearly an independent witness. See also the introduction 1.1.
14 So V. Cf. Schermann, who conforms to E: ἐξ ὅλης σου καρδίας.
15 δευτέρα: V, supported by Syr., reads δευτέρα and A and Mosq., supported by S, read δευτέρα δὲ ἐντολή. Although Lagarde, Pitra and Hilgenfeld prefer δεύτερον, on the basis of E, and Harnack, Funk and Schermann follow them, with further support from the reading of D, the better textual support for K seems to lie with δευτέρα. δέ is probably necessary on stylistic grounds.

3

John said: "Brothers, since we know that we shall have to give an account of what was commanded us, let us not have regard for any person, but if someone should seem to say something which is improper, he should be contradicted." It seemed to all that John should speak first.

4

₁John said: "There are two ways, the one of life and the one of death, and the difference between the two ways is great. ₂For the way of life is this. First you shall love the God who created you with all your heart and you shall glorify him who ransomed you from death. Such is the first commandment. ₃The second: you shall love your neighbour as yourself. Such is the second commandment, on which the whole of the law and the prophets is dependent."

5

Ματθαῖος εἶπεν· Πάντα ὅσα μὴ θέλῃς σοι γενέσθαι, σὺ μηδὲ ἄλλῳ ποιήσῃς·[16] τούτων δὲ τῶν λόγων τὴν διδαχὴν εἰπέ, ἀδελφὲ Πέτρε.

6

₁ Πέτρος εἶπεν· Οὐ φονεύσεις, οὐ μοιχεύσεις, οὐ πορνεύσεις, οὐ παιδοφθορήσεις, οὐ κλέψεις, οὐ μαγεύσεις,[17] οὐ φαρμακεύσεις, οὐ φονεύσεις τέκνον ἐν φθορᾷ οὐδὲ γεννηθὲν ἀποκτενεῖς, οὐκ ἐπιθυμήσεις τὰ τοῦ πλησίον. οὐκ ἐπιορκήσεις,[18] ₂ οὐ ψευδομαρτυρήσεις, οὐ κακολογήσεις, οὐδὲ μνησικακήσεις, οὐκ ἔσῃ δίγνωμος οὐδὲ δίγλωσσος· παγὶς γὰρ θανάτου ἐστιν ἡ διγλωσσία· οὐκ ἔσται ὁ λόγος σου κενὸς οὐδὲ ψευδής. ₃ οὐκ ἔσῃ πλεονέκτης οὐδὲ ἅρπαξ οὐδὲ; ὑποκριτὴς οὐδὲ κακοήθης, οὐδὲ ὑπερήφανος· οὐ λήψῃ βουλὴν πονηρὰν κατὰ τοῦ πλησίον σου· οὐ μισήσεις πάντα ἄνθρωπον, ἀλλ' οὓς μὲν ἐλέγξεις, οὓς δὲ ἐλεήσεις, περὶ ὧν δὲ προσεύξῃ, οὓς δὲ ἀγαπήσεις ὑπὲρ τὴν ψυχήν σου.

16 E here adds: τουτέστιν ὃ σὺ μισεῖς ἄλλῳ μὴ ποιήσῃς, and the addition of these words to K would appear to be supported by Syr. and by S. However, it is possibly a gloss deriving from Tobit 4:16 that entered early into some texts. The phrase does not appear in V, nor in A or Mosq.
17 οὐ πορνεύσεις, οὐ παιδοφθορήσεις, οὐ κλέψεις, οὐ μαγεύσεις do not appear in V; Mosq. has οὐ παιδοφθορήσεις, οὐ κλέψεις, οὐ μαντεύσῃ. Harnack, followed by Schermann, supplied οὐ παιδοφθορήσεις, οὐ κλέψεις, οὐ μαγεύσεις from D, with some justification, since Syr. and S both contain these commandments. Syr. and S., moreover, add the commandment not to fornicate after the commandment not to commit adultery; this commandment is also in D (though in a different position), and the paraphrase in E might lead one to expect such a commandment here and so it is added by Funk in this position, in addition to those supplied by Harnack. The text presented here is thus a retroversion based on the versions. The μαντεύσεις, which Mosq. suggests is possible instead of μαγεύσεις, could equally be a scribal error in that MS.
18 οὐκ ἐπιθυμήσεις τὰ τοῦ πλησίον. οὐκ ἐπιορκήσεις: not in V, but is present in Mosq. and the versions as well as E.

5

Matthew said: "Whatever you would not wish done to you, do to nobody else. State the teaching of these maxims, brother Peter."

6

₁ Peter said: "You shall not murder, you shall not commit adultery, you shall not fornicate, you shall not despoil a child, you shall not steal, you shall not employ charms, you shall not be a sorcerer, you shall not destroy a child through abortion nor kill it once born, you shall not covet what is your neighbour's, ₂ you shall not swear falsely, you shall not bear false witness, you shall not speak evil, you shall not store up wrongs, you shall not be double-minded or double-tongued. For being double-tongued is a snare of death. Your word shall not be empty, nor false. ₃ You shall not be grasping, nor rapacious, nor hypocritical, nor malicious, nor arrogant. You shall not plot evil against your neighbour. You shall not hate any person, but some you shall rebuke, some you shall pity, for some you shall pray, and some you shall love more than your own life."

7

Ἀνδρέας εἶπεν· Τέκνον μου, φεῦγε ἀπὸ παντὸς πονηροῦ καὶ ἀπὸ παντὸς ὁμοίου αὐτοῦ· μὴ γίνου ὀργίλος· ὁδηγεῖ γὰρ ἡ ὀργὴ πρὸς τὸν φόνον. ἔστι γὰρ δαιμόνιον ἀρρενικὸν ὁ θυμός. μὴ γίνου ζηλωτὴς μηδὲ ἐριστικὸς μηδὲ θυμαντικός·[19] ἐκ γὰρ τούτων φόνος γεννᾶται.

8

₁ Φίλιππος εἶπεν· Τέκνον μου, μὴ γίνου ἐπιθυμητής. ὁδηγεῖ γὰρ ἡ ἐπιθυμία πρὸς τὴν πορνείαν και ἕλκει τοὺς ἀνθρώπους πρὸς ἑαυτήν.[20] ἔστι γὰρ θηλυκὸν δαιμόνιον ἡ ἐπιθυμία, καὶ ὃ μὲν μετ' ὀργῆς, ὃ δὲ μεθ' ἡδονῆς[21] ἀπόλλυσι τοὺς εἰσερχομένους αὐτά.[22] ₂ ὁδὸς δὲ πονηροῦ πνεύματος ἁμαρτία ψυχῆς, καὶ ὅταν βραχείαν εἴσδυσιν σχῇ ἐν αὐτῷ,[23]

---

19 θυμαντικός: so V. Although not the most common word in Greek literature, I would agree with Funk that this is the right reading. Harnack and Schermann print θυμώδης, which is the reading of Mosq., but this may be an alteration in the interests of comprehension. Most significantly, E has μανικός, taken as the reading of K by Lagarde and Hilgenfeld. If θυμαντικός stood in κ then the reading of E is more readily understandable than it would be should we seek to see a derivation from θυμώδης. We may also understand that θυμαντικός might derive from the θυμικός of D (and δ?).
20 ἑαυτήν: Funk suggests αὐτήν.
21 καὶ ὃ μὲν μετ' ὀργῆς, ὃ δὲ μεθ' ἡδονῆς: Wilamowitz Moellendorff suggests: καὶ ὁ μὲν θυμὸς μετ' ὀργῆς, ἡ δὲ μεθ' ἡδονῆς; although there is a degree of support in S, the text in S is probably a clarification and there is no need for such extensive emendation.
22 τοὺς εἰσερχομένους αὐτά: V, followed by eds. apart from Harnack, reads: τοὺς εἰσδεχομένους αὐτά. Wilamowitz Moellendorff suggests ἀποδεχομένους. Harnack prefers Mosq.: τοὺς εἰσερχομένους εἰς αὐτήν, and this has some support from Syr., which has ܡܢܗܘܢ ܗܠܝܢ ܕܥܠܝܢ. Here, however, there is ambiguity about whether the spirits or the person affected is making the approach. Certainly, however, on the basis of Mosq. and Syr., the word εἰσερχομένους was present in K, and the text given is an attempt at restoration.
23 Pierre Nautin, in unpublished notes, suggests αὐτῇ. This may well be an improvement.

7

Andrew said: "My child, shun every evil person and all who are like to him. Do not be quick-tempered, for anger leads to murder. For rage is a male demon. Do not be jealous or quarrelsome or ragingly aggressive. For murder is begotten from these."

8

₁ Philip said: "My child, do not be given over to passion. For lust leads to fornication and drags people towards itself. For lust is a female demon, and one with anger, the other with pleasure, destroys those who go close to them. ₂ The way of an evil spirit is a soul's sin, and when it has a narrow place of entry in somebody

πλατύνει αὐτὴν καὶ ἄγει ἐπὶ πάντα τὰ κακὰ τὴν ψυχὴν ἐκείνην καὶ οὐκ ἐᾷ διαβλέψαι τὸν ἄνθρωπον καὶ ἰδεῖν τὴν ἀλήθειαν.²⁴ ₃ ὁ θυμὸς ὑμῶν μέτρον ἐχέτω καὶ ἐν βραχεῖ διαστήματι αὐτὸν ἡνιοχεῖτε καὶ ἀνακρούετε, ἵνα μὴ ἐμβάλλῃ ὑμᾶς εἰς ἔργον πονηρόν. ₄ θυμὸς γὰρ καὶ ἡδονὴ πονηρὰ ἐπὶ πολὺ παραμένουσα κατὰ ἐπίτασιν δαιμόνια γίνεται, καὶ ὅταν ἐπιτρέψῃ αὐτοῖς ὁ ἄνθρωπος, οἰδαίνουσιν ἐν τῇ ψυχῇ αὐτοῦ καὶ γίνονται μείζονες καὶ ἐπάγουσιν αὐτὸν εἰς ἔργα ἄδικα καὶ ἐπιγελῶσιν αὐτῷ καὶ ἥδονται ἐπὶ τῇ ἀπωλείᾳ τοῦ ἀνθρώπου.

9

Σίμων εἶπεν· Τέκνον, μὴ γίνου αἰσχρολόγος μηδὲ ὑψηλόφθαλμος. ἐκ γὰρ τούτων μοιχεῖαι γίνονται.²⁵

10

Ἰάκωβος εἶπεν· Τέκνον μου,²⁶ μὴ γίνου οἰωνοσκόπος, ἐπειδὴ ὁδηγεῖ εἰς τὴν εἰδωλολατρίαν, μηδὲ ἐπαοιδός, μηδὲ μαθηματικὸς μηδὲ περικαθαίρων, μηδὲ θέλε αὐτὰ ἰδεῖν²⁷ μηδὲ ἀκούειν· ἐκ γὰρ τούτων ἁπάντων εἰδωλολατρεῖαι γεννῶνται.

---

24 Mosq. adds: ἐπιγελᾷ δὲ τὸ πονηρὸν πνεῦμα τῷ ἀνθρώπῳ ἐκείνῳ καὶ εὐφραίνεται ἐπὶ τῇ ἀπωλείᾳ αὐτοῦ. This seems misplaced from further below.
25 μοιχεῖαι γίνονται: so V, Lagarde, Hilgenfeld, Funk, Syr., E. Schermann emends to γεννῶνται in order to conform the text to D. There is no reason, however to conform the text to D. Mosq. and A read γεννᾶται μοιχεία, and the Mosq. reading led Harnack to suggest μοιχεία γεννᾶταί, but these readings might come about through a misreading of γίνονται, and thus do not incline us to emend the text of V.
26 μου is not in V, but is supplied from Mosq., supported by Syr. and S, as well as D. The entire phrase is dropped from E. So also Harnack, Funk and Schermann.
27 ἰδεῖν: so Wilamowitz Moellendorff, followed by Funk, Harnack and Schermann. Codd. and other edd. read εἰδέναι.

it expands itself and leads that soul on to all evil things, and does not allow the person to look out and see the truth. ₃Let your rage be measured and rein it in and bring it to a halt in a short distance, so that it cannot lead you to an evil deed. ₄For rage and evil pleasure, when they remain a long time, gain strength to become demons, and when a person yields to them they swell up in his soul and become greater and lead him on to unjust deeds and they mock him and take pleasure in the person's destruction."

9

Simon said: "Child, do not be a speaker of base words, nor immodestly curious.[28] For from these adulteries come about."

10

James said: "My child, do not be an examiner of omens, since this leads to idolatry, nor an enchanter nor an astrologer nor a lustrator, nor desire to see or hear these things. For from all of these are idolatries begotten."

---

28 Literally, "a lifter up of the eyes." The rendition is that of the Patristic Greek Lexicon, drawn to my attention by Allen Brent.

11

₁ Ναθαναὴλ εἶπεν· Τέκνον μου,²⁹ μὴ γίνου ψεύστης, ἐπειδὴ ὁδηγεῖ τὸ ψεῦσμα ἐπὶ τὴν κλοπήν, μηδὲ φιλάργυρος, μηδὲ κενόδοξος· ἐκ τούτων ἁπάντων κλοπαὶ γεννῶνται. ₂ τέκνον μου,³⁰ μὴ γίνου γόγγυσος, ἐπειδὴ ἄγει πρὸς τὴν βλασφημίαν, μηδὲ αὐθάδης, μηδὲ πονηρόφρων· ἐκ γὰρ τούτων ἁπάντων βλασφημίαι γεννῶνται. ₃ ἴσθι δὲ πραΰς, ἐπειδὴ πραεῖς κληρονομήσουσι τὴν βασιλείαν τῶν οὐρανῶν.³¹ ₄ γίνου μακρόθυμος, ἐλεήμων, εἰρηνοποιός, καθαρὸς τῇ καρδίᾳ ἀπὸ παντὸς κακοῦ, ἄκακος καὶ ἡσύχιος, ἀγαθὸς καὶ φυλάσσων καὶ τρέμων τοὺς λόγους οὓς ἤκουσας. ₅ οὐχ ὑψώσεις σεαυτόν, οὐδὲ δώσεις τὴν ψυχήν σου μετὰ ὑψηλῶν ἀλλὰ μετὰ δικαίων καὶ ταπεινῶν ἀναστραφήσῃ. ₆ τὰ δὲ συμβαίνοντά σοι ἐνεργήματα ὡς ἀγαθὰ προσδέξῃ, εἰδὼς ὅτι ἄτερ θεοῦ οὐδὲν γίνεται.

12

₁ Θωμᾶς εἶπεν· Τέκνον,³² τὸν λαλοῦντά σοι τὸν λόγον τοῦ θεοῦ καὶ παραίτιόν σοι γινόμενον τῆς ζωῆς καὶ δόντα σοι τὴν ἐν κυρίῳ σφραγῖδα ἀγαπήσεις ὡς κόρην ὀφθαλμοῦ σου, μνησθήσῃ³³ αὐτοῦ νύκτα καὶ ἡμέραν, τιμήσεις αὐτὸν ὡς τὸν κύριον. ὅθεν γὰρ ἡ κυριότης λαλεῖται, ἐκεῖ κύριός ἐστιν. ₂ ἐκζητήσεις δὲ τὸ πρόσωπον αὐτοῦ καθ' ἡμέραν καὶ τοὺς λοιποὺς ἁγίους, ἵνα ἐπαναπαύσῃ τοῖς λόγοις αὐτῶν· κολλώμενος γὰρ ἁγίους ἅγιος ἁγιασθήσῃ.³⁴ ₃ τιμήσεις δὲ αὐτὸν καθ' ὃ δυνατὸς

---

29 μου is again inserted on the basis of Syr. and S, as well as D, though with less certainty than at the beginning of K10, as there is not the support of Mosq. (which lacks this chapter altogether.)
30 μου is once again inserted on the basis of the versions and D. The entire phrase is omitted from E and the entire chapter from Mosq., thus leaving the text uncertain.
31 τὴν βασιλείαν τῶν οὐρανῶν: S (though unsupported by Ar., Eth.) and D read τὴν γῆν. However Syr. concurs with V in the reading given. τὴν γῆν in S is perhaps an attempt to conform the text to Scripture.
32 On this occasion τέκνον is allowed to stand without μου as at this point, although the versions and D have μου this chapter is contained in Mosq., which reads simply τέκνον.
33 μνησθήσῃ: V and edd. except Funk. Cf. Mosq., A, Funk, μνήσθητι. μνησθήσῃ has support from Syriac.
34 ἁγιασθήσῃ: although E and S read ἁγιασθήσεται, the saying is virtually proverbial, and may therefore have been written from memory.

11

₁ Nathanael said: "My child, do not be a liar, since falsehood leads to theft,[35] nor a lover of money nor vain glory. For from all of these are thefts begotten. ₂ My child, do not be a grumbler, since it leads to blasphemy, nor self-willed nor evil-minded. For from all of these are blasphemies begotten. ₃ Be generous, for the generous will inherit the Kingdom of the Heavens.[36] ₄ Be patient, merciful, a peacemaker, pure in heart from every evil, guileless and peaceable, good and guarding and fearing the words which you heard. ₅ Do not make yourself haughty, nor commit your life to the exalted, but associate with the righteous and lowly. ₆ Whatever befall you, accept these experiences as good, knowing that nothing happens without God."

12

₁ Thomas said: "Child, you shall love as the apple of your eye the one who speaks to you the word of God and is the cause of life to you and gives you the seal of the Lord. You shall remember him night and day, you shall honour him as the Lord. For inasmuch as the dominion is discussed, the Lord is there. ₂ You shall daily seek out his face, as well as the rest of the saints, so that you may find refreshment in their words. For in being cemented with the saints you shall be sanctified as a saint.[37] ₃ You shall honour him as much as you are able

---

35 Cited by Clement, *Strom.* 1.20.
36 Cf. Matt. 5:5.
37 This phrase is cited as scriptural by *1 Clem.* 46.2.

εἴ ἐκ τοῦ ἱδρῶτός σου καὶ ἐκ τοῦ πόνου τῶν χειρῶν σου. εἰ γὰρ ὁ κύριος δι' αὐτοῦ ἠξίωσέν σοι δοθῆναι πνευματικὴν τροφὴν καὶ ποτὸν καὶ ζωὴν αἰώνιον, σὺ ὀφείλεις πολὺ μᾶλλον τὴν φθαρτὴν καὶ πρόσκαιρον προσφέρειν τροφήν. ἄξιος γὰρ ὁ ἐργάτης τοῦ μισθοῦ αὐτοῦ, καὶ βοῦν ἀλοῶντα οὐ φιμώσεις καὶ οὐδεὶς φυτεύει ἀμπελῶνα καὶ ἐκ τοῦ καρποῦ αὐτοῦ οὐκ ἐσθίει.

13

₁ Κηφᾶς εἶπεν· Οὐ ποιήσεις σχίσματα,[38] εἰρηνεύσεις δὲ μαχομένους, κρινεῖς δικαίως, οὐ λήψῃ πρόσωπον ἐλέγξαι ἁμαρτόντα τινὰ[39] ἐπὶ παραπτώματι, οὐ γὰρ ἰσχύει πλοῦτος παρὰ κυρίῳ· οὐ γὰρ ἀξία[40] προσκρίνει οὐδὲ κάλλος ὠφελεῖ, ἀλλ' ἰσότης ἐστὶ πάντων παρ' αὐτῷ. ₂ ἐν προσευχῇ σου μὴ διψυχήσεις πότερον ἔσται ἢ οὔ. ₃ μὴ γίνου πρὸς μὲν τὸ λαβεῖν ἐκτείνων τὰς χεῖρας, πρὸς δὲ τὸ δοῦναι συσπῶν. ἐὰν ἔχῃς διὰ τῶν χειρῶν σου, δώσεις[41] λύτρωσιν τῶν ἁμαρτιῶν σου. οὐ διστάσεις διδόναι[42] οὐδὲ διδοὺς γογγύσεις· γνώσῃ γάρ, τίς ἐστιν

---

38 σχίσματα: Mosq. reads, συνάψαι τινὰ μάχην πρὸς ἕτερον. D and E have σχίσμα.
39 ἁμαρτόντα τινά cf. V and Mosq. τινά. The word is taken from S (Eth., Ar.), which has "the sinner" (ⲁⲫⲉⲣⲛⲟⲃⲉ). It is Arendzen, 76, who suggests that this is the true reading, as Syr. here has a redundant ὄντα, which may in turn be explained by a misreading of ἁμαρτόντα. In addition the τινά here is somewhat harsh. V was left intact in my earlier edition of this text.
40 ἀξία: Such is the emendation offered by Wilamowitz Moellendorff, accepted by Harnack, by Funk and by Schermann. V however reads ἀξίας, and this was likewise clearly read by the Syriac translator; I am thus not entirely confident in the text I have printed here. I would be more confident if οὐ γάρ read οὐδὲ, as Wilamowitz Moellendorff proposed to emend the text.
41 δώσεις: Pitra suggested δός on the basis of Constitutiones apostolorum, a reading which is supported by E and Mosq., but this is insufficient reason to essay an emendation here.
42 διδόναι: so V; cf. Harnack, followed by Schermann, who, on the basis of D and Mosq., amends to δοῦναι.

from your sweat and from the labour of your hands. If the Lord through him has made you worthy to be given spiritual food and drink and eternal life, much the more should you bring him corruptible and temporary food. 'For the workman is worthy of his hire' and 'You shall not muzzle a threshing ox' and 'Nobody plants a vine and does not eat the fruit of it.'"[43]

13

₁ Kephas said: "You shall not make schisms, you shall make peace between those who are disputing, you shall judge justly, you shall not show partiality in rebuking any transgression, for wealth does not count before the Lord. Status does not impress nor does beauty give advantage, for before him all are equal. ₂ In your prayer you shall not be divided in your mind, whether it will be or not. ₃ Do not be one who stretches out hands to take, whilst retracting them to avoid giving. If you have gained through your hands, you shall give a ransom for your sins. Do not hesitate to give, nor grumble in your giving, for you know who is

---

43 The source of these citations is taken to be 1 Tim. 5:18, 1 Cor. 9:7.

ὁ τοῦ μισθοῦ καλὸς ἀνταποδότης.⁴⁴ ₄ οὐκ ἀποστραφήσῃ ἐνδεούμενον, κοινωνήσεις δὲ ἁπάντων⁴⁵ τῷ ἀδελφῷ σου καὶ οὐκ ἐρεῖς ἴδια εἶναι· εἰ γὰρ ἐν τῷ ἀθανάτῳ⁴⁶ κοινωνοί ἐστε, πόσῳ μᾶλλον ἐν τοῖς φθαρτοῖς;⁴⁷

14

₁ Βαρθολομαῖος εἶπεν· Ἐρωτῶμεν ὑμᾶς, ἀδελφοί, ὡς ἔτι καιρός ἐστι καὶ ἔχετε⁴⁸ εἰς οὓς ἐργάζεσθε μεθ' ἑαυτῶν μὴ ἐκλίπητε ἐν μηδενὶ ἐξ οὗ ἂν ἔχητε.⁴⁹ ₂ ἐγγὺς γὰρ ἡ ἡμέρα κυρίου, ἐν ᾗ συναπολεῖται πάντα σὺν τῷ πονηρῷ· ἥξει γὰρ ὁ κύριος καὶ ὁ μισθὸς αὐτοῦ μετ' αὐτοῦ.⁵⁰

---

44   Mosq. concludes here with a doxology. Chapter 14, however, is misplaced and thus Mosq. provides a witness to the chapter.
45   κοινωνήσεις δὲ ἁπάντων: so V and Funk. Cf. Harnack (followed by Schermann) who, on the basis of D and E, emends to συγκοινωνήσεις δὲ πάντα.
46   E reads θάνατῳ, a reading supported by L, though not D. This is probably the reading of κ, since it seems improbable that E would make the error; the originality of the reading is supported by L, which has the same reading. We cannot therefore be sure whether K made the "correction", or whether this results from the scribal tradition, though Syr. clearly implies ἀθανάτοις. D reads ἀθάνατῳ. See Giet, "La Didache", 232–233.
47   φθαρτοῖς: So V, Pitra, Lagarde, Hilgenfeld, Syr., Funk. Cf., again, Harnack and Schermann who, on the basis of D and E, read θνητοῖς. Although the reading here imbalances the clauses, this is explained in the introduction at 1.2.4.1.3.3 as the result of a recollection by K of a different version of the saying.
48   Schermann inserts οὐκ here.
49   ἐξ οὗ ἂν ἔχητε: Such is the conjecture of Lagarde, based on his reading of V as ἐξοῦ ἐὰν ἔχητε. Mosq., however, reads: ἐξουσίαν ἔχητε, which is the manner in which Bickell read V! Thus, with the exception of Lagarde, eds. have given the text as ἐξουσίαν ἐὰν ἔχητε. Apart from being closer to V, Lagarde's conjecture is confirmed by the versions, whereas the version of Mosq. can be understood as a misreading.
50   ὁ μισθὸς αὐτοῦ μετ' αὐτοῦ: So V, Syr., S (with A, Eth.), Funk. Cf., however, Mosq., followed by Harnack and Schermann, ὁ μισθὸς αὐτοῦ. This is the reading of B, but there is no reason to suppose that this was the reading of K, unless under the prior conviction that K is simply following B. The reading of Mosq. is simply a manifestation of the tendency of this MS to abbreviate.

the good dispenser of rewards. ₄ You shall not turn away a beggar. You shall have all things in common with your brother, and you shall not claim anything as your own. For if you are companions in immortality, are you not much more so in what is corruptible?"

14

₁ Bartholomew said: "We ask you, brethren, for as long as there is time, while you have amongst yourselves those for whom to labour, do not withhold anything that you possess. ₂ For the day of the Lord is near, on which all things will perish alongside the evil one. For the Lord will come and his reward with him.

₃ ἑαυτῶν γίνεσθε νομοθέται,⁵¹ ἑαυτῶν γίνεσθε σύμβουλοι ἀγαθοί, θεοδίδακτοι·⁵² φυλάξεις ἃ παρέλαβες μήτε προσθεὶς μήτε ὑφαιρῶν.

15

Πέτρος εἶπεν· Ἀδελφοί, τὰ περὶ τῶν λοιπῶν νουθεσιῶν αἱ γραφαὶ διδάξουσιν,⁵³ ἡμεῖς δὲ ἃ ἐκελεύσθημεν διατάξωμεν. πάντες εἶπαν· Πέτρος λεγέτω.

16

₁ Πέτρος εἶπεν· Ἐὰν ὀλιγανδρία ὑπάρχῃ καὶ μήπου πλῆθος τυγχάνῃ τῶν δυναμένων ψηφίσασθαι περὶ ἐπισκόπου ἐντὸς δεκαδύο ἀνδρῶν, εἰς τὰς πλησίον ἐκκλησίας, ὅπου τυγχάνει πεπηγυῖα, γραφέτωσαν, ὅπως ἐκεῖθεν ἐκλεκτοὶ τρεῖς ἄνδρες παραγενόμενοι δοκιμῇ δοκιμάσαντες⁵⁴ τὸν ἄξιον ὄντα,⁵⁵ εἴ τις φήμην καλὴν ἔχει ἀπὸ τῶν ἐθνῶν, εἰ ἀναμάρτητος ὑπάρχει,⁵⁶ εἰ φιλόπτωχος, εἰ σώφρων, μὴ μέθυσος, μὴ πόρνος, μὴ πλεονέκτης ἢ λοίδορος ἢ προσωπολήπτης καὶ τὰ τούτοις ὅμοια.

---

51 ἑαυτῶν γίνεσθε νομοθέται: these words appear in neither V nor Mosq., but are added by Harnack, Funk and Schermann on the basis of Syr. and S (Ar. Eth.) as well as B. Although B should not figure in any calculation of the text here, the universal witness of the versions is significant.
52 θεοδίδακτοι: So Mosq., Syr. S (Ar., Eth.), Harnack, Funk, Schermann. V has διδακτοί.
53 It is possible that, following Syr. and S, ὑμᾶς should be added to διδάξουσιν.
54 δοκιμάσαντες: Funk, with support from Syr. and S, suggests δοκιμάσωσι. Arendzen, 77, suggests that this might be a correction on the part of the translators, providing a verb after ὅπως, especially as δοκιμῇ is not rendered in either version.
55 S, with some support from Ar. and Eth., adds ⲙ̄ⲡⲉⲓ ⲃⲁⲑⲙⲟⲥ (=τοῦ βαθμοῦ τούτου.)
56 Syr. and S (with Ar., Eth.) add "and not prone to anger." The sole reason not to insert καὶ μὴ ὀργίλος in the text is that this is a negative quality, whereas the other qualities at this point are positive. Hennecke, 242, supports this reading.

₃ Be legislators for yourselves, be good counsellors one to another, taught of God. You shall guard what you have received, neither adding nor subtracting."

15

Peter said: "Brothers, the Scriptures will teach of the remaining exhortations. But let us draw up in order what we have commanded." All said: "Let Peter speak."

16

₁ Peter said: "If there should occur a shortage of men, and there are insufficient competent to elect to the episcopate from among twelve,[57] they should write to the neighbouring churches, where one is established, so that three selected men might come from there carefully to determine[58] which is worthy,[59] whether any has a good reputation among the heathen,[60] being without fault,[61] whether a friend of the poor,[62] whether temperate,[63] not a drunkard,[64] not a fornicator, not grasping or abusive,[65] or a respecter of persons[66] or anything of that nature.

---

57 Cf. Harnack, *Sources*, 7: "and there are not twelve who are competent to vote at the election of a bishop". See the introduction 3.7.1 for some discussion of the phrase.
58 δοκιμῇ δοκιμάσαντες. Cf. 2 Cor. 8:22; 1 Tim. 3:10; *1 Clem.* 42.4, 44.2, 47.4; D15.1.
59 ἄξιον. The word enters ordination rites. See Bradshaw, *Ordination rites*, 23–24. It appears in the qualification list of D15.1.
60 1 Tim. 3:7.
61 Cf. 1 Tim. 3:2; *Didascalia* 2.1.1; *Testamentum Domini* 1.20.
62 Cf. *Testamentum Domini* 1.20.
63 Cf. 1 Tim. 3:2; *Didascalia* 2.2.1.
64 Cf. Tit. 1:7; 1 Tim. 3:3; *Didascalia* 2.2.1.
65 For this list cf. 1 Cor. 5:11. Note also the discussion of these qualifications in the introduction 3.7.1, and in particular the direction here that the bishop should be φιλόπτωχος, which is that which, given the economic office of the bishop in KK, is most authentic and primitive.
66 Cf. Polycarp *Ad Phil.* 61 (of presbyters.) This is demanded frequently of the bishop in the *Didascalia*, so that he should not be partial in exercising judgement. See, e.g., *Didascalia* 2.5.1.

₂ καλὸν μὲν εἶναι ἀγύναιος, εἰ δὲ μή, ἀπὸ μιᾶς γυναικός· παιδείας μέτοχος, δυνάμενος τὰς γραφὰς ἑρμηνεύειν· εἰ δὲ ἀγράμματος, πραΰς ὑπάρχων,⁶⁷ καὶ τῇ ἀγάπῃ εἰς πάντας περισσευέτω, μήποτε περὶ τινος ἐλεγχθεὶς ἐπίσκοπος ἀπὸ τῶν πολλῶν γενηθείη.

17

₁ Ἰωάννης εἶπεν· Ὁ κατασταθεὶς ἐπίσκοπος, εἰδὼς τὸ προσεχὲς καὶ φιλόθεον τῶν σὺν αὐτῷ, καταστήσει οὓς ἂν δοκιμάσῃ πρεσβυτέρους δύο. ₂ πάντες ἀντεῖπον· ὅτι οὐ δύο ἀλλὰ τρεῖς.⁶⁸ εἴκοσι γὰρ καὶ τέσσαρές εἰσι πρεσβύτεροι, δώδεκα ἐξ δεξιῶν καὶ δώδεκα ἐξ εὐωνύμων.

18

₁ Ἰωάννης εἶπεν· Καλῶς ὑπεμνήσατε, ἀδελφοί. οἱ μὲν γὰρ ἐκ δεξιῶν δεχόμενοι ἀπὸ τῶν ἀρχαγγέλων τὰς φιάλας προσφέρουσι τῷ δεσπότῃ, οἱ δὲ ἐξ ἀριστερῶν ἐπέχουσι τῷ πλήθει τῶν ἀγγέλων.

67 δυνάμενος τὰς γραφὰς ἑρμηνεύειν· εἰ δὲ ἀγράμματος, πραΰς ὑπάρχων. So V, versions and eds. However, as noted in the introduction at 3.7.3, this is awkward for a number of reasons. Thus I have conjectured that the text of κκ read: δυνάμενος τὰς γραφὰς ἑρμηνεύειν, εἰ δ' ἦ ἀγράμματος· πραΰς ὑπάρχων. However, in view of the statement (from K?) μήποτε περὶ τινος ἐλεγχθεὶς ἐπίσκοπος, I eventually conclude that the text of K read as printed here. We cannot tell whether the text had already suffered mutilation, or was misread or deliberately recast by K.

68 πρεσβυτέρους δύο. πάντες ἀντεῖπον· ὅτι οὐ δύο ἀλλὰ τρεῖς. Cf. Hilgenfeld, who would emend to πρεσβυτέρους δεκαδύο. πάντες ἀντεῖπον· ὅτι οὐ δεκαδύο ἀλλὰ εἴκοσι καὶ τέσσαρες (κδ΄). This passage is discussed in the introduction at 3.7.2; here we may simply note that Hilgenfeld's emendation, whilst attractive, is hard to explain on orthographical grounds. It is suggested that even had δεκαδύο originally stood in where δύο now stands on the first occasion, the corruption had already occurred by the time the text came into the hand of K.

₂ It is good should he be unmarried,⁶⁹ otherwise he should be of one wife,⁷⁰ having some education,⁷¹ and able to interpret the Scriptures. Even if he is unlettered he should be generous,⁷² and overflowing with love for all,⁷³ so that a bishop should not come under accusation on any account by the many."

17

₁ John said: "The bishop who has been installed, knowing the care and the love of God of those who are with him, should install two presbyters of whom he approves."⁷⁴ ₂ All said in reply: "Not two but three. For there are twenty-four presbyters, twelve on the right and twelve on the left."

18

₁ John said: "You have recalled this well, brothers. For those on the right receive the phials from the archangels and bear them to the master, and those on the left have authority over the company of angels.⁷⁵

69 *Testamentum Domini* 1.20.
70 Cf. 1 Tim. 3:2, Titus 1:6, *Didascalia* 2.2.2. However, the text is slightly distinct in saying "*of*" or "*from*" a single wife. As suggested in the introduction, this may be a redactional alteration indicating that the bishop should either be never-married or widowed, and widowed once.
71 Cf. 1 Tim. 3:2 διδακτικόν and *Didascalia* 2.1.2, possibly reflected in *Constitutiones apostolorum* 2.1.2 πεπαιδευμένος.
72 The text translated is that of K. However, it is suggested that this is a corruption, whether deliberate or accidental, of an earlier text which would read: "... able to interpret the scriptures, even if he is unlettered. He should generous..." For further discussion see the introduction 3.7.3. The scholasticization of the church which becomes apparent in the Pastoral Epistles brought about the requirement that the bishop should some ability in teaching, which is at odds with the duties described. For πραΰς in a qualification list, see D15.1, *Didascalia* 2.1.5.
73 Cf. 1 Thess. 3:12; *Didascalia* 2.3.3.
74 See the introduction 3.7.2 and the textual commentary for the question of whether "two" here is a corruption of "twelve."
75 Cf. Rev. 4:4, 8.

₂ δεῖ οὖν εἶναι⁷⁶ τοὺς πρεσβυτέρους ἤδη κεχρονικότας ἐπὶ τῷ κόσμῳ, τρόπῳ τινὶ ἀπεχομένους τῆς πρὸς γυναῖκας συνελεύσεως, εὐμεταδότους εἰς τὴν ἀδελφότητα, πρόσωπον ἀνθρώπου μὴ λαμβάνοντας, συμμύστας τοῦ ἐπισκόπου καὶ συνεπιμάχους,

76 In keeping with his earlier emendation, Hilgenfeld inserts κδ´ here as well. Pitra notes an erasure in V, and Hilgenfeld so fills it. However, whatever the attraction of the emendation above, it is surely unnecessary here.

₂Therefore the presbyters should have been a long time in the world, having kept themselves to an extent⁷⁷ from congress with women in their lives,⁷⁸ generous towards the brotherhood, not respecters of persons, struggling alongside the bishop and participating in the mysteries together with him,⁷⁹

77 "To an extent" renders τρόπῳ τινί. Whilst slightly odd in the context the phrase is not unknown in statements of qualification, thus: δεῖ δὲ καὶ τοὺς διακόνους ὄντας μυστηρίων Ἰησοῦ Χριστοῦ κατὰ πάντα τρόπον πᾶσιν ἀρέσκειν (Ignatius *Trall.* 2.3) and τὸν ποιμένα τὸν καθιστάμενον ἐπίσκοπον... οὐκ ἔλαττον ἐτῶν πεντήκοντα, ὅτι τρόπῳ τινὶ τὰς νεωτερικὰς ἀταξίας... ἐκπεφευγὼς ὑπάρχει *(Constitutiones apostolorum* 2.1.1). Here it means something like "to some extent" (or in Ignatius, to the entire possible extent); in the light of the *Constitutiones apostolorum* parallel, where time has put some distance between the ordinand and his *folies de jeunesse*, possibly in K it indicates the time since he last spoke to a woman. That is to say a presbyter is to be an older man, who has long abandoned the company of women. Heid, *Celibacy*, 108, also cites *Constitutiones apostolorum* 3.1.1: χήρας δὲ καθιστᾶτε μὴ ἔλαττον ἐτῶν ἑξήκοντα, ἵνα τρόπῳ τινὶ τὸ τῆς διγαμίας αὐτῶν ἀνύποπτον βέβαιον ὑμῖν διὰ τῆς ἡλικίας ὑπάρχῃ. This is less relevant, since it is addressed to bishops, who are to have assurance "to a certain extent" that the widows will not remarry. Heid takes this to mean "so that in a certain manner she will not be tempted to marry again", which is not what the Greek says. The *Didascalia* does not assist with interpretation here.
78 Cf. the translation of Heid, *Celibacy*, 109: "they refrain from relations with their wives." For discussion see the introduction 4.4.
79 This may be a reference to Wisdom 8:4, μύστις γὰρ ἐστι τῆς τοῦ Θεοῦ ἐπιστήμης stating in effect that the presbyter is to share with the bishop in having knowledge of God; Ignatius *Eph.* 12.2. uses the term of the Ephesians, as fellow-initiates with Paul. Arendzen, 69, suggests that the term simply means that the presbyters concelebrate the eucharist with the bishop; although it is hard to see ordination as meaning initiation, the presbyters, as argued in the introduction. But, as suggested in the introduction, this would probably refer to some form of spiritual insight shared by bishop and presbyters. The presbyters are less liturgical officers than spiritual athletes.

συναθροίζοντας τὸ πλῆθος, προσθυμουμένους τὸν[80] ποιμένα.

3 οἱ[81] ἐκ δεξιῶν πρεσβύτεροι προνοήσονται τῶν ἐπισκοπούντων[82] πρὸς τὸ θυσιαστήριον, ὅπως τιμήσωσι καὶ ἐντιμηθῶσιν[83] εἰς ὃ ἂν δέῃ. οἱ ἐξ ἀριστερῶν πρεσβύτεροι προνοήσονται τοῦ πλήθους ὅπως εὐσταθήσῃ καὶ ἀθόρυβον ᾖ,[84] πρῶτον μεμαθηκὸς ἐν πάσῃ ὑποταγῇ.[85]

4 εἰ δέ τις νουθετούμενος αὐθάδως ἀποκριθῇ, τὸ[86] ἕν ποιήσαντες[87] οἱ ἐπὶ τῷ θυσιαστηρίῳ τὸν τοιοῦτον μετὰ ἴσης βουλῆς, ὃ ἂν ᾖ ἄξιον, δικασάτωσαν, ἵνα καὶ οἱ λοιποὶ φόβον ἔχωσι, μήποτε ἑνὸς πρόσωπον λάβωσι,

80 προσθυμουμένους τόν: so V. Syr., however, inserts ܠܘܬ here and, as Arendzen, 77, remarks, it seems that some preposition is needed in the Greek. The obvious preposition would be πρός, but this is stylistically awkward after προσθυμουμένους.
81 Funk suggests οἱ δέ.
82 ἐπισκοπούντων: V has τῶν ἐπισκόπων whereas the oriental versions indicate that the word present was κοπιόντων, a reading supported by Hennecke, 242-243. ἐπισκοπούντων is thus a conjecture intended to account for both possible readings. If the conjecture is not accepted, then I must suggest that of the two existing readings, that of the Greek text is the less probable, as there is no basis in K (or κκ) for a plurality of bishops.
83 ἐντιμηθῶσιν: Syr. and S (Ar., Eth.) imply a reading of ἐπιτιμήσωσιν. The acceptance of the reading depends to a great extent on the interpretation of the passage. It seems to me that Harnack is right in seeing the focus on the distribution of gifts, and thus it is possible that the versions had misunderstood the passage, leading to the reading which they present. ἐπιτιμήσωσιν is supported by Hennecke, 243-244.
84 εὐσταθήσῃ καὶ ἀθόρυβον ᾖ: so Lagarde, and all subsequent edd. V has εὐσταθὴς ᾖ καὶ ἀθόρυβον εἴη.
85 Arendzen, 77, suggests on the basis of Syr. and S that an infinitive, probably ὑπάρχειν, has fallen out here. Although this would be an improvement in the text, it may be that the versions are making such an improvement, whereas the somewhat awkward Greek is original.
86 ἀποκριθῇ, τὸ: So V and edd. except Pitra, who conjectures ἀποκριθήτω.
87 ἓν ποιήσαντες: So V, followed by edd. Syr. and S imply ἓν νοήσαντες, a reading supported by Arendzen. However, this is to an extent made redundant by μετὰ ἴσης βουλῆς. Pitra conjectured ἐμποιήσαντες.

gathering the people and devoted to the pastor.[88]

₃ The presbyters on the right are to assist those who oversee[89] the altar, so that they may distribute the gifts of honour and receive them as necessary.[90] The presbyters on the left are to assist the congregation, so that it may be peaceful and without disturbance, once it has been instructed in all submission. ₄ But if anyone who has been warned should respond rashly, those at the altar, acting in concert, should pronounce a like decision, as is deserved, so that the rest might be in fear, and so that they do not accept any person,

88 As Maclean, *The ancient church orders*, 68, n., observes, the use of the term "shepherd" absolutely to refer to the bishop is not common in church order literature, but is found most prominently in *Testamentum Domini*, as well as occasionally in the *Didascalia* and *Constitutiones apostolorum*. This is to be considered alongside other indications of a common interest between *Testamentum Domini* and K/κκ.
89 Following the conjecture made opposite. This, as does the reading of the oriental versions, solves the difficulty regarding the sudden plurality of bishops, and balance the functions of the presbyters on the left and the right.
90 The interpretation of Harnack, *Sources*, 13-14, who sees the verbs as referring to the distribution and receipt of gifts, is followed. According to this reading the meaning of the passage is that the gifts are received at the altar, and that they are distributed according to need to the congregation. This task is that of the bishop and deacons, who are assisted (and perhaps overseen) in this task by the presbyters on the right (if the term presbyters does not indeed refer to deacons as well.) There is one difference with the interpretation of Harnack, who felt that the subject was the bishops. However, as the result of an emendation, these bishops have disappeared, and so the task is that of "those who oversee the altar". Funk, 64, however, suggested that the subject was the πλῆθος, and that the verbs referred to the giving of gifts, rather than the distribution thereof; the πλῆθος, however, does not appear in this sentence. See also Hennecke, "Zur apostolischen Kirchenordnung", 243-244.

καὶ ἐπὶ πλεῖον νεμηθῇ <τὸ κακὸν> ὡς γάγγραινα, καὶ αἰχμαλωτισθῶσιν οἱ πάντες.⁹¹

19

Ἰάκωβος εἶπεν· Ἀναγνώστης καθιστανέσθω πρῶτον δοκιμῇ δεδοκιμασμένος,⁹² μὴ γλωσσοκόπος, μὴ μέθυσος μήτε γελωτολόγος, εὔτροπος, εὐπειθής, εὐγνώμων, ἐν ταῖς κυριακαῖς συνόδοις πρῶτος σύνδρομος, εὐήκοος, διηγητικός, εἰδὼς ὅτι εὐαγγελιστῶν τόπον ἐργάζεται. ὁ γὰρ ἐμπιπλῶν ὦτα μὴ νοοῦντος ἔγγραφος λογισθήσεται παρὰ τῷ θεῷ.

91 μήποτε ἑνὸς πρόσωπον λάβωσι, καὶ ἐπὶ πλεῖον νεμηθῇ <τὸ κακὸν> ὡς γάγγραινα, καὶ αἰχμαλωτισθῶσιν οἱ πάντες: I have supplied τὸ κακόν as something is clearly missing here, but I have been as conservative as possible in supplying a noun as Lat. commences here, and supports the text of V. For this reason I reject the far more extensive restoration proposed by Arendzen, largely on the basis of Syr., as an attempt by the Syriac translator to make sense of a text which he did not understand. Arendzen's proposed restoration is: μήποτε ἐὰν πρόσωπον λάβωσιν τολμήσωσιν οἱ ἀδικοῦντες καὶ ἐπὶ πλεῖον νεμηθῇ τὸ κακὸν καὶ νομὴν σχῇ ὡς γάγγραινα.
92 δοκιμῇ δεδοκιμασμένος: both Lat. (probatione omni probatus) and Syr. ܟܠܗ ܒܒܘܚܪܢܐ imply that some word intervened between the two, but there is no agreement as to which.

and so that the evil[93] might not spread further like a cancer and all be infected."[94]

19

James said: "A reader should be appointed after careful testing. He should not be a babbler, or a drunkard, or a jester. He should be of upstanding life, submissive, well-intentioned, taking the lead in the assemblies on the Lord's days,[95] who is good to listen to and is able to construct a narrative, aware that he labours in the place of an evangelist.[96] For whoever fills the ears of the ignorant shall be reckoned enrolled in the presence of God."

---

93 The word "evil" here is not in the text but is supplied to make sense.
94 For this imagery cf. *Didascalia* 2.42.1, and 2.46.6, 2.47.1.
95 Cf. *Canones Hippolyti* 37.
96 Cf. 2 Tim. 4:5.

20

₁ Ματθαῖος εἶπεν· Διάκονοι καθιστάσθωσαν <τρεῖς>·⁹⁷ γέγραπται· ἐπὶ τριῶν σταθήσεται πᾶν ῥῆμα κυρίου. ₂ ἔστωσαν δεδοκιμασμένοι πάσῃ διακονίᾳ, μεμαρτυρημένοι παρὰ τοῦ πλήθους, μονόγαμοι, τεκνοτρόφοι, σώφρονες, ἐπιεικεῖς, ἥσυχοι, μὴ γόγγυσοι, μὴ δίγλωσσοι, μὴ ὀργίλοι, ὀργὴ γὰρ ἀπόλλυσι ἄνδρα φρόνιμον, μὴ πρόσωπον πλουσίου⁹⁸ λαμβάνοντες μηδὲ πένητα καταδυναστεύοντες μηδὲ οἴνῳ πολλῷ χρώμενοι, εὔσκυλτοι· ₃ τῶν κρυφίων ἔργων καλοὶ προτρεπτικοί, ἐπαναγκάζοντες τοὺς ἔχοντας τῶν ἀδελφῶν ἁπλοῦν τὰς χεῖρας, καὶ αὐτοὶ εὐμετάδοτοι, κονωνικοί, πάσῃ τιμῇ καὶ ἐντροπῇ καὶ φόβῳ τιμώμενοι ἀπὸ τοῦ πλήθους, ἐπιμελῶς προσέχοντες τοῖς ἀτάκτως περιπατοῦσιν, οὓς μὲν νουθετοῦντες, οὓς δὲ παρακαλοῦντες, οὓς δὲ ἐπιτιμῶντες, τοὺς δὲ καταφρονοῦντας τελέως παραπεμπόμενοι, εἰδότες ὅτι οἱ ἀντίλογοι καὶ καταφρονηταὶ καὶ λοίδοροι Χριστῷ ἀντετάξαντο.

97 Bickell and Funk supply the number τρεῖς, following whom it is supplied here; whereas Harnack suggests that the number has been deliberately omitted by K, Hauler (apparatus reproduced in Tidner, 106) suggests that the omission is accidental, and that γ΄ fell out before γέγραπται. The issue is discussed in the introduction at 3.7.4, where an accidental explanation of the absence of the number in V is preferred, on the basis that K would more probably insert, rather than omit, the number here. The number is present in Syriac but not in the other versions. The introduction also canvasses the possibility that the number seven stood in κκ at some point.
98 πλουσίου; Schermann prints πλησίου.

20

₁ Matthew said: "Three[99] deacons should be appointed. It is written: "Every matter of the Lord shall be established by three."[100] ₂ They should be proven in every ministry, with witness borne by the congregation,[101] married once,[102] educating their children,[103] temperate,[104] fair,[105] peaceable, not grumblers, not double-tongued, not irascible,[106] for anger distracts a reasonable man,[107] who neither accept the persons of the rich nor oppress the poor, not given to much use of wine,[108] intelligent, ₃ good at exhorting to secret works, as they oblige the brothers who have possessions to open their hands, and themselves generous, communicative, honoured by the congregation with all honour, esteem and fear, carefully mindful of those who are conducting themselves in a disorderly manner, warning some, encouraging others, threatening others, but leaving the scoffers entirely alone, mindful that those opposed to reason, the scoffers and the abusive have resisted Christ."

---

99   The appearance of this number is not absolutely certain. See the discussion in the introduction at 3.7.3.
100 Deut 19:15; Matt. 18:16; 2 Cor. 8:1. Since none of these passages are exactly cited, it is not clear which is intended. Faivre, "Apostolicité", 43–44, interestingly suggest that, in view of the disciplinary context, Deuteronomy 17 lies behind this provision.
101 Cf. 1 Clem. 44.3; D15.1; *Testamentum Domini* 1.33.
102 Cf. 1 Tim. 3:12. *Testamentum Domini* 1.33.
103 Cf. 1 Tim. 3:12.
104 Cf. 1 Tim. 3:2.
105 Cf. 1 Tim. 3:3.
106 Cf. Titus 1:7.
107 Prov. 15:1. Whereas this may look like a later gloss, the same text is quoted, in the same context (though with regard to the appointment of bishops rather than deacons) by *Didascalia* 2.3.
108 Cf. 1 Tim. 3:8; Titus 1:7.

21

₁ Κηφᾶς εἶπεν· Χῆραι καθιστανέσθωσαν τρεῖς· αἱ δύο προσμένουσαι τῇ προσευχῇ περὶ πάντων τῶν[109] ἐν πείρᾳ καὶ πρὸς τὰς ἀποκαλύψεις περὶ οὗ ἂν δέῃ. ₂ μία δὲ παρεδρεύσουσα ταῖς ἐν ταῖς νόσοις πειραζομέναις· εὐδιάκονος ᾖ, νηπτική, τὰ δέοντα ἀπαγέλλουσα τοῖς πρεσβυτέροις, μὴ αἰσχροκερδής, μὴ οἴνῳ πολλῷ προσέχουσα, ἵνα δύνηται νήφειν πρὸς τὰς νυκτερινὰς ὑπηρεσίας καὶ εἴ τις ἕτερα[110] βούλοιτο ἐργαγαθεῖν. καὶ γὰρ ταῦτα πρῶτα κυρίου[111] θησαυρίσματά εἰσιν ἀγαθά.

109 τῶν: Not in V and supplied by Lagarde.
110 ἕτερα: The accentuation here (reading a neuter plural) is that implied by the Syriac translation and as given by Hilgenfeld (who attributes the reading to E. Bochmer) and Harnack. Serious consideration, however should be given to accenting the word with Lagarde, followed by Funk and Schermann, and also in accordance with the reading of Lat. and S (with A, Eth), as ἑτέρα (feminine singular). In this event the translation would read: "If another wished to perform good works, and indeed these are the good treasures of the Lord." This could well be an expansion by K, as part of his response to the proper ministries of women, and coheres, moreover, with the statement at K29. It is, however, difficult to make sense of the clause, as it seems incomplete. S (with Ar., Eth.) expands the clause, adding, "let her act in accordance with her heart." It is quite possible, however, that this expansion is a rationalizing addition by the translator. Thus the accentuation as given is, after due consideration, preferred on the grounds of sense, and rendered in the translation, but the suspicion remains that the text read otherwise. For discussion see Gryson, *Ministry of women*, 46, who prefers the accentuation as given here.
111 πρῶτα κυρίου: So V, Lagarde, Hilgenfeld, Harnack, Funk. Schermann omits πρῶτα. Pitra's conjecture of παρὰ τῷ κυρίῳ should, however, be given serious consideration, though unsupported by the versions.

21

₁ Kephas said: "Three widows should be appointed. Two are to continue in prayer[112] for all who are in temptation and for revelations concerning whatever is necessary. ₂ One is to assist women who are being troubled by sickness.[113] She is to be a good minister, discreet in communicating what is necessary to the presbyters,[114] not avaricious, not fond of much wine, so that she may be sober in her service during the night,[115] and in whatever other acts of charity[116] she desires to perform. These foremost treasures of the Lord are good."

---

112 Cf. 1 Tim. 5:5.
113 Cf. *Canones Hippolyti* 9: widows are to pray, to care for the sick and to fast.
114 Cf. *Didascalia* 2.44.3 (of the deacon and the bishop).
115 Soranus *Gyn.* 2.32 suggests the same of a wet nurse.
116 Cf. 1 Tim. 5:10.

22

₁ Ἀνδρέας εἶπεν· Διάκονοι ἐργάται τῶν καλῶν ἔργων. νυχθήμερον ἐπελεύσονται¹¹⁷ πανταχοῦ, μήτε πένητα ὑπεροπτεύοντες μήτε πλούσιον προσωποληπτοῦντες, ἐπιγνώσονται τὸν θλιβόμενον καὶ ἐκ τῆς λογίας οὐ παραπέμψονται, ₂ ἐπαναγκάσουσι δὲ τοὺς δυναμένους ἀποθησαυρίζειν εἰς ἔργα ἀγαθά, προορῶντας τοὺς λόγους τοῦ διδασκάλου ἡμῶν· εἴδετέ με πεινῶντα καὶ οὐκ ἐθρεψατέ με. οἱ γὰρ καλῶς διακονήσαντες καὶ ἀμέμπτως τόπον ἑαυτοῖς περιποιοῦνται¹¹⁸ τὸν ποιμενικόν.

23

₁ Φίλιππος εἶπεν· Ὁ λαϊκὸς τοῖς λαϊκοῖς προστάγμασι¹¹⁹ περιπειθέσθω¹²⁰ ὑποτασσόμενος τοῖς παρεδρεύσι τῷ θυσιαστηρίῳ. ₂ ἕκαστος τῷ ἰδίῳ τόπῳ ἀρεσκέτω τῷ θεῷ¹²¹ μὴ φιλεχθροῦντες ἀλλήλοις περὶ τῶν τεταγμένων, ἕκαστος ἐν ᾧ ἐκλήθη

---

117 ἐπελεύσονται: V reads ἐπελεύσοντε, and Bickell gave ἐπελεύσοντες which, as Harnack, *Sources*, 21, remarks, "is no word at all." M. Schmidt (apud Hilgenfeld) proposed ἐπιλεύσοντες, but I can make no sense of this suggestion, though it is accepted by Schermann. Harnack suggested instead ἐπιλεύσσοντες, though he was not sure of the emendation, as the word is purely Homeric (though λεύσσω without a prefix is more widespread.) The emendation proposed is that of Funk. It represents only a minor change in the text of V and, most importantly, is entirely coherent with the versions, all of which agree in having "going around."
118 περιποιοῦνται: Funk reads προσποιοῦνται, but there seems no good reason to make the emendation.
119 προστάγμασι: So Lat., Syr., S (with Ar., Eth.), Hennecke, 242, Schermann. V, followed by other edd., has πράγμασι.
120 περιπειθέσθω: So Lagarde and subsequent edd. except Hilgenfeld, who suggests περιτιθέσθω or περιπλεκέσθω. V has περιποιθέσθω. M. Schmidt, apud Hilgenfeld, suggests ἐπιτερπέσθω.
121 θεῷ: So V and S. Lat. and Syr., however, agree in having κυρίῳ.

22

₁ Andrew said: "Deacons perform noble deeds; they go around everywhere, night and day, neither looking down upon the poor or paying undue attention to the wealthy, recognizing any who is oppressed and not excluding him from the collections, ₂ obliging those who are able to put something aside for good works, having in mind the words of our teacher: 'You saw me hungry, and fed me not.'[122] Those who serve nobly and blamelessly set aside for themselves the position of the pastorate."

23

₁ Philip said: "The layman should be content to concern himself with matters pertaining to the laity,[123] submitting to whose who attend to the altar. ₂ Each should please God in his own position,[124] not striving with each other in the matter of rank, each in that to which he was called and

---

122   Matt. 25:42.
123   Cf. 1 Clement 40.5.
124   Cf. 1 Clement 41.1.

παρατεθεὶς ὑπὸ Χριστοῦ.¹²⁵ ₃ ὁ ἕτερος τοῦ ἑτέρου τὸν δρόμον μὴ παρατεμνέτω·¹²⁶ οὐδὲ γὰρ οἱ ἄγγελοι παρὰ τὸ διατεταγμένον αὐτοῖς οὐδὲν ἕτερον ἐξελίσσουσιν.

24

Ἀνδρέας εἶπεν· Εὔχρηστόν ἐστιν, ἀδελφοί, ταῖς γυναιξὶ διακονίαν καταστῆσαι.

25

Πέτρος εἶπεν· Ἐφθάσαμεν τάξαντες· περὶ δὲ τῆς προσφορᾶς τοῦ σώματος καὶ τοῦ αἵματος ἀκριβῶς μηνύσωμεν.

---

125 ἕκαστος ἐν ᾧ ἐκλήθη παρατεθεὶς ὑπὸ Χριστοῦ: The last three words are conjectural. Cf. V: ἕκαστος ἐν ᾧ ἐκλήθη παρὰ τῷ θεῷ. Harnack, *Sources*, 24 suggests that ἐν τούτῳ μενέτω θεέτω has fallen out before παρὰ τῷ θεῷ. The addition of ἐν τούτῳ μενέτω would conform the text to 1 Cor. 7:24, but there is no reason to suspect such a conformity. The further addition of θεέτω is suggested in the light of S (Ar., Eth.) and in the light of the δρόμος which appears below, and may indeed fall out in proximity to θεῷ, but there is no support in Syr., though Arendzen, 78, supports the thrust of Harnack's argument (nonetheless noting that Harnack's additional words would appear to be in the wrong place.) However the passage is difficult, and, even with Harnack's emendation, the dative after παρά is difficult. Latin reads: quae singulis decreta sunt loca, unusquisque in quo vocatus est a Christo. There are thus two deviations from V, namely the explicit mention of an allotted place and the term Christo rather than θεῷ. The conjectural emendation is thus made in order to account for these two points, as well as the dative after παρά and the mention of a δρόμος (the term παρατίθημι being understood as placement in a lane or course, which would lead the Latin translator to infer the idea of an allotted place), and suggests that παρὰ τοῦ θεῷ is a misreading of παρατεθείς, leading to the loss of the final words as redundant. Such a misreading might be the result of a homoiarctic or a homoioteleutic error, reading παρὰ τῷ θεῷ from 19 above, or 29 below. The corruption had already occurred by the time that the text came before the Syriac translator, whereas the Sahidic translator freely adapts in order to make sense of the passage.

126 παρατεμνέτω: V has παρατεμνεῖτο. Funk reads παρατεμνέσθω.

is placed by Christ.[127] ₃ None should obstruct the path of another, for neither do the angels anything contrary to their station,[128] or take another's route."

24

Andrew said: "It would be useful, brothers, to establish ministries for the women."

25

Peter said: "We have previously legislated. Let us carefully explain regarding the offering of the Body and the Blood."

---

127 The text has been extensively conjecturally emended at this point. If the emendation is not accepted the phrase would read: "in that in which he was called beside God."
128 Cf. 1 Clement 34.5.

26

Ἰωάννης εἶπεν· Ἐπελάθεσθε, ἀδελφοί, ὅτε ᾔτησεν ὁ διδάσκαλος τὸν ἄρτον καὶ τὸ ποτήριον καὶ ηὐλογήσεν αὐτὰ λέγων· τοῦτο ἐστι τὸ σῶμα μου· καὶ τὸ αἷμα, ὅτι οὐκ ἐπέτρεψε ταύταις συστῆναι ἡμῖν. Μάρθα εἶπεν· διὰ Μαριάμ, ὅτι εἶδεν αὐτὴν μειδιῶσαν· Μαρία εἶπεν· οὐχ ὅτι[129] ἐγέλασα· προέλεγε γὰρ ἡμῖν, ὅτε ἐδίδασκεν, ὅτι τὸ ἀσθενὲς διὰ τοῦ ἰσχυροῦ σωθήσεται.

27

Κηφᾶς εἶπεν· Ἐνίων μεμνῆσθαι δεῖ ὅτι ταῖς γυναιξὶ μὴ ὀρθαῖς προσεύχεσθαι,[130] ἀλλὰ ἐπὶ[131] τῆς γῆς καθεζομέναις.[132]

---

129 οὐχ ὅτι is read with Lat. The emendation was suggested by Wilamowitz Moellendorff without reference to the (as yet undiscovered) Latin text. Cf. V and eds. οὐκέτι.
130 ἐνίων μεμνῆσθαι δεῖ ὅτι ταῖς γυναιξὶ μὴ ὀρθαῖς προσεύχεσθαι: Cf. V ἐνίων μέμνησθε δὲ ὅτι... The emendation is made following a suggestion of Arendzen, derived from Syr. In order to make better sense of the unemended text, and to conform it in some way to Lat., which reads: aliquantorum memores estis, quoniam hoc iubebat mulieribus... Hauler and Schermann supplied προσέταξεν after ὅτι, and Pitra, Lagarde, Hilgenfeld, Harnack and Funk similarly supplied πρέπει after ὀρθαῖς; this is unnecessary once the δέ is emended, as the force of iubebat may be contained within δεῖ, and as δεῖ explains the infinitive.
131 ἐπί is given following the suggestion of Wilamowitz Moellendorff, Funk and Harnack. V, however has ἀπό, accepted by Schermann, and Latin has de, whereas the other versions offer no guidance.
132 The entire phrase is questioned by Maclean, *The ancient church orders*, 28, who prefers the rendering of the Syriac that women should approach the sacrifice with heads covered. He suggests a misreading of προσέρχεσθαι as προσεύχεσθαι. Whereas it is possible that there was some misreading here, it would surely be a misreading by the Syriac translator. As noted in the comments to the translation, Maclean in part prefers the reading because it is paralleled elsewhere in the church orders.

26

John said: "You are forgetting, brothers, that when the teacher requested the bread and the cup and blessed them saying: 'This is my Body and Blood',[133] he did not permit the women to stand alongside us. Martha said it was on account of Mary because he saw her smiling. Mary said: 'I did not laugh at this. Previously he said to us, when he was teaching, that the weak would be saved through the strong'.[134]"

27

Kephas said: "Some things should be remembered: that women should not pray upright but seated on the ground."[135]

---

133 This is clearly a loose paraphrase. This in turn indicates, however, that there is no established use of the words of institution in the liturgy.
134 For the punctuation here, assigning the entire speech to John, see the introduction 3.4.2, and for an alternative view Ernst, *Martha*, 243, n. 27, 248–249.
135 For discussion of this *agraphon* see the introduction, 3.4.4.

28

Ἰάκωβος εἶπεν· Πῶς οὖν δυνάμεθα περὶ γυναικῶν διακονίαν[136] ὁρίσαι, εἰ μή τι διακονίαν ἵνα ἐπισχύσωσι[137] ταῖς ἐνδεομέναις;

29

Φίλιππος εἶπεν· Τοῦτο, ἀδελφοί, περί τῆς μεταδόσεως· ὁ ποιῶν ἔργον καλὸν ἑαυτῷ θησαυρὸν περιποιεῖται·[138] ὁ γὰρ θησαυρίζων ἐν τῇ βασιλείᾳ ἔγγραφος ἐργάτης λογισθήσεται παρὰ τῷ θεῷ.

30

Πέτρος εἶπεν· Ταῦτα, ἀδελφοί, οὐχ ὡς ἐξουσίαν τινὸς ἔχοντες πρὸς ἀνάγκην, ἀλλ᾽ ἐπιταγὴν ἔχοντες παρὰ κυρίου. ἐρωτῶμεν ὑμᾶς, φυλάξαι τὰς ἐντολὰς μηδὲν ἀφαιροῦντας ἢ προστιθέντας ἐν τῷ ὀνόματι τοῦ κυρίου ἡμῶν,[139] ᾧ ἡ δόξα εἰς τοὺς αἰῶνας. ἀμήν.

---

136 διακονίαν: V, Lat., Lagarde, Hilgenfeld, Schermann; cf. Harnack and Funk, who read διακονίας.
137 ἐπισχύσωσι: Wilamowitz Moellendorff suggests ἐπισχήσωσι, Lagarde ἐπισχῶσι. I cannot see that any emendation is necessary. Hilgenfeld, Harnack, Funk and Schermann leave the text so.
138 ἔργον καλὸν ἑαυτῷ θησαυρόν περιποιεῖται: so Lagarde. Cf. V and all versions and eds. except Lagarde, ἔργον ἑαυτῷ θησαυρὸν καλόν περιποιεῖται. Something certainly seems to be missing before or after ἔργον in V and versions, particularly in the light of the manner in which this saying mirrors 22.2 above (ἀποθησαυρίζειν εἰς ἔργα ἀγαθά), to which, it is suggested in the introduction, it is redactionally related. Moreover, καλόν is redundant in the light of the second part of the saying. Lagarde's conjecture is accepted on this basis.
139 κυρίου ἡμῶν: Lat., Syr, S, add Ἰησοῦ Χριστοῦ. Although loath to leave the text as it is against the unanimous versional witness, doxologies are so prone to alteration that I have left the text as it stands.

28

James said: "How then can we establish ministries for the women, except the ministry of supporting women in need?"[140]

29

Philip said: "This, brothers, concerning sharing. Whoever does a noble deed gathers for himself a store.[141] Whoever lays up a store in the Kingdom is reckoned a labourer enrolled in the presence of God."[142]

30

Peter said: "Brothers, we do not command these things as those who have the power to compel, but as having a command from the Lord. We ask you to keep the commandments, neither detracting from them or adding, in the name of Our Lord, to whom be glory for ever. Amen."

---

140 This may also be translated as "Support those who are in chains." If this translation is followed, then this must refer to some form of exorcistic ministry, as no kind of persecution is apparently envisaged. But a ministry of healing and evangelism, rather than social support, hardly seems to be what K is envisaging for women. See, for discussion, though with a different conclusion, Faivre, "Apostolicité", 60–61.
141 Note that this has been subjected to a conjectural emendation. See the textual commentary ad loc.
142 On this statement, and the related statements elsewhere in K, see the introduction, 3.7.

Appendices

1. Three epitomae of TWT material found in K
2. The eschatological conclusions of K and B
3. The TWT in D, K, E, and B

Note: In the first edition of this text, Schermann's text of E was reprinted. This is omitted on this occasion, as the entire text is to be found in the synoptic tables.

Appendix 1
Three epitomae of TWT as found in K
This first synopsis includes E, alongside Mosq. and A.

E: Cod. Ottob. gr. 408, f. 88v, Cod. Parisiensis gr. 1555A, f. 178v, Cod. Neapolitanus II C34 (olim 35), f. 83v (ed. T. Schermann, *Eine Elfapostelmoral oder die X-Rezension der "beiden Wege"* (Munich: Lentner, 1903), 14–18.)

A: Athous, Koutloumousiou 39 f. 79va, l. 16-79vb, l. 3 (ed. David Lincicum, "An Excerpt from the Apostolic Church Order (CPG 1739)" *Sacris Erudiri* 57 (2018), 439-444.)

M: Cod. Mosquensis 125, f. 284, (ed. O. von Gebhardt, A. von Harnack, and T. Zahn, *Patrum apostolicorum opera* 1.2 (Leipzig: Hinrichs, 1878), xxix-xxxi.)

E	Mosq.	A
ἐπιτομὴ ὅρων τῶν ἁγίων ἀποστόλων καθολικῆς παραδόσεως	ἐκ τῶν διατάξεων τῶν ἁγίων ἀποστόλων	ἐκ τῶν διατάξεων τῶν ἁγίων ἀποστόλων
1: Ἰωάννης εἶπεν· ὁδοὶ δύο εἰσί, μία τῆς ζωῆς καὶ μία τοῦ θανάτου, καὶ διαφορὰ πολλὴ τῶν δύο. ἡ οὖν τῆς ζωῆς ἐστιν αὕτη· πρῶτον ἀγαπήσεις τὸν θεὸν τὸν ποιήσαντά σε ἐξ ὅλης σου καρδίας·	1: ὁδοὶ δύο εἰσί, μία τῆς ζωῆς καὶ μία τοῦ θανάτου καὶ ἡ μὲν τῆς ζωῆς ὁδὸς αὕτη ἐστίν. πρῶτον πάντων ἀγαπήσεις, τέκνον, τὸν θεὸν σου ἐξ ὅλης τῆς καρδίας σου καὶ δοξάσεις αὐτὸν τὸν λυτρωσάμενόν σε ἐκ θανάτου. ὅ ἐστιν	1: Ἰωάννης εἶπεν ὁδοὶ δύο εἰσὶν, μία τῆς ζωῆς καὶ μία τοῦ θανάτου. καὶ ἡ μὲν τῆς ζωῆς ὁδός ἐστὶν, πρῶτον ἀγαπήσεις κύριον τὸν θεόν σου ἐξ ὅλης τῆς καρδίας σου, καὶ δοξάσεις αὐτὸν τὸν λυτρωσάμενόν σε ἐκ θανάτου, ἥτις ἐστὶν
δεύτερον ἀγαπήσεις τὸν πλησίον σου ὡς	ἐντολὴ πρώτη. δευτέρα δὲ ἐντολή ἐστιν· ἀγαπήσεις τὸν πλησίον σου ὡς	ἐντολὴ πρώτη. δευτέρα δὲ ἐντολή ἐστιν, ἀγαπήσεις τὸν πλησίον σου ὡς

ἑαυτόν.	ἑαυτόν.	ἑαυτόν, ἐν οἷς ὅλος ὁ νόμος καὶ οἱ προφῆται κρέμανται.
2: Ματθαῖος εἶπεν· πᾶν ὃ μὴ θέλῃς γενέσθαι σοι, μηδὲ σὺ ἄλλῳ ποιήσῃς, τουτέστιν ὃ σὺ μισεῖς ἄλλῳ μὴ ποιήσῃς.	2: Ματθαῖος εἶπεν· πάντα ὅσα ἂν μὴ θέλῃς σοι γίνεσθαι, μηδὲ σὺ ἄλλῳ ποιήσῃς. τούτων δὲ τῶν λόγων τὴν διδαχὴν εἰπέ, ἀδελφὲ Πέτρε.	2: Ματθαῖος εἶπεν· πάντα ὅσα μὴ θέλῃς σοι γενέσθαι, μὴ δὲ σὺ ἄλλῳ ποιήσεις. τούτων δὲ τῶν λόγων τὴν διδαχήν, εἰπέ, ἀδελφὲ Πέτρε.
3: Πέτρος εἶπεν· οὐ φονεύσεις, οὐ ποιήσεις ἁμαρτίαν τινὰ τῇ σαρκί σου, οὐ κλέψεις, οὐ μαγεύσεις, οὐ φαρμακεύσεις,	3: Πέτρος εἶπεν· οὐ φονεύσεις, οὐ μοιχεύσεις, οὐ πορνεύσεις, οὐ παιδοφθορήσεις, οὐ κλέψεις, οὐ μαντεύσῃ, οὐ φαρμακεύσεις, οὐ φονεύσεις τέκνον εἰς φθοράν, οὐδὲ γεννηθὲν ἀποκτείνεις·	
οὐκ ἐπιθυμήσεις τὰ τοῦ πλησίον σου. οὐκ ἐπιορκήσεις, οὐ ψευδομαρτυρήσεις, οὐ κακολογήσεις, οὐδὲ μνησικακήσεις, οὐκ ἔσῃ δίγνωμος οὐδὲ δίγλωσσος· οὐκ ἔσται σοι λόγος κενός, οὐκ ἔσῃ πλεονέκτης, οὐχ ἅρπαξ οὐδὲ ὑποκριτής, οὐκ ἔσῃ κακοήθης, οὐχ ὑπερήφανος· οὐ λήψῃ	οὐκ ἐπιθυμήσεις τὰ τοῦ πλησίον· οὐκ ἐπιορκήσεις, ἀλλ' οὐδὲ ὀμόσεις ὅλως. οὐ ψευδομαρτυρήσεις, οὐ κακολογήσεις τινά οὐδὲ μνησικακήσεις· οὐκ ἔσῃ δίγνωμος οὐδὲ δίγλωσσος· παγὶς γὰρ θανάτου ἐστὶν ἡ διγλωσσία. οὐκ ἔσται ὁ λόγος σου κενὸς οὐδὲ ψευδής· οὐκ ἔσῃ ἅρπαξ οὐδὲ ὑποκριτής, οὐδὲ κακοήθης οὐδὲ ὑπερήφανος· οὐ λάβῃς	

βουλὴν πονηρὰν κατὰ τὸν πλησίον σου· οὐ μισήσεις πάντα ἄνθρωπον, ἀλλ' οὓς μὲν ἐλέγξεις, περὶ ὧν δὲ καὶ προσεύξῃ, οὓς δὲ ἀγαπήσεις ὑπὲρ τὴν ψυχήν σου.

4: Ἀνδρέας εἶπε· φεῦγε ἀπὸ παντὸς κακοῦ καὶ ἀπὸ παντὸς ὁμοίου αὐτοῦ. μὴ γίνου ὀργίλος μήτε ζηλωτής, μὴ ἐριστικὸς μηδὲ μανικός· ὁδηγεῖ γὰρ ταῦτα πρὸς τὸν φόνον.

5: Φίλιππος εἶπε· μὴ γίνου ἐπιθυμητής, ὁδηγεῖ γὰρ πρὸς τὴν πορνείαν.

βουλὴν πονηρὰν κατὰ τὸν πλησίον σου, οὐ μισήσεις οἷον δήποτε ἄνθρωπον ἀλλὰ τοὺς μὲν ἐλέγξεις πταίοντας, τοὺς δὲ ἐλεήσεις, καὶ ὑπὲρ ἄλλων προσεύξῃ, τινὰς δὲ καὶ ὑπὲρ τὴν ψυχήν σου ἀγαπήσεις.

4: καὶ ὁ Ἀνδρέας εἶπε· τέκνον μου, φεῦγε ἀπὸ παντὸς πονηροῦ καὶ ἀπὸ παντὸς ὁμοίου αὐτῶν· μὴ γίνου ὀργίλος, ὁδηγεῖ γὰρ ἡ ὀργὴ πρὸς τὸν φόνον. μὴ γίνου ζηλεύων, μὴ ἐριστικὸς μηδὲ θυμώδης· ἐκ γὰρ τούτων φόνος γίνεται.

5: Φίλιππος εἶπεν· τέκνον μου, μὴ γίνου ἐπιθυμητής. ὁδηγεῖ γὰρ ἡ ἐπιθυμία πρὸς τὴν πορνείαν καὶ ἕλκει τοὺς ἀνθρώπους πρὸς ἑαυτήν καὶ μεθ' ἡδονῆς ἀπόλλυσι τοὺς εἰσερχομένους εἰς αὐτήν. ὁδὸς δὲ πονηροῦ πνεύματος ἁμαρτία ψυχῆς, καὶ ὅταν βραχείαν εἴσδυσιν σχῇ ἐπὶ πλεῖον πλατύνει αὐτὴν καὶ ἄγει

ἐπὶ πάντα τὰ κακὰ τὴν
ψυχὴν ἐκείνην καὶ οὐκ ἐᾷ
διαβλέψαι τὸν ἄνθρωπον
καὶ ἰδεῖν τὴν ἀλήθειαν.
ἐπιγελᾷ δὲ τὸ πονηρὸν
πνεῦμα τῷ ἀνθρώπῳ
ἐκείνῳ καὶ εὐφραίνεται
ἐπὶ τῇ ἀπωλείᾳ αὐτοῦ

6: Σίμων εἶπεν· μὴ γίνου αἰσχρολόγος μηδὲ ὑψηλόφθαλμος. ἐκ γὰρ τούτων μοιχεῖαι γίνονται.

6: Σίμων εἶπε· τέκνον, μὴ γίνου αἰσχρολόγος μηδὲ ὑψηλόφθαλμος. ἐκ γὰρ τούτων γεννᾶται μοιχεῖα.

3: Σίμων εἶπεν· τέκνον, μὴ γίνου αἰσχρολόγος, μὴ δὲ ὑψηλόφθαλμος. ἐκ γὰρ τούτων γεννᾶται μοιχεία.

7: Ἰάκωβος εἶπεν·
μὴ γίνου
οἰωνοσκόπος,

μὴ
ἐπαοιδός, μὴ μαθητικὸς
μήτε ἃ ἐρεῖ περικαθαίρων,
μήτε θέλε αὐτὰ εἰδέναι
μηδὲ ἀκούειν· ἐκ γὰρ
τούτων ἁπάντων
εἰδωλολατρίαι γίνονται.

7: Ἰάκωβος εἶπεν· τέκνον
μου, μὴ γίνου
οἰωνοσκόπος ἐπειδὴ
ὁδηγεῖ εἰς τὴν
εἰδωλολατρίαν· μηδὲ
ἐπαοιδός, μηδὲ μαθητικὸς
μηδὲ περικαθαίρων,
μηδὲ θέλε αὐτὰ εἰδέναι
μηδὲ ἀκούειν· καὶ γὰρ ἐκ
τούτων ἁπάντων
εἰδωλολατρίαι γίνονται.

8: Ναθαναὴλ εἶπεν· μὴ γίνου ψεύστης, μηδὲ φιλάργυρος, μηδὲ κενόδοξος· ἐκ τούτων ἁπάντων κλοπαὶ γίνονται· μὴ γίνου γόγγυσος, μὴ θυμώδης, μὴ αὐθάδης, μήτε πονηρόφρων· ἐκ γὰρ τούτων ἁπάντων βλασφημίαι γίνονται. ἴσθι

8: Βαρθολομαῖος εἶπεν· ἐρωτῶμεν ὑμᾶς, ἀδελφοί, ὡς ἔτι καιρός ἐστι καὶ ἔχετε εἰς οὓς ἐργάζεσθε μεθ᾽ ἑαυτῶν, μὴ ἐκλείπητε ἐν μηδενί, ἐξουσίαν ἔχητε. ἐγγὺς γὰρ ἡ ἡμέρα κυρίου ἐν ᾗ συναπολοῦνται πάντα σὺν τῷ πονηρῷ· ἥξει γὰρ ὁ κύριος καὶ ὁ

δὲ πραΰς, ἐπειδὴ πραεῖς κληρονομήσουσι τὴν βασιλείαν τοῦ θεοῦ. γίνου μακρόθυμος, ἐλεήμων, εἰρηνοποιός, καθαρὸς τὴν καρδίαν, ἄκακος, ἥσυχος, ἀγαθός, φυλάσσων καὶ τρέμων τοὺς λόγους τοῦ θεοῦ. οὐχ ὑψώσεις σεαυτόν, οὐ δώσεις τῇ ψυχῇ σου θράσος, οὐδὲ κολληθήσῃ τῇ ψυχῇ σου μετὰ ὑψηλῶν· ἀλλὰ μετὰ δικαίων καὶ ταπεινῶν. τὰ συμβαίνοντά σοι ἐνεργήματα ὡς ἀγαθὰ προσδέξαι, εἰδὼς ὅτι ἄτερ τοῦ θεοῦ οὐδὲν γίνεται.

μισθὸς αὐτοῦ. ἑαυτῶν γίνεσθε σύμβουλοι ἀγαθῶν, θεοδίδακτοι. ἃ παρελάβετε, μήτε προσθήσετε μήτε ὑφέλετε ἀπ' αὐτῶν.

9: Θωμᾶς εἶπεν· τὸν λαλοῦντά σοι τὸν λόγον τοῦ θεοῦ καὶ παραίτιόν σοι γινόμενον τῆς ζωῆς καὶ δόντα σοι τὴν ἐν κυρίῳ σφραγῖδα ἀγαπήσεις αὐτὸν ὡς κόρην ὀφθαλμοῦ σου, μνησθήσῃ αὐτοῦ νυκτὸς καὶ ἡμέρας, τιμήσεις δὲ αὐτὸν ὡς κύριον, ὅθεν γὰρ ᾽Ιησοῦς Χριστὸς λαλεῖται, ἐκεῖ κύριος ἐστιν. ἐκζητήσεις δὲ αὐτὸν καὶ τοὺς λοιποὺς ἁγίους, ἵνα ἐπαναπαυσθῇς

9: Θωμᾶς εἶπεν· τέκνον, τὸν λαλοῦντά σοι τὸν λόγον τοῦ θεοῦ

ἀγαπήσεις ὡς κόρην ὀφθαλμοῦ. μνήσθητι δὲ αὐτοῦ ἡμέραν καὶ νύκτα καὶ τῶν λοιπῶν τῶν ἁγίων

4: Θωμᾶς εἶπεν· τέκνον, τὸν λαλοῦντά σοι τὸν λόγον τοῦ θεοῦ,

ἀγαπήσεις ὡς κόρην ὀφθαλμοῦ. μνήσθητι δὲ αὐτοῦ νύκτα καὶ ἡμέραν.

ἐκζητήσεις δὲ τὸ πρόσωπον αὐτοῦ καθημέραν.

τοῖς λόγοις αὐτῶν·
κολλώμενος γὰρ ἁγίους
ἅγιος ἁγιασθήσεται. ὁ γὰρ
κύριος ἠξίωσέ σε δι' αὐτοῦ
δοθῆναι πνευματικὴν
τροφὴν καὶ ζωὴν αἰώνιον.

10: Κηφᾶς εἶπεν· οὐ
ποιήσεις σχίσμα,

εἰρηνεύσεις δὲ
μαχομένους, κρινεῖς
δικαίως, οὐ λήψῃ
πρόσωπον ἐλέγξαι τινὰ
ἐπὶ παραπτώματι, ἰσότης
γὰρ ἐστι παρὰ θεῷ· ἐν
προσευχῇ σου μὴ
διψυχήσης. ἐὰν ἔσται
ἔχειν σε ἀπὸ τῶν χειρῶν
σου, δὸς εἰς ἄφεσιν
ἁμαρτιῶν σου.

οὐκ
ἀποστραφήσῃ
ἐνδεούμενον,
συγκοινωνήσεις δὲ πάντα
τοῖς ἀδελφοῖς σου καὶ οὐκ
ἐρεῖς ἴδια εἶναι· εἰ γὰρ ἐν
τῷ θανάτῳ κοινωνοί ἐστε,
πόσῳ μᾶλλον ἐν τοῖς
θνητοῖς;

κολλώμενος γὰρ ἁγιοῖς
ἅγιος ἁγιασθήσῃ. τιμήσεις
δὲ αὐτοὺς καθ' ὃ δυνατὸς
εἶ ἐκ τοῦ ἱδρῶτός σου καὶ
ἐκ τοῦ πόνου τῶν χειρῶν
σου.

10: Πέτρος εἶπεν· οὐ
ποιήσεις συνάψαι τινὰ
μάχην πρὸς ἕτερον,
εἰρηνεύσεις δὲ
μαχομένους, κρινεῖς
δικαίως, οὐ λήψῃ
πρόσωπον ἐλέγξαι τινὰ
ἐπὶ παραπτώματι,

ἐὰν
ἔχῃς διὰ τῶν χειρῶν
σου, δὸς εἰς λύτρον τῶν
ἁμαρτιῶν σου. οὐ
διστάσεις δοῦναι οὐδὲ
δοὺς γογγύσεις. οὐκ
ἀποστραφήσῃ
ἐνδεούμενον, λήψῃ γὰρ
τὸν ἄξιον μισθὸν παρὰ τοῦ
φιλανθρώπου θεοῦ.
ᾧ ἡ δόξα εἰς τοὺς αἰῶνας.
ἀμήν.

11: Βαρθολομαῖος εἶπεν· οὐκ ἄρῃς τὴν χεῖρά σου ἀπὸ τοῦ υἱοῦ οὐδὲ ἀπὸ τῆς θυγατρός σου, ἀλλ' ἅμα ἀπὸ νεότητος διδάξεις αὐτοὺς τὸν φόβον τοῦ κυρίου. ἐξομολογήσῃ τὰ παραπτώματά σου, οὐκ ἐγκαταλείψῃ ἐντολὰς κυρίου, οὐ προσελεύσῃ ἐν προσευχῇ σου ἐν συνειδήσει πονηρᾷ, μισήσεις πᾶσαν ὑπόκρισιν καὶ πᾶν ὃ μὴ ἀρέσκει κυρίῳ, φυλάξῃ δὲ ἃ παρέλαβες μήτε προστιθεὶς μήτε ὑφαιρῶν. αὕτη ἐστὶν ἡ ὁδὸς τῆς ζωῆς.

Cf 8 *supra*:
Βαρθολομαῖος εἶπεν·
ἐρωτῶμεν ὑμᾶς, ἀδελφοί,
ὡς ἔτι καιρός ἐστι καὶ ἔχετε
εἰς οὓς ἐργάζεσθε μεθ'
ἑαυτῶν, μὴ ἐκλείπητε ἐν
μηδενί, ἐξουσίαν ἔχητε.
ἐγγὺς γὰρ ἡ ἡμέρα κυρίου
ἐν ᾗ συναπολοῦνται πάντα
σὺν τῷ πονηρῷ· ἥξει γὰρ ὁ
κύριος καὶ ὁ μισθὸς αὐτοῦ.
ἑαυτῶν γίνεσθε σύμβουλοι
ἀγαθῶν, θεοδίδακτοι.

ἃ
παρελάβετε, μήτε
προσθήσετε μήτε ὑφέλετε
ἀπ' αὐτῶν.

Appendix 2

The eschatological conclusions of K and B

K	B
Βαρθολομαῖος εἶπεν·	καλὸν οὖν ἐστὶν μαθόντα τὰ δικαιώματα τοῦ κυρίου, ὅσα γέγραπται, ἐν τούτοις περιπατεῖν. ὁ γὰρ ταῦτα ποιῶν ἐν τῇ βασιλείᾳ τοῦ θεοῦ δοξασθήσεται· ὁ ἐκεῖνα ἐκλεγόμενος μετὰ τῶν ἔργων αὐτοῦ συναπολεῖται. διὰ τοῦτο ἀνάστασις, διὰ τοῦτο ἀνταπόδομα.
ἐρωτῶμεν ὑμᾶς, ἀδελφοί, ὡς ἔτι καιρός ἐστι καὶ ἔχετε εἰς οὓς ἐργάζεσθε μεθ' ἑαυτῶν μὴ ἐκλίπητε ἐν μηδενί, ἐξ οὗ ἂν ἔχητε. ἐγγὺς γὰρ ἡ ἡμέρα κυρίου, ἐν ᾗ συναπολεῖται πάντα σὺν τῷ πονηρῷ· ἥξει γὰρ ὁ κύριος καὶ ὁ μισθὸς αὐτοῦ μετ' αὐτοῦ. ἑαυτῶν γίνεσθε νομοθέται, ἑαυτῶν γίνεσθε σύμβουλοι ἀγαθοί,	ἐρωτῶ τοὺς ὑπερέχοντας, εἴ τινά μου γνώμης ἀγαθῆς λαμβάνετε συμβουλίαν· ἔχετε μεθ' ἑαυτῶν εἰς οὓς ἐργάσησθε τὸ καλόν· μὴ ἐλλείπητε. ἐγγὺς ἡ ἡμέρα ἐν ᾗ συναπολεῖται πάντα τῷ πονηρῷ. ἐγγὺς ὁ κύριος καὶ ὁ μισθὸς αὐτοῦ. ἔτι καὶ ἔτι ἐρωτῶ ὑμᾶς· ἑαυτῶν γίνεσθε νομοθέται ἀγαθοί, ἑαυτῶν μένετε σύμβουλοι πιστοί, ἄρατε ἐξ ὑμῶν πᾶσαν ὑπόκρισιν. ὁ δὲ θεός, ὁ τοῦ παντὸς κόσμου κυριεύων, δῴη ὑμῖν σοφίαν, σύνεσιν, ἐπιστήμην, γνῶσιν τῶν δικαιωμάτων αὐτοῦ, ὑπομονήν. γίνεσθε
θεοδίδακτοι· φυλάξεις ἃ παρέλαβες μήτε προσθεὶς μήτε ὑφαιρῶν.	δὲ θεοδίδακτοι, ἐκζητοῦντες τί ζητεῖ κύριος ἀφ' ὑμῶν, καὶ ποιεῖτει ἵνα εὑρεθῆτε ἐν ἡμέρᾳ κρίσεως.

Appendix 3

A synoptic arrangement of TWT material in D, K, E, B[1]

D	K	E	B
ὁδοὶ δύο εἰσί, μία τῆς ζωῆς καὶ μία τοῦ θανάτου, διαφορὰ δὲ πολλὴ μεταξὺ τῶν δύο ὁδῶν.	Ἰωάννης εἶπεν· ὁδοὶ δύο εἰσί, μία τῆς ζωῆς καὶ μία τοῦ θανάτου, διαφορὰ δὲ πολλὴ μεταξὺ τῶν δύο ὁδῶν.	Ἰωάννης εἶπεν· ὁδοι δύο εἰσί, μία τῆς ζωῆς καὶ μία τοῦ θανάτου, καὶ διαφορὰ πολλὴ τῶν δύο.	B18.1b-2 ὁδοὶ δύο εἰσὶν διδαχῆς καὶ ἐξουσίας, ἥ τε τοῦ φωτὸς καὶ ἡ τοῦ σκότους. διαφορὰ δὲ πολλὴ τῶν δύο ὁδῶν. ἐφ' ἧς μὲν γάρ εἰσιν τεταγμένοι φωταγωγοὶ ἄγγελοι τοῦ θεοῦ, ἐφ' ἧς δὲ ἄγγελοι του σατανᾶ. καὶ ὁ μέν ἐστιν κύριος ἀπ' αἰώνων καὶ εἰς τοὺς αἰῶνας, ὁ δὲ ἄρχων καιροῦ τοῦ νῦν τῆς ἀνομίας.
ἡ μὲν οὖν τῆς ζωῆς ἐστιν αὕτη· πρῶτον ἀγαπησεις τὸν θεὸν τὸν ποιήσαντά σε,	ἡ μὲν γὰρ ὁδὸς τῆς ζωῆς ἐστιν αὕτη· πρῶτον ἀγαπήσεις τὸν θεὸν τὸν ποιήσαντά σε ἐξ ὅλης τῆς καρδίας σου καὶ δοξάσεις τὸν λυτρωσάμενόν σε ἐκ θανάτου, ἥτις ἐστὶν	πρῶτον ἀγαπήσεις τὸν θεὸν τὸν ποιήσαντά σε ἐξ ὅλης σου καρδίας·	B19.2a ἀγαπήσεις τὸν ποιήσαντά σε, φοβηθήσῃ τόν σε πλασαντα, δοξάσεις τόν σε λυτρωσάμενον ἐκ θανάτου·

1 As noted in the introduction, the order of topics in B is significantly different from that of D/K. This synopsis follows the order of D/K/E and shows verbal parallels with B by re-organizing and disordering the B material.

185

δεύτερον τὸν πλησίον σου ὡς σεαυτόν·	ἐντολὴ πρώτη. δευτέρα δέ· ἀγαπήσεις τὸν πλησίον σου ὡς ἑαυτόν, ἥτις ἐστὶν ἐντολὴ δευτέρα, ἐν οἷς ὅλος ὁ νόμος κρέμαται καὶ προφῆται.	δεύτερον ἀγαπήσεις τὸν πλησίον σου ὡς ἑαυτόν.	B19.5c ἀγαπήσεις τὸν πλησίον σου ὑπὲρ τὴν ψυχήν σου.
πάντα δὲ ὅσα ἐὰν θελήσῃς μὴ γίνεσθαί σοι, καὶ σὺ ἄλλῳ μὴ ποίει.	Ματθαῖος εἶπεν· πάντα ὅσα μὴ θέλῃς σοι γενέσθαι, σὺ μηδὲ ἄλλῳ ποιήσῃς.	Ματθαῖος εἶπεν· πάντα ὅσα μὴ θέλῃς σοι γενέσθαι, μὴ δὲ σὺ ἄλλῳ ποιήσεις.	
τούτων δὲ τῶν λόγων ἡ διδαχή ἐστιν αὕτη· εὐλογεῖτε τοὺς καταρωμένους ὑμῖν καὶ προσεύχεσθε ὑπὲρ τῶν ἐχθρῶν ὑμῶν, νηστεύετε δὲ ὑπὲρ τῶν διωκότων ὑμᾶς· ποία γὰρ χάρις, ἐὰν ἀγαπᾶτε τοὺς ἀγαπῶντας ὑμᾶς; οὐχὶ καὶ τὰ ἔθνη τὸ αὐτὸ ποιοῦσιν; ὑμεῖς δὲ ἀγαπᾶτε τοὺς μισοῦντας ὑμᾶς, καὶ οὐχ ἕξετε ἐχθρόν.	τούτων δὲ τῶν λόγων τὴν διδαχὴν εἰπέ, ἀδελφὲ Πέτρε.		

ἀπέχου τῶν
σαρκικῶν καὶ
σωματικῶν
ἐπιθυμιῶν· ἐὰν τίς
σοι δῷ ῥάπισμα εἰς
τὴν δεξιὰν σιαγόνα,
στρέψον αὐτῷ καὶ
τὴν ἄλλην, καὶ ἔσῃ
τέλειος· ἐὰν
ἀγγαρεύσῃ σέ τις
μίλιον ἕν, ὕπαγε
μετ' αυτοῦ δύο· ἐὰν
ἄρῃ τις τὸ ἱμάτιόν
σου, δὸς αὐτῷ καὶ
τὸν χιτῶνα· ἐὰν
λάβῃ τις ἀπὸ σοῦ τὸ
σόν, μὴ ἀπαίτει·
οὐδὲ γὰρ δύνασαι.
παντὶ τῷ αἰτοῦντί
σε δίδου καὶ μὴ
ἀπαίτεν· πᾶσι γὰρ
θέλει δίδοσθαι ὁ
πατὴρ ἐκ τῶν ἰδίων
χαρισμάτων.
μακάριος ὁ διδοὺς
κατὰ τὴν ἐντολήν·
ἀθῶος γάρ ἐστιν.
οὐαὶ τῷ λαμβάνοντι
τις, ἀθῶος ἔσται· ὁ
δὲ μὴ χρείαν ἔχων
ἔχων δώσει δίκην,
ἱνατί ἔλαβε καὶ εἰς τί·
ἐν συνοχῇ δὲ
γενόμενος

ἐξετασθήσεται περὶ ὧν ἔπραξε, καὶ οὐκ ἐξελεύσεται ἐκεῖθεν, μέχρις οὗ ἀποδῷ τὸν ἔσχατον κοδράντην. ἀλλὰ καὶ περὶ τούτου δὲ εἴρηται· Ἰδρωσάτω ἡ ἐλεημοσύνη σου εἰς τὰς χεῖρας σου, μέχρις ἂν γνῷς τίνι δῷς.			
οὐ φονεύσεις, οὐ μοιχεύσεις, οὐ παιδοφθορήσεις, οὐ πορνεύσεις, οὐ κλέψεις, οὐ μαγεύσεις, οὐ φαρμακεύσεις, οὐ φονεύσεις τέκνον ἐν φθορᾷ, οὐδὲ γεννηθὲν ἀποκτενεῖς,	Πέτρος εἶπεν· οὐ φονεύσεις, οὐ μοιχεύσεις, οὐ πορνεύσεις, οὐ παιδοφθορήσεις, οὐ κλέψεις, οὐ μαγεύσεις, οὐ φαρμακεύσεις, οὐ φονεύσεις τέκνον ἐν φθορᾷ οὐδὲ γεννηθὲν ἀποκτενεῖς,	Πέτρος εἶπεν· οὐ φονεύσεις, οὐ ποιήσεις ἁμαρτίαν τινὰ τῇ σαρκί σου, οὐ κλέψεις, οὐ μαγεύσεις, οὐ φαρμακεύσεις,	B19.4a οὐ πορνεύσεις, οὐ μοιχεύσεις, οὐ παιδοφθορήσεις. οὐ φονεύσεις τέκνον ἐν φθορᾷ, οὐδὲ πάλιν γεννηθὲν ἀνελεῖς.
οὐκ ἐπιθυμήσεις τὰ τοῦ πλησίον. οὐκ ἐπιορκήσεις, οὐ ψευδομαρτυρήσεις, οὐ κακολογήσεις, οὐ μνησικακήσεις.	οὐκ ἐπιθυμήσεις τὰ τοῦ πλησίον. οὐκ ἐπιορκήσεις, οὐ ψευδομαρτυρήσεις, οὐ κακολογήσεις, οὐδὲ μνησικακήσεις,	οὐκ ἐπιθυμήσεις τὰ τοῦ πλησίον σου. οὐκ ἐπιορκήσεις, οὐ ψευδομαρτυρήσεις, οὐ κακολογήσεις, οὐδὲ μνησικακήσεις,	B19.6a οὐ μὴ γένῃ ἐπιθυμῶν τὰ τοῦ πλησίον σου, B19.4e οὐ μνησικακήσεις τῷ ἀδελφῷ σου.

			B19.7a
οὐκ ἔσῃ διγνώμων οὐδὲ δίγλωσσος· παγὶς γὰρ θανάτου ἡ διγλωσσία. οὐκ ἔσται ὁ λόγος σου ψευδής, οὐ κενός, ἀλλὰ μεμεστωμένος πράξει. οὐκ ἔσῃ πλεονέκτης οὐδὲ ἅρπαξ οὐδὲ ὑποκριτὴς οὐδὲ κακοήθης οὐδὲ ὑπερήφανος. οὐ λήψῃ βουλὴν πονηρὰν κατὰ τοῦ πλησίον σου. οὐ μισήσεις πάντα ἄνθρωπον, ἀλλὰ οὓς μὲν ἐλέγξεις, περὶ δὲ ὧν προσεύξῃ, οὓς δὲ ἀγαπήσεις ὑπὲρ τὴν ψυχήν σου.	οὐκ ἔσῃ δίγνωμος οὐδὲ δίγλωσσος· παγὶς γὰρ θανάτου ἐστιν ἡ διγλωσσία· οὐκ ἔσται ὁ λόγος σου κενὸς οὐδὲ ψευδής. οὐκ ἔσῃ πλεονέκτης οὐδὲ ἅρπαξ οὐδὲ ὑποκριτὴς οὐδὲ κακοήθης, οὐδὲ ὑπερήφανος· οὐ λήψῃ βουλὴν πονηρὰν κατὰ τοῦ πλησίον σου· οὐ μισήσεις πάντα ἄνθρωπον, ἀλλ' οὓς μὲν ἐλέγξεις, οὓς δὲ ἐλεήσεις, περὶ ὧν δὲ προσεύξῃ, οὓς δὲ ἀγαπήσεις ὑπὲρ τὴν ψυχήν σου.	οὐκ ἔσῃ δίγνωμος οὐδὲ δίγλωσσος· οὐκ ἔσται σοι λόγος κενός, οὐκ ἔσῃ πλεονέκτης, οὐχ ἅρπαξ οὐδὲ ὑποκριτής, οὐκ ἔσῃ κακοήθης, οὐχ ὑπερήφανος· οὐ λήψῃ βουλὴν πονηρὰν κατὰ τὸν πλησίον σου· οὐ μισήσεις πάντα ἄνθρωπον, ἀλλ' οὓς μὲν ἐλέγξεις, περὶ ὧν δὲ καὶ προσεύξῃ, οὓς δὲ ἀγαπήσεις ὑπὲρ τὴν ψυχήν σου.	οὐκ ἔσῃ διγνώμων οὐδὲ δίγλωσσος· παγὶς γὰρ θανάτου ἐστὶν ἡ διγλοσσία. B19.6b οὐ μὴ γένῃ πλεονέκτης. B19.3bβ οὐ λήμψῃ βουλὴν πονηρὰν κατὰ τοῦ πλησίον σου B19.5c ἀγαπήσεις τὸν πλησίον σου ὑπὲρ τὴν ψυχήν σου.
τέκνον μου, φεῦγε ἀπὸ παντὸς πονηροῦ καὶ ἀπὸ παντὸς ὁμοίου αὐτου. μὴ γίνου ὀργίλος, ὁδηγεῖ γὰρ ἡ ὀργὴ πρὸς τὸν φόνον,	τέκνον μου, φεῦγε ἀπὸ παντὸς πονηροῦ καὶ ἀπὸ παντὸς ὁμοίου αὐτοῦ. μὴ γίνου ὀργίλος, ὁδηγεῖ γὰρ ἡ ὀργὴ πρὸς τὸν φόνον. ἔστι γὰρ δαιμόνιον ἀρρενικὸν	φεῦγε ἀπὸ παντὸς κακοῦ καὶ ἀπὸ παντὸς ὁμοίου αὐτοῦ. μὴ γίνου ὀργίλος	μήτε

μηδὲ ζηλωτὴς μηδὲ ἐπιστικὸς μηδὲ θυμικός· ἐκ γὰρ τούτων ἁπάντων φόνοι γεννῶνται.	ὁ θυμός. μὴ γίνου ζηλωτὴς μήδὲ ἐριστικὸς μηδὲ θυμαντικός· ἐκ γὰρ τούτων φόνος γεννᾶται.	ζηλωτής, μὴ ἐριστικὸς μηδὲ μανικός· ὁδηγεῖ γὰρ ταῦτα πρὸς τὸν φόνον.	
τέκνον μου, μὴ γίνου ἐπιθυμητής, ὁδηγεῖ γὰρ ἡ ἐπιθυμία πρὸς τὴν πορνείαν,	Φίλιππος εἶπεν· τέκνον μου, μὴ γίνου ἐπιθυμητής. ὁδηγεῖ γὰρ ἡ ἐπιθυμία πρὸς τὴν πορνείαν καὶ ἕλκει τοὺς ἀνθρώπους πρὸς ἑαυτήν. ἔστι γὰρ θηλυκὸν δαιμόνιον ἡ ἐπιθυμία, καὶ ὃ μὲν μετ' ὀργῆς, ὃ δὲ μεθ' ἡδονῆς ἀπόλλυσι τοὺς εἰσερχομένους αὐτά. ὁδὸς δὲ πονηροῦ πνεύματος ἁμαρτία ψυχῆς, καὶ ὅταν βραχείαν εἴσδυσιν σχῇ ἐν αὐτῷ, πλατύνει αὐτὴν καὶ ἄγει ἐπὶ πάντα τὰ κακὰ τὴν ψυχὴν ἐκείνην καὶ οὐκ ἐᾷ διαβλέψαι τὸν ἄνθρωπον καὶ ἰδεῖν τὴν ἀλήθειαν. ὁ θυμὸς ὑμῶν μέτρον	Φίλιππος εἶπεν· μὴ γίνου ἐπιθυμητής, ὁδηγεῖ γὰρ πρὸς τὴν πορνείαν.	

	ἐχέτω καὶ ἐν βραχεῖ διαστήματι αὐτὸν ἡνιοχεῖτε καὶ ἀνακρούετε, ἵνα μὴ ἐμβάλλῃ ὑμᾶς εἰς ἔργον πονηρόν. θυμὸς γὰρ καὶ ἡδονὴ πονηρὰ ἐπὶ πολὺ παραμένουσα κατὰ ἐπίτασιν δαιμόνια γίνεται, καὶ ὅταν ἐπιτρέψῃ αὐτοῖς ὁ ἄνθρωπος, οἰδαίνουσιν ἐν τῇ ψυχῇ αὐτοῦ καὶ γίνονται μείζονες καὶ ἐπάγουσιν αὐτὸν εἰς ἔργα ἄδικα καὶ ἐπιγελῶσιν αὐτῷ καὶ ἥδονται ἐπὶ τῇ ἀπωλείᾳ τοῦ ἀνθρώπου.		
μηδὲ αἰσχρολόγος μηδὲ ὑψηλόφθαλμος· ἐκ γὰρ τούτων ἁπάντων μοιχεῖαι γεννῶνται.	Σίμων εἶπεν· τέκνον, μὴ γίνου αἰσχρολόγος μηδὲ ὑψηλόφθαλμος· ἐκ γὰρ τούτων μοιχεῖαι γίνονται.	Σίμων εἶπεν· μὴ γίνου αἰσχρολόγος μηδὲ ὑψηλόφθαλμος· ἐκ γὰρ τούτων μοιχεῖαι γίνονται.	
τέκνον μου, μὴ γίνου οἰωνοσκόκος,	Ἰάκωβος εἶπεν· τέκνον μου, μὴ γίνου οἰωνοσκόπος,	Ἰάκωβος εἶπεν· μὴ γίνου οἰωνοσκόπος,	

| ἐπειδὴ ὁδηγεῖ εἰς τὴν εἰδωλολατρίαν, μηδὲ ἐπαοιδὸς μηδὲ μαθηματικὸς μηδὲ περικαθαίρίαν, μηδὲ θέλε αὐτὰ βλέπειν· ἐκ γὰρ τούτων ἁπάντων εἰδωλολατρία γεννᾶται. | ἐπειδὴ ὁδηγεῖ εἰς τὴν εἰδωλολατρίαν, μηδὲ ἐπαοιδός, μηδὲ μαθηματικὸς μηδὲ περικαθαίρων, μηδὲ θέλε αὐτὰ ἰδεῖν μηδὲ ἀκούειν· ἐκ γὰρ τούτων ἁπάντων εἰδωλολατρεῖαι γεννῶνται. | μὴ ἐπαοιδός, μὴ μαθητικὸς μήτε ἃ ἐρεῖ περικαθαίρων, μήτε θέλε αὐτὰ εἰδέναι μηδὲ ἀκούειν· ἐκ γὰρ τούτων ἁπάντων εἰδωλολατρίαι γίνονται. | | |
| τέκνον μου, μὴ γίνου ψεύστης, ἐπειδὴ ὁδηγεῖ τὸ ψεῦσμα εἰς τὴν κλοπήν, μηδὲ φιλάργυρος μηδὲ κενόδοξος· ἐκ γὰρ τούτων ἁπάντων κλοπαὶ γεννῶνται. τέκνον μου, μὴ γίνου γόγγυσος, ἐπειδὴ ὁδηγεῖ εἰς τὴν βλασφημίαν, μηδὲ αὐθάδης μηδὲ πονηρόφρων· ἐκ γὰρ τούτων ἁπάντων βλασφημίαι γεννῶνται. ἴσθι δὲ πραΰς, ἐπεὶ οἱ | Ναθαναὴλ εἶπεν· τέκνον μου, μὴ γίνου ψεύστης, ἐπειδὴ ὁδηγεῖ τὸ ψεῦσμα ἐπὶ τὴν κλοπήν, μηδὲ φιλάργυρος, μηδὲ κενόδοξος· ἐκ τούτων ἁπάντων κλοπαὶ γεννῶνται. τέκνον μου, μὴ γίνου γόγγυσος, ἐπειδὴ ἄγει πρὸς τὴν βλασφημίαν, μηδὲ αὐθάδης, μηδὲ πονηρόφρων· ἐκ γὰρ τούτων ἁπάντων βλασφημίαι γεννῶνται. ἴσθι δὲ πραΰς, ἐπειδὴ | Ναθαναὴλ εἶπεν· μὴ γίνου ψεύστης, μηδὲ φιλάργυρος, μηδὲ κενόδοξος· ἐκ τούτων ἁπάντων κλοπαὶ γίνονται· μὴ γίνου γόγγυσος, μὴ θυμώδης, μὴ αὐθάδης, μήτε πονηρόφρων· ἐκ γὰρ τούτων ἁπάντων βλασφημίαι γίνονται. ἴσθι δὲ πραΰς, ἐπειδὴ | B19.4d πραΰς | ἔσῃ |

πραεῖς κληρονομήσουσιν τὴν γῆν. γίνου μακρόθυμος καὶ ἐλεήμων καὶ	πραεῖς κληρονομήσουσι τὴν βασιλείαν τῶν οὐρανῶν. γίνου μακρόθυμος, ἐλεήμων, εἰρηνοποιός, καθαρὸς τῇ καρδίᾳ ἀπὸ παντὸς κακοῦ,	πραεῖς κληρονομήσουσι τὴν βασιλείαν τοῦ θεοῦ. γίνου μακρόθυμος, ἐλεήμων, εἰρηνοποιός, καθαρὸς τὴν καρδίαν,	
ἄκακος καὶ ἡσύχιος καὶ ἀγαθὸς καὶ τρέμων τοὺς λόγους διὰ παντός, οὓς ἤκουσας.	ἄκακος καὶ ἡσύχιος, ἀγαθὸς καὶ φυλάσσων καὶ τρέμων τοὺς λόγους οὓς ἤκουσας.	ἄκακος, ἥσυχος, ἀγαθός, φυλάσσων καὶ τρέμων τοὺς λόγους τοῦ θεοῦ.	ἔσῃ ἡσύχιος, ἔσῃ τρέμων τοὺς λόγους οὓς ἤκουσας. B19.3a-b
οὐχ ὑψώσεις σεαυτὸν	οὐχ ὑψώσεις σεαυτόν,	οὐχ ὑψώσεις σεαυτόν,	οὐχ ὑψώσεις σεαυτόν, ἔσῃ δὲ ταπεινόφρων κατὰ πάντα· οὐκ ἀρεῖς ἐπὶ σεαυτὸν δόξαν. οὐ λήμψῃ βουλὴν πονηρὰν κατὰ τοῦ πλησίον σου, οὐ
οὐδὲ δώσεις τῇ ψυχῇ σου θράσος.	οὐδὲ δώσεις τὴν ψυχήν σου	οὐ δώσεις τῇ ψυχῇ σου θράσος,	δώσεις τῇ ψυχῇ σου θράσος. B19.6b-c οὐ μὴ γένῃ πλεονέκτης
οὐ κολληθήσεται ἡ ψυχή σου μετὰ ὑψηλῶν, ἀλλὰ μετὰ δικαίων καὶ ταπεινῶν	μετὰ ὑψηλῶν ἀλλὰ μετὰ δικαίων καὶ ταπεινῶν	οὐδὲ κολληθήσῃ τῇ ψυχῇ σου μετὰ ὑψηλῶν· ἀλλὰ μετὰ δικαίων καὶ ταπεινῶν. τὰ	οὐδὲ κολληθήσῃ ἐκ ψυχῆς σου μετὰ ὑψηλῶν, ἀλλὰ μετὰ ταπεινῶν καὶ δικαίων

ἀναστραφήσῃ. τὰ συμβαίνοντά σοι ἐνεργήματα ὡς ἀγαθὰ προσδέξῃ, εἰδὼς ὅτι ἄτερ θεοῦ οὐδὲν γίνεται.	ἀναστραφήσῃ. τὰ δὲ συμβαίνοντά σοι ἐνεργήματα ὡς ἀγαθὰ προσδέξῃ, εἰδὼς ὅτι ἄτερ θεοῦ οὐδὲν γίνεται.	συμβαίνοντά σοι ἐνεργήματα ὡς ἀγαθὰ προσδέξαι, εἰδὼς ὅτι ἄτερ τοῦ θεοῦ οὐδὲν γίνεται.	ἀναστραφήσῃ, τὰ συμβαίνοντά σοι ἐνεργήματα ὡς ἀγαθὰ προσδέξῃ, εἰδὼς ὅτι ἄνευ θεοῦ οὐδὲν γίνεται.
τέκνον μου, τοῦ λαλοῦντός σοι τὸν λόγον τοῦ θεοῦ	Θωμᾶς εἶπεν· τέκνον, τὸν λαλοῦντά σοι τὸν λόγον τοῦ θεοῦ καὶ παραίτιόν σοι γινόμενον τῆς ζωῆς καὶ δόντα σοι τὴν ἐν κυρίῳ σφραγῖδα ἀγαπήσεις ὡς κόρην ὀφθαλμοῦ σου,	Θωμᾶς εἶπεν· τὸν λαλοῦντά σοι τὸν λόγον τοῦ θεοῦ καὶ παραίτιόν σοι γινόμενον τῆς ζωῆς καὶ δόντα σοι τὴν ἐν κυρίῳ σφραγῖδα ἀγαπήσεις αὐτὸν ὡς κόρην ὀφθαλμοῦ σου,	B19.9b-10 ἀγαπήσεις ὡς κόρην τοῦ ὀφθαλμοῦ σου πάντα τὸν λαλοῦντά σοι τὸν λόγον κυρίου.
μνησθήσῃ νυκτὸς καὶ ἡμέρας, τιμήσεις δὲ αὐτὸν ὡς κύριον· ὅθεν γὰρ ἡ κυριότης λαλεῖται, ἐκεῖ κύριός ἐστιν. ἐκζητήσεις δὲ καθ' ἡμέραν τὰ πρόσωπα τῶν ἁγίων, ἵνα ἐπαναπαῇς τοῖς	μνησθήσῃ αὐτοῦ νύκτα καὶ ἡμέραν, τιμήσεις αὐτὸν ὡς τὸν κύριον. ὅθεν γὰρ ἡ κυριότης λαλεῖται, ἐκεῖ κύριός ἐστιν. ἐκζητήσεις δὲ τὸ πρόσωπον αὐτοῦ καθ' ἡμέραν καὶ τοὺς λοιποὺς ἁγίους, ἵνα ἐπαναπαύσῃ τοῖς	μνησθήσῃ αὐτοῦ νυκτὸς καὶ ἡμέρας, τιμήσεις δὲ αὐτὸν ὡς κύριον, ὅθεν γὰρ Ἰησοῦς Χριστὸς λαλεῖται, ἐκεῖ κύριος ἐστιν. ἐκζητήσεις δὲ αὐτὸν καὶ τοὺς λοιποὺς ἁγίους, ἵνα ἐπαναπαυσθῇς τοῖς	μνησθήσῃ ἡμέραν κρίσεως νυκτὸς καὶ ἡμέρας καὶ ἐκζητήσεις καθ' ἑκάστην ἡμέραν τὰ πρόσωπα τῶν ἁγίων, ἢ διὰ

λόγοις αὐτῶν.	λόγοις αὐτῶν· κολλώμενος γὰρ ἁγίους ἅγιος ἁγιασθήσῃ. τιμήσεις δὲ αὐτὸν καθ' ὃ δυνατὸς εἶ ἐκ τοῦ ἱδρῶτός σου καὶ ἐκ τοῦ πόνου τῶν χειρῶν σου. εἰ γὰρ ὁ κύριος δι' αὐτοῦ ἠξίωσέν σοι δοθῆναι πνευματικὴν τροφὴν καὶ ποτὸν καὶ ζωὴν αἰώνιον, σὺ ὀφείλεις πολὺ μᾶλλον τὴν φθαρτὴν καὶ πρόσκαιρον προσφέρειν τροφήν. ἄξιος γὰρ ὁ ἐργάτης τοῦ μισθοῦ αὐτοῦ, καὶ βοῦν ἀλοῶντα οὐ φιμώσεις καὶ οὐδεὶς φυτεύει ἀμπελῶνα καὶ ἐκ τοῦ καρποῦ αὐτοῦ οὐκ ἐσθίει.	λόγοις αὐτῶν· κολλώμενος γὰρ ἁγίους ἅγιος ἁγιασθήσεται. ὁ γὰρ κύριος ἠξίωσέ σε δι' αὐτοῦ δοθῆναι πνευματικὴν τροφὴν καὶ ζωὴν αἰώνιον.	λόγου κοπιῶν καὶ πορευόμενος εἰς τὸ παρακαλέσαι καὶ μελετῶν εἰς τὸ σῶσαι ψυχὴν τῷ λόγῳ...
οὐ ποιήσεις σχίσμα, εἰρηνεύσεις δὲ μαχομένους·	Κηφᾶς εἶπεν· οὐ ποιήσεις σχίσματα, εἰρηνεύσεις δὲ μαχομένους,	Κηφᾶς εἶπεν· οὐ ποιήσεις σχίσμα, εἰρηνεύσεις δὲ μαχομένους,	B19.12a οὐ ποιήσεις σχίσμα, εἰρηνεύσεις δὲ μαχομένους συναγαγών.

			B19.11d
κρινεῖς δικαίως,	κρινεῖς δικαίως,	κρινεῖς δικαίως,	κρινεῖς δικαίως.
			B19.4c
οὐ λήψῃ	οὐ λήψῃ	οὐ λήψῃ	οὐ λήμψῃ
πρόσωπον ἐλέγξαι	πρόσωπον ἐλέγξαι	πρόσωπον ἐλέγξαι	πρόσωπον ἐλέγξαι
ἐπὶ	ἁμαρτόντα τινὰ ἐπὶ	τινὰ ἐπὶ	τινὰ ἐπὶ
παραπτώμασιν. οὐ	παραπτώματι, οὐ	παραπτώματι,	παραπτώματι.
	γὰρ ἰσχύει πλοῦτος	ἰσότης γάρ ἐστι	
	παρὰ κυρίῳ· οὐ γὰρ	παρὰ θεῷ·	
	ἀξία προσκρίνει		
	οὐδὲ κάλλος ὠφελεῖ,		
	ἀλλ' ἰσότης ἐστι		
	πάντων παρ' αὐτῷ.		B19.5a
	ἐν προσευχῇ σου μὴ	ἐν προσευχῇ σου μὴ	οὐ μὴ
διψυχήσεις, πότερον	διψυχήσεις πότερον	διψυχήσῃς.	διψυχήσῃς, πότερον
ἔσται ἢ οὔ.	ἔσται ἢ οὔ.		ἔσται ἢ οὔ.
			B19.9a
μὴ γίνου πρὸς μὲν	μὴ γίνου πρὸς μὲν		μὴ γίνου πρὸς μὲν
τὸ λαβεῖν ἐκτείνων	τὸ λαβεῖν ἐκτείνων		τὸ λαβεῖν ἐκτείνων
τὰς χεῖρας, πρὸς δὲ	τὰς χεῖρας, πρὸς δὲ		τὰς χεῖρας, πρὸς μὲν
			τὸ λαβεῖν ἐκτείνων
			τὰς χεῖρας, πρὸς δὲ
τὸ δοῦναι συσπῶν.	τὸ δοῦναι συσπῶν.		τὸ δοῦναι συσπῶν.
			B19.10c-11a
ἐὰν ἔχῃς	ἐὰν ἔχῃς	ἐὰν ἔσται ἔχειν σε	...ἢ
διὰ τῶν χειρῶν σου,	διὰ τῶν χειρῶν σου,	ἀπὸ τῶν χειρῶν σου,	διὰ τῶν χειρῶν σου
δώσεις λύτρωσιν	δώσεις λύτρωσιν	δὸς εἰς ἄφεσιν	ἐργάσῃ εἰς λύτρον
ἁμαρτιῶν σου.	τῶν ἁμαρτιῶν σου.	ἁμαρτιῶν σου.	ἁμαρτιῶν σου.
οὐ διστάσεις δοῦναι	οὐ διστάσεις διδόναι		οὐ διστάσεις δοῦναι
οὐδὲ διδοὺς	οὐδὲ διδοὺς		οὐδὲ διδοὺς
γογγύσεις· γνώσῃ	γογγύσεις· γνώσῃ		γογγύσεις, γνώσῃ
γάρ, τίς ἐστιν ὁ τοῦ	γάρ, τίς ἐστιν ὁ τοῦ		δὲ τίς ὁ τοῦ
μισθοῦ καλὸς	μισθοῦ καλὸς		μισθοῦ καλὸς
ἀνταποδότης. οὐκ	ἀνταποδότης. οὐκ	οὐκ	ἀνταποδότης.

ἀποστραφῇς τὸν ἐνδεόμενον, συγκοινωνήσεις δὲ πάντα τῷ ἀδελφῷ σου καὶ οὐκ ἐρεῖς ἴδια εἶναι· εἰ γὰρ ἐν τῷ ἀθανάτῳ κοινωνοί ἐστε, πόσῳ μᾶλλον ἐν τοῖς θνητοῖς;	ἀποστραφῇ ἐνδεούμενον, κοινωνήσεις δὲ ἁπάντων τῷ ἀδελφῷ σου καὶ οὐκ ἐρεῖς ἴδια εἶναι· εἰ γὰρ ἐν τῷ ἀθανάτῳ κοινωνοί ἐστε, πόσῳ μᾶλλον ἐν τοῖς φθαρτοῖς;	ἀποστραφῇ ἐνδεούμενον, συγκοινωνήσεις δὲ πάντα τοῖς ἀδελφοῖς σου καὶ οὐκ ἐρεῖς ἴδια εἶναι· εἰ γὰρ ἐν τῷ θανάτῳ κοινωνοί ἐστε, πόσῳ μᾶλλον ἐν τοῖς θνητοῖς;	B19.8a κοινωνήσεις ἐν πᾶσιν τῷ πλησίον σου καὶ οὐκ ἐρεῖς ἴδια εἶναι· εἰ γὰρ ἐν τῷ ἀφθάρτῳ κοινωνοί ἐστε, πόσῳ μᾶλλον ἐν τοῖς φθαρτοῖς;
οὐκ ἀρεῖς τὴν χεῖρα σου ἀπὸ τοῦ υἱοῦ σου ἢ ἀπὸ τῆς θυγατρός σου, ἀλλὰ ἀπὸ νεότητος διδάξεις τὸν φόβον τοῦ θεοῦ. οὐκ ἐπιτάξεις δούλῳ σου ἢ παιδίσκῃ, τοῖς ἐπὶ τὸν αὐτὸν θεὸν ἐλπίζουσιν, ἐν πικρίᾳ σου, μήποτε οὐ μὴ φοβηθήσονται τὸν ἐπ' ἀμφοτέροις θεόν· οὐ γὰρ ἔρχεται κατὰ πρόσωπον καλέσαι, ἀλλ' ἐφ' οὓς τὸ πνεῦμα ἡτοίμασεν.	Βαρθολομαῖος εἶπεν· ἐρωτῶμεν ὑμᾶς, ἀδελφοί, ὡς ἔτι καιρός ἐστι καὶ ἔχετε εἰς οὓς ἐργάζεσθε μεθ' ἑαυτῶν μὴ ἐκλίπητε ἐν μηδενί ἐξ οὗ ἂν ἔχητε. ἐγγὺς γὰρ ἡ ἡμέρα κυρίου, ἐν ᾗ συναπολεῖται πάντα σὺν τῷ πονηρῷ· ἥξει γὰρ ὁ κύριος καὶ ὁ μισθὸς αὐτοῦ μετ' αὐτοῦ. ἑαυτῶν γίνεσθε νομοθέται, ἑαυτῶν γίνεσθε σύμβουλοι ἀγαθοί, θεοδίδακτοι·	Βαρθολομαῖος εἶπεν· οὐκ ἄρῃς τὴν χεῖρά σου ἀπὸ τοῦ υἱοῦ οὐδὲ ἀπὸ τῆς θυγατρός σου, ἀλλ' ἅμα ἀπὸ νεότητος διδάξεις αὐτοὺς τὸν φόβον τοῦ κυρίου.	B19.5e οὐ μὴ ἄρῃς τὴν χεῖρά σου ἀπὸ τοῦ υἱοῦ σου ἢ ἀπὸ τῆς θυγατρός σου, ἀλλὰ ἀπὸ νεότητος διδάξεις φόβον θεοῦ. B19.7c οὐ μὴ ἐπιτάξῃς δούλῳ σου ἢ παιδίσκῃ ἐν πικρίᾳ, τοῖς ἐπὶ τὸν αὐτὸν θεὸν ἐλπίζουσιν, μή ποτε οὐ μὴ φοβηθήσονται τὸν ἐπ' ἀμφοτέροις θεόν· ὅτι ἦλθεν οὐ κατὰ πρόσωπον καλέσαι, ἀλλ' ἐφ' οὓς τὸ πνεῦμα ἡτοίμασεν.

ὑμεῖς δὲ οἱ δοῦλοι ὑποταγήσεσθε τοῖς κυρίοις ὑμῶν ὡς τύπῳ θεοῦ ἐν αἰσχύνῃ καὶ φόβῳ.			B19.7b ὑποταγήσῃ κυρίοις ὡς τύπῳ θεοῦ ἐν αἰσχύνῃ καὶ φόβῳ· B19.2d-f
μισήσεις πᾶσαν ὑπόκρισιν καὶ πᾶν ὃ μὴ ἀρεστὸν τῷ κυρίῳ. οὐ μὴ ἐγκαταλίπῃς ἐντολὰς κυρίου,			μισήσεις πᾶν, ὃ οὐκ ἔστιν ἀρεστὸν τῷ θεῷ, μισήσεις πᾶσαν ὑπόκρισιν· οὐ μὴ ἐγκαταλιπῃς ἐντολὰς κυρίου. B19.11b
φυλάξεις δὲ ἃ παρέλαβες, μήτε προστιθεὶς μήτε ἀφαιρῶν. ἐν ἐκκλησίᾳ ἐξομολογήσῃ τὰ παραπτώματά σου,	φυλάξεις ἃ παρέλαβες μήτε προσθεὶς μήτε ὑφαιρῶν.	Cf. below ἐξομολογήσῃ τὰ παραπτώματά σου, οὐκ ἐγκαταλείψῃ ἐντολὰς κυρίου, οὐ	φυλάξεις ἃ παρέλαβες, μήτε προστιθεὶς μήτε ἀφαιρῶν. B19.12b-c ἐξομολογήσῃ ἐπὶ ἁμαρτίαις σου. οὐ
καὶ οὐ προσελεύσῃ ἐπὶ προσευχήν σου ἐν συνειδήσει πονηρᾷ·		προσελεύσῃ ἐν προσευχῇ σου ἐν συνειδήσει πονηρᾷ, μισήσεις πᾶσαν ὑπόκρισιν καὶ πᾶν ὃ	προσήξεις ἐπὶ προσευχὴν ἐν συνειδήσει πονηρᾷ.
	Cf also K30: φυλάξαι τὰς ἐντολὰς μηδὲν ἀφαιροῦντας ἢ προστιθέντας	μὴ ἀρέσκει κυρίῳ, φυλάξῃ δὲ ἃ παρέλαβες μήτε προστιθεὶς μήτε	
αὕτη ἐστὶν ἡ ὁδὸς τῆς ζωῆς.		ὑφαιρῶν. αὕτη ἐστὶν ἡ ὁδὸς τῆς ζωῆς.	αὕτη ἐστὶν ἡ ὁδὸς τοῦ φωτός.

Bibliography

Aland, K. "The problem of anonymity and pseudonymity in Christian literature of the first two centuries", *JTS* 12 (1961), 39–49.
Arendzen, J.P. "An entire Syriac text of the 'Apostolic Church Order'", *JTS* 3 (1901), 59–80.
Audet, J-P. "Affinités littéraires et doctrinales du 'Manuel de discipline'", *Revue Biblique* 59 (1952), 219–238.
Barnard, L.W. "The Dead Sea scrolls, Barnabas, the Didache and the later history of the 'two ways'", in *Studies in the Apostolic Fathers and their Background* (Oxford: Blackwell, 1966), 87–107.
Barnes, T.D. "The date of the Council of Gangra", *JTS* 40 (1989), 121–124.
Bartlet, J.V. *Church-Life and Church-Order during the First Four Centuries* (Oxford: Blackwell, 1943).
Bartsch, H.-W. *Die Anfänge urchristlicher Rechtsbildungen. Studien zu den Pastoralbriefen* (ThF 34; Hamburg: Evangelischer, 1965).
Baumstark, Anton "Alte und neue Spuren eines ausserkanonischen Evangeliums", *ZNW* 14 (1913), 232–247.
Bestmann, C. *Geschichte der christlichen Sitte* II (Nördlinger: Beck, 1885).
Bickell, Johann Wilhelm *Geschichte des Kirchenrechts* 1 (Giessen: Heyer, 1843).
Bovon, François "Mary Magdalene in the *Acts of Philip*", in F.S. Jones (ed.), *Which Mary: The Marys of Early Christian Tradition* (Atlanta: SBL, 2002), 75–89.
Bradshaw, P.F. *The Search for the Origins of Christian Worship: Sources and Methods for the Study of Early Liturgy* (New York: Oxford University Press, ²2002 [1993]).
Bradshaw, P.F. *Ordination Rites of the Ancient Churches of East and West* (New York: Pueblo, 1990).
Brock, Ann Graham "Peter, Paul and Mary: canonical vs non-canonical portrayals of apostolic witnesses", in *SBL 1999 Seminar Papers* (Atlanta: SBL, 1999), 173–202.
Brock, Ann Graham "What's in a name: the competition for authority in early Christian texts", *SBL 1998 Seminar Papers I* (Atlanta: Scholars, 1998), 106–124.
Butler, B.C. "The 'two ways' in the Didache", *JTS* 12 (1961), 27–38.
Carleton Paget, James *The Epistle of Barnabas: Outlook and Background* (WUNT 2.64; Tübingen: Mohr-Siebeck, 1994).

Cavalieri, Pio Franchi di   *I martiri di S. Theodoto di Ancira e di S. Ariadne* (Studi e testi 6; Rome: Biblitheca Vaticana, 1900).
Cerrato, J.A.   *Hippolytus Between East and West* (Oxford: Oxford University Press, 2002).
Clark, G.   *The letters of Cyprian* 4 (New York: Newman, 1989).
Connolly, R.H.   *Didascalia apostolorum* (Oxford: Clarendon, 1929).
Connolly, R.H.   "The use of the *Didache* in the *Didascalia*", *JTS* 24 (1923), 147–157.
Cooper, James, & Arthur J. Maclean   *The Testament of Our Lord* (Edinburgh: T&T Clark, 1902).
Daniélou, J.   *The Ministry of Women in the Early Church* (London: Faith, 1961).
Denzey, Nicola   "What did the Montanists read", *HTR* 94 (2001), 427–448.
Dibelius, Martin   *Der Hirt des Hermas* (Tübingen: Mohr-Siebeck, 1923).
Draper, J.A.   "Barnabas and the riddle of the Didache revisited", *JSNT* 58 (1995), 89–113.
Duchesne, L.   Untitled review of Harnack, *Quellen*, in *Bulletin Critique* 7 (1886), 361–370.
Ernst, Allie M.   *Martha from the Margins: The Authority of Martha in Early Christian Tradition* (Leiden: Brill, 2009).
Faivre, Alexandre   "Apostolicité et pseudo-apostolicité dans la 'Constitution ecclésiastique des apôtres': L'art de faire parler les origines", *Revue des sciences religieuses* 66 (1992), 19–67.
Faivre, Alexandre   "Le texte grec de la Constitution ecclésiastique des apôtres 16–20 et ses sources", *Revue des sciences religieuses* 55 (1981), 31–42.
Faivre, Alexandre   "La documentation canonico-liturgique de l'église ancienne", *Revue des sciences religieuses* 54 (1980), 204–219, 273–297.
Faivre, Alexandre, & C. Faivre   "La place des femmes dans le rituel eucharistique des marcosiens. déviance ou archaïsme?", *Revue des sciences religieuses* 71 (1997), 310–328.
Frazee, Charles A.   "Anatolian asceticism in the fourth century: Eustathios of Sebastea and Basil of Caesarea", *Catholic Historical Review* 66 (1980), 16–33.
Funk, F.X.   *Doctrina duodecim apostolorum* (Tübingen: Laupp, 1887).
Gamble, H.Y.   *Books and Readers in the Early Church* (New Haven: Yale University Press, 1995).
Gebhardt, O., et al.   *Patrum apostolicorum opera* 1.2 (Leipzig: Hinrichs, 1878).
Giet, Stanislaus   "La Didache: enseignement des douze apôtres?", *Melto* 3 (1967), 223–236.

Goodrich, John K. "Overseers as stewards and the qualifications for leadership in the Pastoral Epistles", *ZNW* 104 (2013), 77–97.

Goodspeed, E.J. "The Didache, Barnabas and the Doctrina", *Anglican Theological Review* 27 (1945), 228–247.

Gryson, R. *The Ministry of Women in the Early Church* (Collegeville: Liturgical, 1976).

Hanson, R.P.C. *Eucharistic Offering in the Early Church* (Bramcote: Grove, 1979).

Harris, William V. *Ancient Literacy* (Cambridge, MA: Harvard University Press, 1989).

Harnack, Adolf *Die Apostellehre und die jüdischen beiden Wege* (Lepizig: Hinrichs, 1886).

Harnack, Adolf *Die Lehre der zwölf Apostel nebst Untersuchungen zur ältesten Geschichte der Kirchenverfassung und des Kirchenrechts* (TU 2.1; Leipzig: Hinrichs, 1886).

Harnack, Adolf *The Sources of the Apostolic Canons* (ETr; London: Norgate, 1895 [German: 1886]).

Hatch, E. *The Organization of the Early Christian Churches* (London: Longman, 1881).

Heid, Stefan *Celibacy in the Early Church. The Beginnings of a Discipline of Obligatory Continence for Clerics in East and West* (ETr; San Francisco: Ignatius, 2000 [German: 1997]).

Henne, Philippe *L'unité du Pasteur d'Hermas* (Paris: Gabalda, 1992).

Hennecke, E. "Zur apostolischen Kirchenordnung", *ZNW* 20 (1921), 241–248.

Hennecke, E. "Die Grundschrift der Didache und ihre Recensionen", *ZNW* 2 (1901), 58–72.

Hilgenfeld, A. *Novum Testamentum extra canonem receptum* 4 (Leipzig: Weigel, 1864).

Hill, C.E. "The *Epistula apostolorum*: an Asian tract from the time of Polycarp", *JECS* 7 (1999), 1–53.

Horner, G. *The statutes of the apostles or canones ecclesiastici* (London: Williams and Norgate, 1904).

Jensen, A. *God's Self-Confident Daughters* (Kampen: Kok Pharos, 1996).

Kateusz, Ally *Mary and Early Christian Women: Hidden Leadership* (Cham, Switzerland: Palgrave Macmillan, 2019).

Kelly, J.N.D. *Early Christian Creeds* (London: Longmans, 1950).

Koester, H. "Überlieferung und Geschichte der frühchristlichen Evangelienliteratur", in W. Haase (ed.) *ANRW* II.25.2 (Berlin: de Gruyter, 1984), 1463–1542.

Kraft, R.A. *The Apostolic Fathers 3: Barnabas and the Didache* (New York: Nelson, 1965).

Krawutzcky, A. "Über das altkirchliche Unterrichtsbuch 'Die zwei Wege oder die Entscheidung des Petrus'", *ThQ* 64 (1882), 359–445.

Lagarde, P. *Aegyptiaca* (Göttingen: Hoyer, 1883).

Lagarde, P. *Reliquiae iuris ecclesiastici antiquissimae* (Leipzig: Teubner, 1856).

Lemoine, Bernadette "Étude de la notice sur l'évêque dans la 'Constitution ecclésiastique des apôtres' (C.E.A.)", *Questions liturgiques* 80 (1999), 5–23.

Leutholf, Hiob, (Ludolfus) *Iobi Ludolfi alias Leutholf dicti ad suam Historiam Aethiopicam antehac commentarius* (Frankfurt am M: Zunner, 1691).

Lietzmann, Hans "Zur altchristlichen Verfassungsgeschichte", in *Kleine Schriften* I (TU 67; Berlin: Akademie, 1958), 141–185.

Lincicum, David "An excerpt from the Apostolic Church Order (CPG 1739)", *Sacris Erudiri* 57 (2018), 439–444.

Maclean, A.J. *The Ancient Church Orders* (Cambridge: Cambridge University Press, 1910).

Martimort, A.G. *Deaconesses: An Historical Study* (San Francisco: Ignatius, 1986).

Massebieau, Init. "Title", *Revue d'Histoire des religions* No (1884), pp.

Methuen, Charlotte "Widows, bishops and the struggle for authority in the *Didascalia apostolorum*", *JEH* 46 (1995), 197–213.

Niederwimmer, K. *Die Didache* (Göttingen: Vandenhoek & Ruprecht, ²1993 [1989]).

Parrott, Douglas M. "Gnostic and orthodox disciples in the second and third centuries", in C.W. Hedrick and R. Hodgson (eds.), *Nag Hammadi, Gnosticism and Early Christianity* (Peabody: Hendrickson, 1986), 193–219.

Paschke, Boris A. "The cura morum of the Roman censors as historical background for the bishop and deacon lists of the Pastoral Epistles", *ZNW* 98 (2007), 105–119.

Peterson, Erik "Beiträge zur Interpretation der Visionen im 'Pastor Hermae'", in *Frühkirche Judentum und Gnosis* (Rome: Herder, 1959), 254–270.

Peterson, Erik "Die Häretiker der Philippus-Akten", *ZNW* 31 (1932), 97–111.

Pitra, J.B. *Iuris ecclesiastici Graecorum historia et monumenta* I (Rome: Collegium Urbani, 1864).

Powell, D.L. "Ordo Presbyterii", *JTS* ns 26 (1975), 290–328.

Powell, D.L. "Tertullianists and Cataphrygians", *VigChr* 29 (1975), 33–54.

Prostmeier, F.R. *Der Barnabasbrief* (Göttingen: Vandenhoeck und Ruprecht, 1999).
Rordorf, W., & A. Tuilier *La doctrine des douze apôtres* (Paris: Cerf, 1998).
Rudolph, K. "Der gnostische Dialog als literarisches Genus", in Peter Nagel (ed.), *Probleme der koptischen Literatur* (Halle: Wiss. B. Univ. Halle, 1968), 85–107.
Sandt, Huub van de "James 4,1–4 in the Light of the Jewish Two Ways Tradition 3,1–6", *Biblica* 88 (2007), 38–63.
Sandt, Huub van de, & D. Flusser *The Didache: its Jewish Sources and its Place in Early Judaism and Christianity* (Assen: Van Gorcum, 2002).
Schermann, Theodor *Die allgemeine Kirchenordnung, frühchristliche Liturgien und kirchliche Überlieferung* I (Paderborn: Schöningh, 1914).
Schermann, Theodor *Eine Elfapostelmoral oder die x-Rezension der "beiden Wege"* (Veröffentlichungen aus dem Kirchenhistorischen Seminar München 2.2; Munich: Lentner, 1903).
Schöllgen, G. "Der Abfassungszweck der frühchristlichen Kirchenordnungen", *JbAC* 40 (1997), 55–77.
Schöllgen, G. "Pseudapostolizität und Schriftgebrauch in den ersten Kirchenordnungen", in G. Schöllgen & C. Scholten (eds.), *Stimuli: Exegese und ihre Hermeneutik in Antike und Christentum* (JbAC Ergänzungsband 23; Münster: Aschendorff, 1996), 96–121.
Schmidt, Carl *Gespräche Jesu mit seinen Jüngern nach der Auferstehung* (TU 43; Leipzig: Hinrichs, 1919).
Smith, Julien C.H. "The Epistle of Barnabas and the two ways of teaching authority", *VigChr* 68 (2014), 465–497.
Smith, Yancy *The Mystery of Anointing: Hippolytus' Commentary on the Song of Songs in Social and Critical Contexts* (Piscataway: Gorgias, 2015).
(Sperry-)White, G. *Daily prayer and Its Ascetic Context in the Syriac and Ethiopic Testamentum Domini* (Joensuu: University of Joensuu, 2002).
(Sperry-)White, G. "The Imagery of Angelic Praise and Heavenly Topography in the Testament of our Lord", *Ecclesia orans* 19 (2002), 315–332.
(Sperry-)White, G. *The Testamentum Domini: A Text for Students* (Bramcote: Grove, 1991).
Steimer, Bruno *Vertex Traditionis* (Berlin: de Gruyter, 1992).
Stewart(-Sykes), Alistair "The ordination prayers in *Traditio apostolica*: the search for a Grundschrift" *SVTQ* 64 (2020), 11–24.
Stewart(-Sykes), Alistair "The deaconess in *Testamentum Domini*: a window on women's ministry in fourth-century Asia", in *Masculum et feminam creavit eos (Gen. 1,27): Paradigmi del maschile e femminile nel cristianesimo antico* (Studia Ephemeridis Augustinianum 157; Lugano: Nerbini, 2020), 175–183.

Stewart(-Sykes), Alistair *The Testament of the Lord: An English Version* (Yonkers: St Vladimir's Seminary Press, 2018).

Stewart(-Sykes), Alistair *The Original Bishops: Office and Order in the First Christian Communities* (Grand Rapids: Baker Academic, 2014).

Stewart(-Sykes), Alistair *On the Two Ways, Life or Death, Light or Darkness: Foundational Texts in the Tradition* (Yonkers NY: St Vladimir's Seminary, 2011).

Stewart(-Sykes), Alistair "Deacons in the Syrian church order tradition: a search for origins", in *Diakonia, Diaconiae, Diaconato: Semantica e storia nei padri della chiesa* (Studia Ephemeridis Augustinianum 117; Rome: Institutum patristicum Augustinianum, 2010), 111–120.

Stewart(-Sykes), Alistair *The Didascalia apostolorum: An English Version with Introduction and Annotation* (Turnhout: Brepols, 2009).

Stewart(-Sykes), Alistair "The domestic origin of the liturgy of the word", in F.M. Young et al. (eds.), *Studia patristica* 40 (Leuven: Peeters, 2006), 115–120.

Stewart(-Sykes), Alistair *The Life of Polycarp: An Anonymous vita from Third-Century Smyrna* (ECS 4; Sydney: St Paul's, 2002).

Stewart(-Sykes), Alistair "Bread, fish, water and wine: the Marcionite menu and the maintenance of purity", in G. May & K. Greschat (eds.), *Marcion und seine kirchengeschichtliche Wirkung* (TU 150; Berlin: de Gruyter, 2002), 207–220.

Stewart(-Sykes), Alistair *Hippolytus: On the Apostolic Tradition* (Crestwood: Saint Vladimir's Seminary, 2001).

Stewart(-Sykes), Alistair *The Lamb's High Feast: Melito*, Peri Pascha *and the Quartodeciman paschal liturgy at Sardis* (Leiden: Brill, 1998).

Stewart(-Sykes), Alistair "The Asian origin of *Epistula apostolorum* and of the new prophecy", *VigChr* 51 (1997), 416–438.

Tabbernee, William "Revelation 21 and the Montanist New Jerusalem", *ABR* 37 (1989), 52–60.

Theissen, G. *The Social Setting of Pauline Christianity* (Philadelphia: Fortress, 1982).

Tidner, Erik *Didascaliae apostolorum, canonum ecclesiasticorum, traditionis apostolicae versiones Latinae* (TU 75; Berlin: Akademie, 1963).

Torjeson, K.J. *When Women were Priests* (San Francisco: Harper, 1993).

Trevett, Christine "'Angelic visitations and speech she had': Nanas of Kotiaeion", in Pauline Allen et al. (eds.), *Prayer and Spirituality in the Early Church* 2 (Brisbane: Centre for early Christian studies, 1999), 259–277.

Trevett, Christine "Spiritual authority and the 'heretical' woman: Firmilian's word to the church in Carthage", in J.W. Drijvers & J.W. Watt (eds.), *Portraits of Spiritual Authority: Religious Power in Early*

	Christianity, Byzantium and the Christian Orient (Leiden: Brill, 1999), 45–62.
Trevett, Christine	*Montanism: Gender, Authority and the New Prophecy* (Cambridge: Cambridge University Press, 1996).
Vilela, A.	*La condition collegiale des prêtres au IIIe siècle* (Paris: Beauchesne, 1971).
Wengst, K.	*Schriften des Urchristentums* II (Darmstadt: Wissenschaftliche Buchgesellschaft, 1984).
Wilamowitz Moellendorff, U. von	"In libellum ΠΕΡΙ ΥΨΠΟΥΣ coniectanea", *Hermes* 10 (1876), 334–346.
Wilhite, Shawn J.	*"One of Life and one of Death": Apocalypticism and the Didache's Two Ways* (Piscataway NJ: Gorgias, 2019).
Wills, Lawrence	"The form of the sermon in Hellenistic Judaism and early Christianity", *HTR* 77 (1984), 277–299.
Wilson, W.T.	*The Mysteries of Righteousness: The Literary Composition and Genre of the Sentences of Pseudo-Phocylides* (Tübingen: Mohr-Siebeck, 1994).
Zahn, Theodor	*Forschungen zur Geschichte des neutestamentlichen Kanons und der altkirchlichen Literatur* 6.1 (Leipzig: Deichert, 1900).

Bibliographical note: the unpublished notes of Pierre Nautin

The reader will find several references to the unpublished work of Pierre Nautin; these citations result from an examination of Nautin's notes which I made in January 2005 in Aix en Provence.

It is clear that Nautin was planning a book on K much like this, having announced his identification of an ancient church order lying behind K in *Annuaire de l'École pratique des hautes Études, V^e section: sciences religieuses* 90 (1981–1982), 335–339.

However, the only part which reached completion was a translation into French. I have compared my own translation to his. For the rest there are notes, frequently re-written, in which we see Nautin struggling to make sense, as do we all, of the contradictions and tensions within the text. However, it is clear that Nautin had reached provisional conclusions at various points since these are repeated frequently in various ways within his notes as sections were re-written, and it is these conclusions to which reference is made.

Indices

1. Ancient authors[1]

1.1 Scripture

Deut 19:15	165
Proverbs 7:2	34
15:1	165
Wisdom 8:4	159
Tobit 4:16	142
Matt 5:5	149
18:16	165
25:42	169
Acts 4:13	123
1 Cor 1:12-17	44
5:11	155
7.24	170
8:6	32
9:7	151
11:3	77
2 Cor 8:1	165
8:22	155
1 Thess 3:12	157
1 Tim 2:5-6	32
3:2	59, 82, 83, 155, 157
3:3	82, 155, 165
3:7	82
3:8	165
3:10	155
3:12	82, 165
5:5	167
5:10	167
5:18	151
2 Tim 4:5	163
Titus 1:6	59, 157
1:7	82, 165
1:8	82
Rev. 1:3	95
4:4	60, 157
4:8	157

1.2 Early Jewish literature

Babylonian Talmud	
Yebamoth 47A-B	25
Dead Sea scrolls:	
1QS 3.1-4	89
1QS 3.13-4.26	38
1QS 8.16-19	88
4Q560	42
Testaments of the twelve patriarchs:	
Levi 19	3
Asher 1	3
Reuben 3	42
Dan 2-3	42
Test Solomon 1.7	42
4.1	42

1.3 Early Christian literature

1 Clem. 34.1-6	117
34.5	171
40.5	169
41.1	169
42.4	155
44.2	155

---

1   References to TWT material in the introduction are not included here, nor are references to K itself.

44.3	165	2.3.3	157
46.2	33, 149	2.5.1	155
47.4	155	2.6.1	115
63	90	2.26.4	34
65	90	2.32.3	34
Acta Philippi 8.2	74	2.36.4	88
Acta Thomae 1	109	2.42.1	128, 163
Canones Concilii Gangrae 4	130	2.44.3	167
7	130	2.46.6	128, 163
Canones Concilii Laodiceni 11	74	2.47.1	128, 163
46	115	2.57.5-7	100-101, 129
Canones Hippolyti 9	167		
37	97, 163	6.6.9	71
ps-Clem.		6.22.2	69
Hom. 9.9	42	*Epistula apostolorum* 2	47-49
11.36	89	*Ep. Barnabae* 4.9	81
Rec. 3.66	89	*Eusebius HE* 1.12	46
6.15	89	3.1	109
Clement Alex. *Strom.* 1.20	149	5.16.10	109
3.63	43	5.17.3	72
3.91	42	5.18.2	73
4.8	117	5.18.5	49
Const. App.		5.24.2	72
2.1.1	159	6.43.8-9	90
2.1.2	157	7.24	121
2.47	78	*Ev. Jud.* 34	75-76
3.1.1	159	*Ev. Phil.* 61a	43
Cyprian Ep. 29.1.2	98	*Ev. Thom.* 114	65
74.4	108	Hermas *Vis.* 1.3.4	78
75.10.5	69, 72	*Mand.* 1.1	25-26
Didache 3.7-8	115	Hippolytus (*school of*)	
10.7	72	*Haer.* 8.19	76
15.1	155, 157, 165	*In cant.* 25.2	66
		Traditio apostolica 11	98
Didascalia 2.1.1	155	Ignatius	
2.1.2	157	*Eph.* 12.2	159
2.1.3-5	51, 125-126	*Smyrn.* 8.2	45
2.1.5	115, 157	*Trall.* 2.3	159
2.2.1	155	3.1	117
2.2.2	157	Justin *I Apol.*1.67	88
2.3	165	*Passio Theodoti* 13	120

ps Pionius *VitPol* 17	118	Bickell, Johann		
Polycarp *Ad Phil.* 6.1	155	Wilhelm	1, 152, 164, 168	
Quaestiones		Bovon, François	66, 74	
Bartholomaei 2.1-14	77-78	Bradshaw, P.F.	115-116, 155	
Rufinus *Expositiones in*		Brock, Ann Graham	68, 78	
symbol. Apost. 38	11-12, 96	Butler, B.C.	23	
Tertullian *De praescriptione*		Carleton Paget,		
haer. 41	95	James	19, 41	
Testamentum Domini 1.16	52, 72	Cavalieri,		
1.17	52	Pio Franchi di	120	
1.19	71, 74, 103	Cerrato, J.A.	66	
1.20	90, 131, 155, 157	Clark, G.	108	
1.21	52	Connolly, R.H.	34, 59, 68, 118, 125, 126, 127, 129	
1.22	113, 114	Cooper, James	131	
1.23	71, 74	Daniélou, J.	70	
1.31	52, 112	Denzey, Nicola	76	
1.33	165	Dibelius, Martin	31	
1.34	89, 93, 102, 114	Draper, J.A.	18-20, 25, 38	
1.37	103	Duchesne, L.	51, 87, 90, 99	
		Ernst, Allie M.	65, 68, 75, 76, 173	
		Faivre, Alexandre	55, 65, 72, 84, 85, 87, 88, 89, 95, 106, 110, 115, 119, 122, 123, 128, 165, 175	

1.4 Classical literature

Aristotle *Rhetorica* 3.13.1-3	96-97	Flusser, D.	3, 16, 17, 18, 19, 21, 23, 36, 37, 39
3.17.3-5	97		
Dionysius Thrax, *De arte*		Frazee, Charles A.	120
grammatica 1	96	Funk, F.X.	17, 34, 35, 47, 49, 56, 92, 93, 94, 96, 100, 108, 136, 140, 142, 144, 146, 148, 150, 152, 154, 160, 161, 164, 166, 168, 170, 172, 174
Quintilian *Institutio*			
oratoria 2.4.1	96		
Soranus *Gyn.* 2.32	167		

2. Modern authors

Aland, K.	124		
Audet, J-P.	3	Gamble, H.Y.	97-98
Barnard, L.W.	29	Gebhardt, O.	15
Barnes, T.D.	120	Giet, Stanislaus	47, 152
Bartlet, J.V.	57-64	Goodrich, John K.	82, 83
Bartsch, H.-W.	82	Goodspeed, E.J.	16, 18-20, 49
Baumstark, Anton	46, 66	Gryson, R.	70, 166
Bestmann, C.	19	Hanson, R.P.C.	69

Harris, William V.	96	Peterson, Erik	78, 120
Harnack, Adolf	1-3, 5, 6, 7, 17, 27, 29, 35, 41, 46, 47, 49, 54-57, 61, 62, 64, 65, 66, 77, 82, 85, 86, 88, 90, 92, 93, 94, 96, 97, 98, 99, 101, 102, 104, 106, 107-111, 116-122, 132, 140, 142, 144, 146, 150, 12, 154, 155, 160, 161, 164, 166, 168, 170, 172, 174	Powell, D.L.	73, 100
		Prostmeier, F.R.	31
		Rordorf, W.	3
		Rudolph, K.,	67
		Sandt, Huub van de	3, 16, 17, 18, 19, 21, 23, 36, 37, 39
		Schermann, Theodor	1, 5, 7, 10-13, 46, 81, 140, 142, 144, 146, 150, 152, 154, 164, 166, 168, 172, 174
		Schöllgen, G.	123, 124
		Schmidt, Carl	46-49
Hatch, E.	88	Smith, Julien C.H.	26
Heid, Stefan	58, 113, 159,	Smith, Yancy	66
Henne, Philippe	25, 31,	(Sperry-)White, G.	52, 53, 112-113, 122, 131
Hennecke, E.	16, 27-28, 36-37, 49, 121, 154, 160, 161, 168	Steimer, Bruno	1, 124
		Stewart(-Sykes), Alistair	38, 45, 48, 49, 53, 71, 72, 74, 84, 86, 95, 116, 130
Hilgenfeld, A.	92, 136, 140, 144, 146, 152, 156, 158, 166, 168, 172, 174		
Hill, C.E.	48	Tabbernee, William	73
Jensen, A.	73, 74	Theissen, G.	44-45
Kateusz, Ally	76	Tidner, Erik	102, 164
Kelly, J.N.D.	32	Torjeson, K.J.	74
Koester, H.	67	Trevett, Christine	72, 73
Kraft, R.A.	20-21	Vilela, A.	87, 90, 99, 109
Krawutzcky, A.	1, 29, 92	Wengst, K.	4, 6, 10, 11, 14, 25
Lemoine, Bernadette	2, 84, 108-109	Wilamowitz Moellendorff, U. von	140, 144, 146, 150, 172, 174
Leutholf, Hiob (Ludolfus)	1		
Lietzmann, Hans	85-86		
Lincicum, David	15	Wilhite, Shawn J.	39
Maclean, A.J.	48, 78, 131, 161, 172	Wills, Lawrence	97
		Zahn, Theodor	74
Martimort, A.G.	77		
Methuen, Charlotte	71		
Niederwimmer, K.	3, 11, 20-25, 36		
Parrott, Douglas M.	109-110		
Paschke, Boris A.	82, 83		

www.ingramcontent.com/pod-product-compliance
Lightning Source LLC
Chambersburg PA
CBHW071730080526
44588CB00013B/1968